IMAGES
of America

DANVILLE

On the cover: Please see page 90. (Hendricks County Museum.)

IMAGES
of America

DANVILLE

Jeffrey K. Baldwin on behalf of the
Hendricks County Museum

ARCADIA
PUBLISHING

ISBN 978-0-7385-7700-5

Published by Arcadia Publishing
Charleston, South Carolina

Printed in the United States of America

Library of Congress Control Number: 2009925392

For all general information contact Arcadia Publishing at:
Telephone 843-853-2070
Fax 843-853-0044
E-mail sales@arcadiapublishing.com
For customer service and orders:
Toll-Free 1-888-313-2665

Visit us on the Internet at www.arcadiapublishing.com

To the residents of Danville, past, present, and future,
who have made our town a unique and wonderful place
to live, work, and raise a family.

Contents

Acknowledgments 6

Introduction 7

1. Agriculture and Business 13

2. Government and Politics 55

3. Transportation 77

4. Danville Schools and Central Normal College 89

5. Homes, Churches, Suburban Life, and Other Interruptions 109

ACKNOWLEDGMENTS

I have heard that writing a book is a lonely business. That is true in regard to the moments when words are taken to the page. In that regard I am responsible for any errors that may exist in this book. Researching a book, on the other hand, is people-intensive—and many people deserve thanks for their assistance and the interest that they have shown in this book. To sound like a lawyer, they include, but are not necessarily limited to, the board of directors of the Friends of the Hendricks County Historical Museum, Inc. I must give special thanks to Judy Pingel, who opened up her personal collection of photographs to me, and to Phyllis Walters, who assisted me greatly with the Plainfield Library Collection. Additionally, my thanks go to Susan Carter and Reann Poray, who have a wonderful Indiana Room at the Plainfield-Guilford Township Public Library. At the Danville Public Library, Cindy Rutledge has been of immeasurable help to me, and she was ably assisted by Rose Ann Sigborn. People in the community have been wonderful in their interest in the book and their desire to help. There are many more pictures that I would have loved to include in the book, and every contribution has been valuable. Therefore my thanks to John Bowden, Terri Bowden-Balon, the Danville Conservation Club, the Danville Community School Corporation, Dr. Denis Ward, Pat Fuson, Mike Peters, P. J. Hamann, Tina Carlton, Suzy Freeman, Hendricks County, the county commissioners, Judy Wyeth, Judge Jeff Boles, the Danville Republican, Betty Weesner, Betty Bartley, Lynda Morgan, Robert and Gloria Higgins, Dave Kersey, Marilyn Barber, Verna Barber, Robert Kelly, Cheryl Phillips, Bill Micheli, Robert Davidson, Owen and Lucille Stamper, Hendricks Regional Health, Aimee Ketterer, Kathy and Larry Witte, Danville Chamber of Commerce, Amanda Jensen, Clayton Public Library, Walter and Loretta Anderson, and my special thanks to the many people who have said that they want to buy this book.

My particular thanks to Anna Wilson and Arcadia Publishing for guiding me through the route of author "want-to-be" to author. Your imprint fills a very deep and deserving need in American history.

My deepest thanks go to my parents, Keith and Ann Baldwin, for their love and support in any project that I undertake, and a special thanks to them for instilling in me at a young age my love for history. My thanks, also, to my children and their families, Matthew (and his wife, Christy, and their children Nathan and Jennifer), Dr. Katy (and her husband, Brian, and my "grand-animals"), Tim, and Philip (without whose technical help this book would not have been completed).

And, of course, my greatest love and thanks to my wife, Pat, who will (I hope) frown and cheerfully bear the burden if I ever attempt to write another book!

INTRODUCTION

This book is not intended as a comprehensive history of Danville. This book is intended, however, to highlight some of the people, places, and events that have transpired here as told from the point of view of someone who, other than while away from Danville to attend college, has lived his whole life and raised a family in Danville.

I started walking to school in first grade. As I ventured away from the street where my home was located I realized that some of the other homes in Danville looked very different from mine, which was a recently built three-bedroom ranch home.

Many of the homes had two or two and a half stories, several of them had multiple doors, and they looked like places where more than one family could live. As I asked questions I was surprised to find that Danville had once been the home to a college, and that these homes around town were where students lived with the families of Danville.

As my range expanded I found the vestiges of the college as part of the Danville High School whose east end bore the name of Hargrave Hall. I began to hear stories of the days when Danville had lots of restaurants around the public square and all were full of faculty and students and staff and Danville residents. This was difficult to comprehend as my elementary-aged eyes saw only the Coffee Cup and Waffle House on the square. We were thrilled in the late 1960s to finally get a Burger Chef in Danville! Not only could we get "the greatest 15 cent hamburger," but the driveway that circled around was a great way for the teenagers with cars to show how cool they were by "buzzing the Burger Chef!"

And so, I discovered, the architecture hints at our history.

Danville is an amazing town with an amazing history. The purpose of this book is to show some of that history with photographs that I have been able to find that illustrate snapshots of lives of some of the people who have lived here and some of the events that have happened here.

This book covers the time span of 1824 to yesterday. Danville was created in 1824 to be the county seat of Hendricks County. The site was chosen because the place to be called Danville was near the center of the land that had been set aside to call Hendricks County. And Danville is still important today as the seat of county government in Hendricks County.

The court was an important place in 1824. By 2009, the number of courts in Hendricks County has multiplied to a circuit court and five superior courts, and three towns in the county have town courts. Perhaps even more important are all the other offices that have come to be involved in county government. I suspect that hundreds of people deal with county government every week.

But surrounding this small center of government agriculture developed. The farmers needed a place to sell their surplus crops and get them to a market, and there was a necessity to have a place to buy the things that they needed on the farm that they could not make for themselves. Therefore, commerce developed around the courthouse square.

An 1865 map of the town of Danville available on Hendricks County's Web site lists the businesspeople of Danville at the time. They included three medical doctors; a dentist; five grocers; seven lawyers; a druggist; a newspaper publisher; at least two manufacturers and dealers in boots and shoes; a tanner and dealer in hides and leathers; a carpenter; a plasterer; a photographer; a hotel proprietor; two millers; a woolen factory; a marble (tombstone) dealer; an undertaker (who also manufactured furniture and chairs); a dealer in stoves, tin, copper, iron, and hardware; a pastor; a livery stable owner; a builder and repairer of carriages; a postmaster and book store owner; a dealer in all kinds of stock, including livestock; a dealer and manufacturer of harness and saddlery; a resident farmer; and the collector of internal revenue. Much has changed today!

In 1865, most of the businesses were on the courthouse square on the streets surrounding the courthouse or within close proximity. In 2009, Danville has spread out considerably, especially to the east and west along the present U.S. Highway 36.

Very few of the businesses that served a very self-sufficient horse-drawn community are even in existence today, let alone existing in the middle of town. Tombstones can be bought in town, but there is no public place to peruse your purchase other than the east or south cemeteries.

Krogers is in its third building since leaving the courthouse square in my youth, and it is far east of the downtown. IGA survived on the south side of the square until it had a fire and it, too, built a building on the outskirts of town to the west. It is no longer in existence at all. As modes of transportation changed and as the country changed, Danville changed too.

The reader should be able to get a glimpse of understanding of Danville today by looking carefully at its past, much of which is preserved in bits and pieces throughout the community. The business fronts on the courthouse square downtown have changed many times, but similarities can still be seen to those of years ago.

Several years ago I was at a national meeting of the Circus Historical Society. One of the renowned scholars of the organization asked me where I was from. Upon being told he immediately inquired as to whether I knew of John Hanson Craig, a resident of Danville, who at one time was the heaviest man alive and appeared with the circus.

Upon learning that I did know of Craig, this scholar wanted to know if Danville identified with him, much as Baraboo, Wisconsin, does today with the Ringling Brothers.

He could hardly believe it when I told him that Danville did not identify with the circus nor this man of the circus. I told him that Danville identified with Central Normal College.

Actually, Danville identifies with education. Danville was founded in 1824. Some sources say that by 1829 the Danville Seminary building was being constructed at what would later become the site of Central Normal College, Danville High School, and Danville Middle School. By 1860, the Danville Academy was adding on to the building previously constructed for the seminary. And in 1878, Danville brought Central Normal College from Ladoga.

But these were not Danville's only schools. Many who lived close to Danville went to one-room schools out in the township. Danville had a succession of schools, and that succession continues to this day. Danville residents have always valued a good education.

The presence of Central Normal College gave many Danville residents a lifestyle that we now would call upscale. The college had a decided effect on how all of Danville lived. There were no dormitories or fraternity houses. Therefore, students roomed with families. To make college affordable, students' room and board was a very low cost as they lived in spare bedrooms of houses all over town. In addition to their small rent, students served as house help for their landlords as they cleaned houses, washed dishes, cooked meals, helped care for the children, worked in the garden, and essentially functioned as a college-age family member. Accordingly, the effective lifestyle of Danville residents was enriched.

Accordingly, Danville residents built many beautiful homes and churches. Some of these are still in existence, and there are some wonderful pictures of some that have not stood the test of time. Some of those people, homes, and churches are highlighted here. Due to the constraints of time and space there are many that could and should have been presented but are absent from this volume.

A Central Normal College catalog early in the 20th century described Danville as follows: "Danville, the county seat of Hendricks County, is in every respect a model college town. There is not a more healthful locality anywhere. One may visit a hundred health resorts without finding water equal in its medical qualities to that of the city from the Danville overflowing wells. In Summer, Danville's beautiful streets and luxurious shade trees present a picture to be proud of. Its morality, hospitality and intelligence make it peculiarly fitted for a college town. Parents who send their sons and daughters here may know that there is no place where they could be more free from temptations and distracting influence."

There have been, however, interruptions to this nirvana of the Midwest. One such interruption was on Good Friday of 1948 when a tornado swept toward Danville from the southwest, flattening everything in its path. Large portions of Danville were devastated, including many residential areas, the Catholic church, and the Christian church.

Yet another interruption put Danville in the national news in both print and on television. This interruption was not as devastating as the tornado, but it hit the suburban commuters of Danville where they lived most—on U.S. 36 coming into the center of town from the east—at rush hour. And this interruption created a mystery that has not been solved to this day.

It is hoped that every reader learns something about Danville that was not known before, even if the reader has lived in town for their whole life. However, if the person exists who knows everything about Danville that is disclosed in this book it is hoped that the recollection will bring to the reader's lips a smile in recognition of a wonderful memory.

But what makes Danville different? It is nothing that you can see or touch or smell. It is something that you feel! You feel it in your heart when you are greeted warmly on the street. You can sense the deep roots of some of the residents in ancestors from centuries long past. They are related to practically everybody! But they, too, warmly greet someone who has been in town for only a week. This is not a town of suburbanites who have recently moved in. This is a town with a core of people who have lived here for a long, long time. However, when you move in to live and work and raise your family they welcome you like an old friend, and they are happy to have you be a resident of Danville.

As you visit Danville by way of this book please let me extend my greetings to you. Welcome to Danville!

One

Agriculture and Business

This land was called the "New Eden." People came from Virginia, the Carolinas, Pennsylvania, Ohio, and all over the east looking for more land. More land was the secret to success. With more land people could raise more crops. If people raised more crops they could sell them for more money. If they made more money they could buy more things for their families.

And so people came to Hendricks County, a place in central Indiana where the soil was good (at least in many areas), the weather was tolerable, and the threat of Native Americans was minimal.

Danville had been designated as the county seat. And so they settled on the farmland around Danville, and they raised their crops and their livestock, and when they needed something that they could not make or when they were ready to sell what they had produced they went into town.

The shopkeepers were no fools, either. They had figured out what a farmer would buy and they had figured out what a farmer would sell, and when the farmer and his family came into town the shopkeepers were ready to serve.

At first when the farmers came to town they rode their horses and drove their carriages. As time went on they started buying cars and trucks, and stores developed in town that catered to the needs of cars and trucks. The livery stable and the carriage dealer went away. Gradually the needs of the families in the area grew less agrarian and more suburban, and the business community changed to follow the needs of the community. This is reflected in the changing business around the courthouse square. Reflected, too, are the styles of the day in such business dressings as awnings on the buildings and streetlamps to light the night.

The flow of business is a reflection of the flow of the changing times.

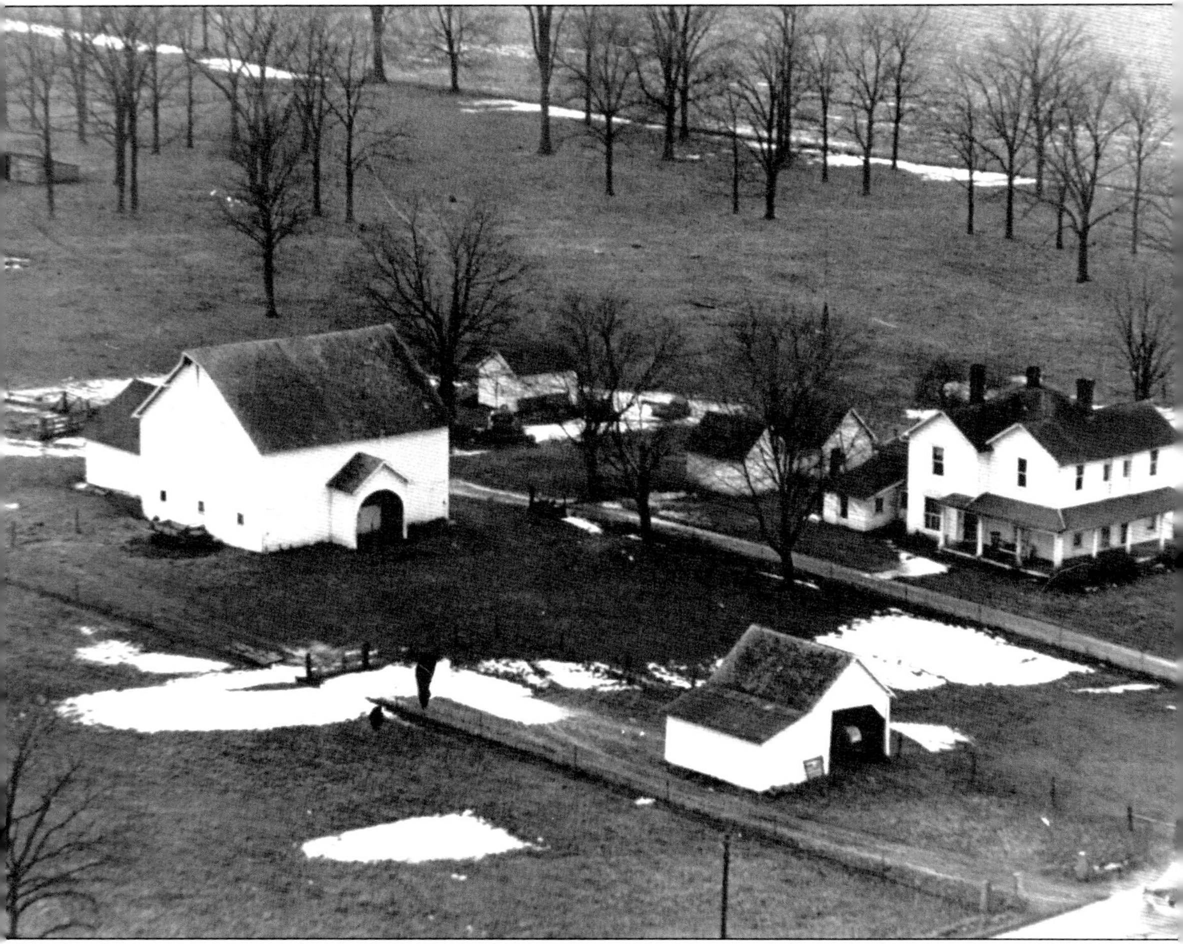

Many of the residents of the Danville area today trace their roots to ancestors who were early farmers in the area around the new county seat. This aerial view shows the farmstead of Harvey and Elsie McLane Higgins. The house was lit by gaslight before being converted to electricity. Marble fireplaces adorned many of the rooms. The porch surrounded three sides of the house. Outbuildings included the barn, the scale shed, a coal shed, a wood shed, and a smokehouse. Of course, other sheds and barns were added as needed. This house, like many farmsteads, even had a windmill at one time. Farm children tried to avoid "being taken to the wood shed." (Robert and Gloria Higgins.)

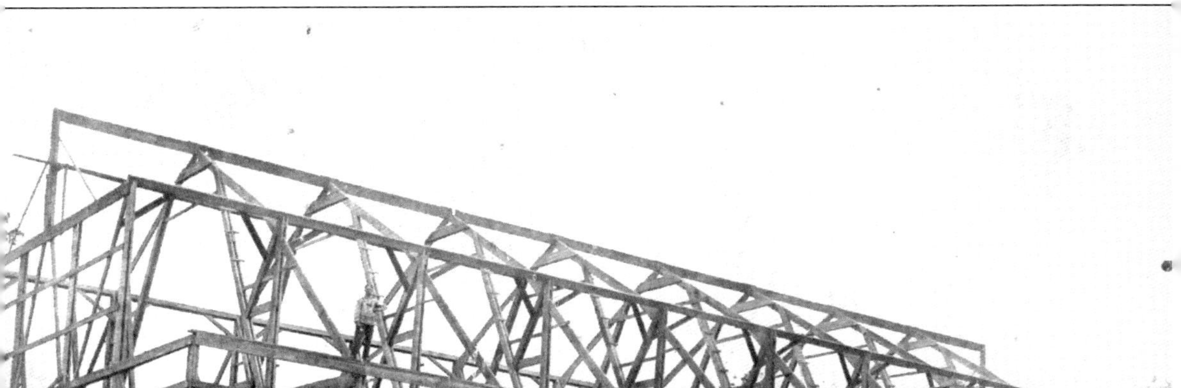

Barns were built using an inside skeleton of lumber. Several of the barns in the Danville area were built by Charles E. McLane, an ancestor of Robert Higgins of Danville. This picture does not show a large number of men working on the project, but usually that was the case. The work went much faster and safer if there were a large number of men to handle the load of weight that building a large barn entailed. (Robert and Gloria Higgins.)

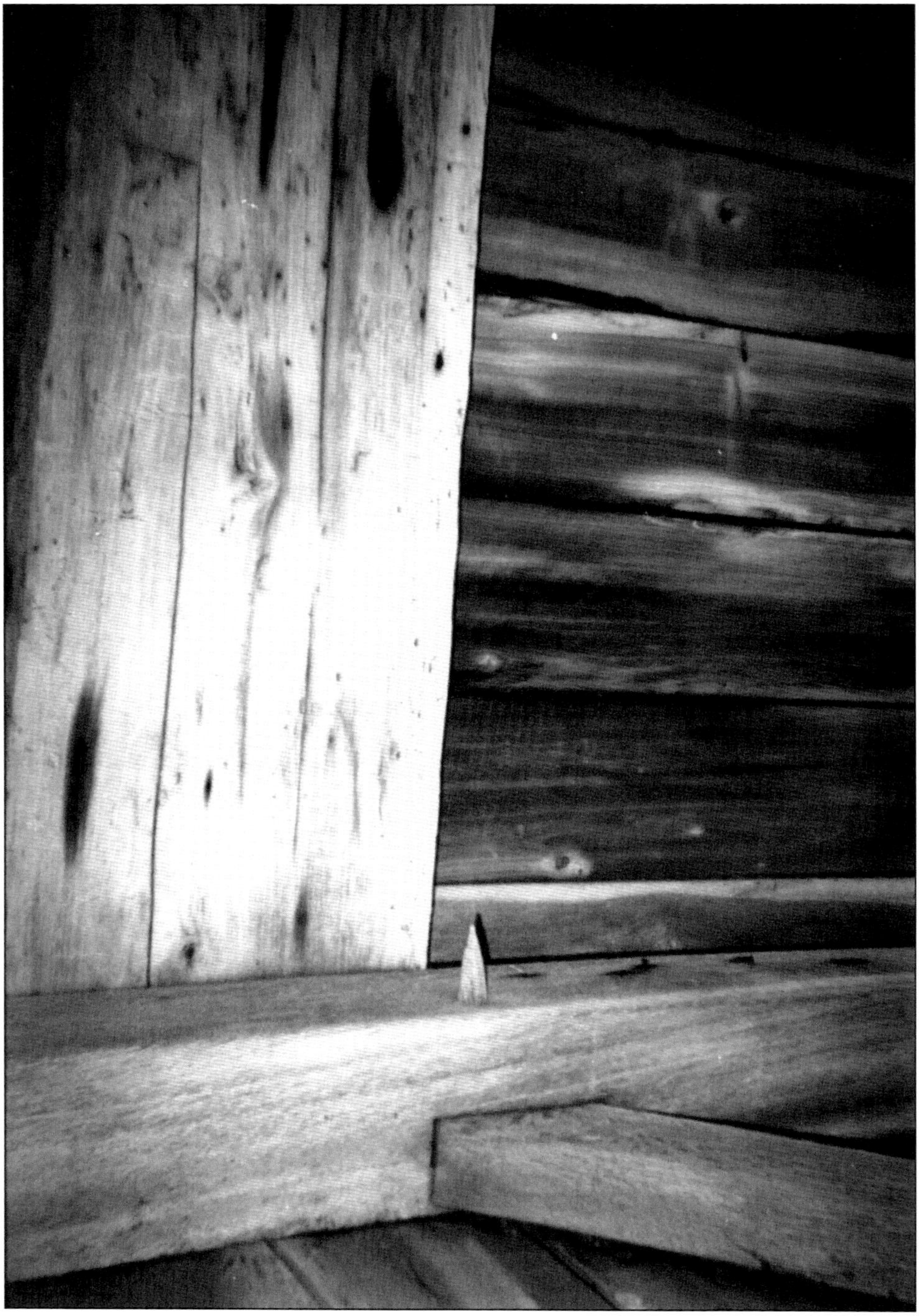

The superstructure or skeleton of the barn was fastened together using pegs. This picture shows the peg, which is a foot long, coming through the beam that is notched into place and through the support beam, protruding out the bottom of the support beam. In more modern days of barn construction, nails, screws, and bolts would commonly be used to make connections in the wood. However, as one can see, the pegs were utilitarian and long-lasting. (Robert and Gloria Higgins.)

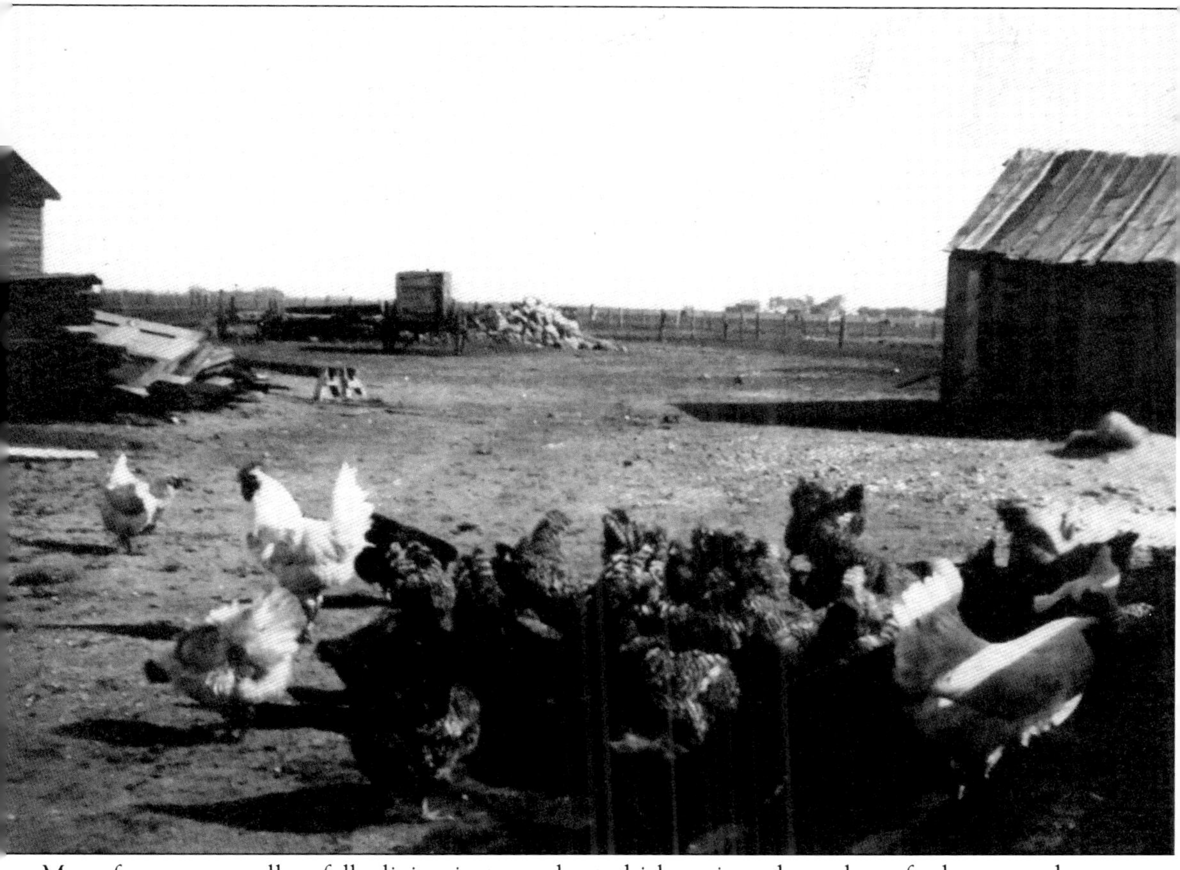

Many farmers, as well as folks living in town, kept chickens in order to have fresh eggs and the occasional fresh fried chicken or fresh chicken and noodles. In many of the restaurants in Danville early in the 20th century their Sunday lunch special was fried chicken. (Judy Pingel.)

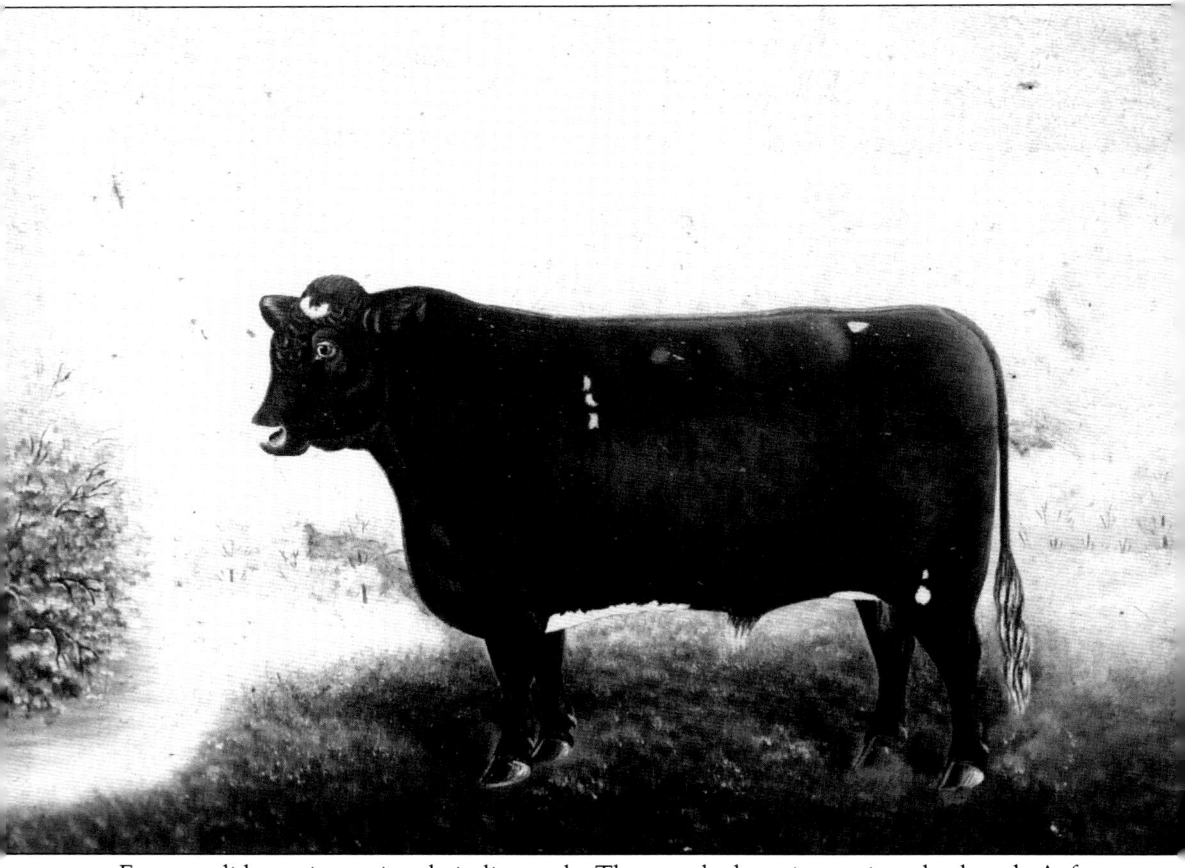

Farmers did not just raise their livestock. They worked on improving the breed. A farmer whose livestock became renowned stood to make a substantial income from selling breeding livestock to improve other herds. And when a particular animal made for a good payday every once in a while farmers wanted to have that animal's picture. This image is of a shorthorn bull belonging to Charles E. McLane. He must have had great affection for this animal. (Robert and Gloria Higgins.)

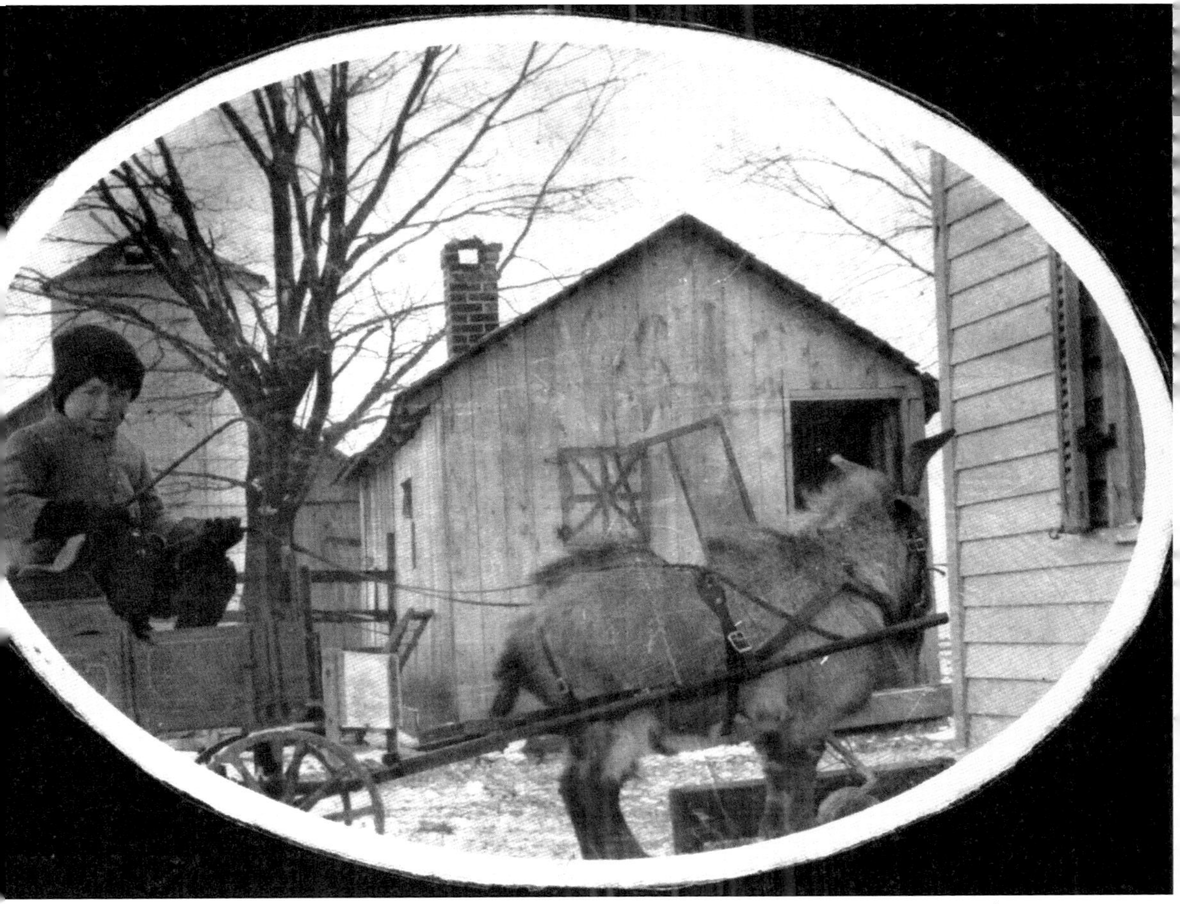

Children who lived on the farm were trained to be productive helpers at a young age. In the age of the horse, however, children did not start to learn how to drive a horse by using one of the horses but by using a goat attached to a goat cart. In this picture the youngster is wrapped up for winter but the lessons in driving were still underway. (Judy Pingel.)

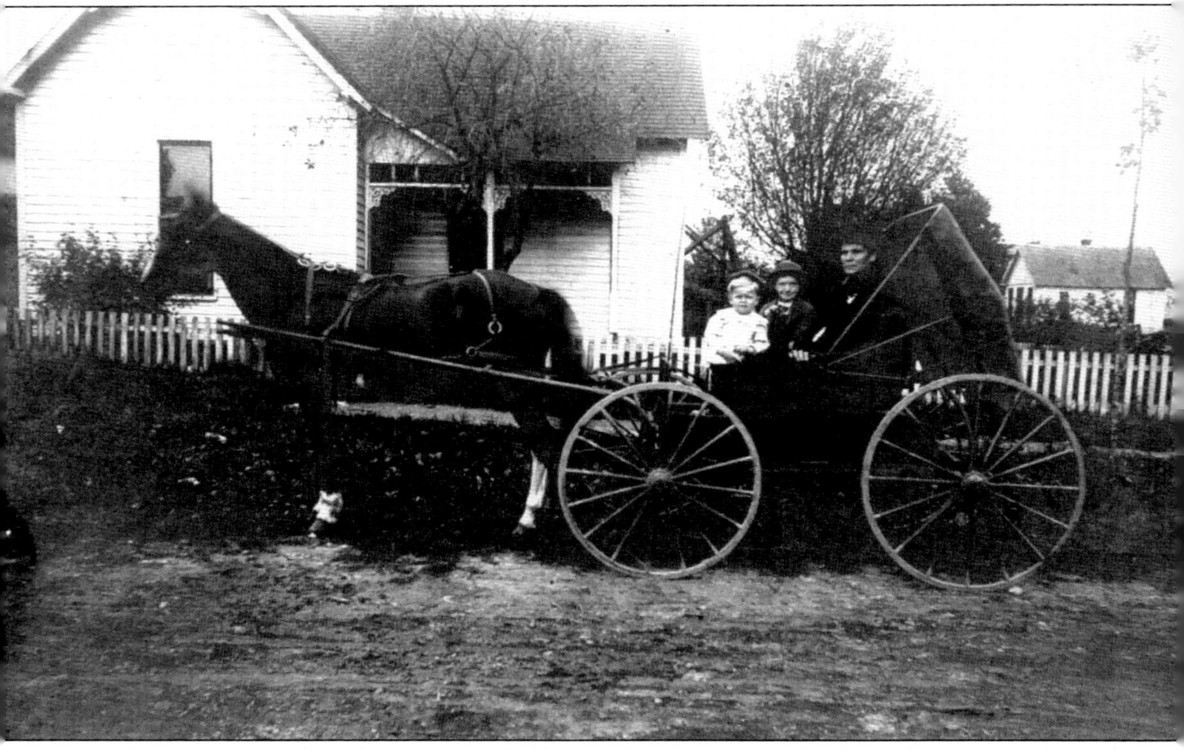

Horses were used for locomotion of all sorts. In this picture the horse has been pulling the buggy containing Mary Silery and her son Oral. The blonde boy is Floyd Parker. (Owen and Lucille Stamper.)

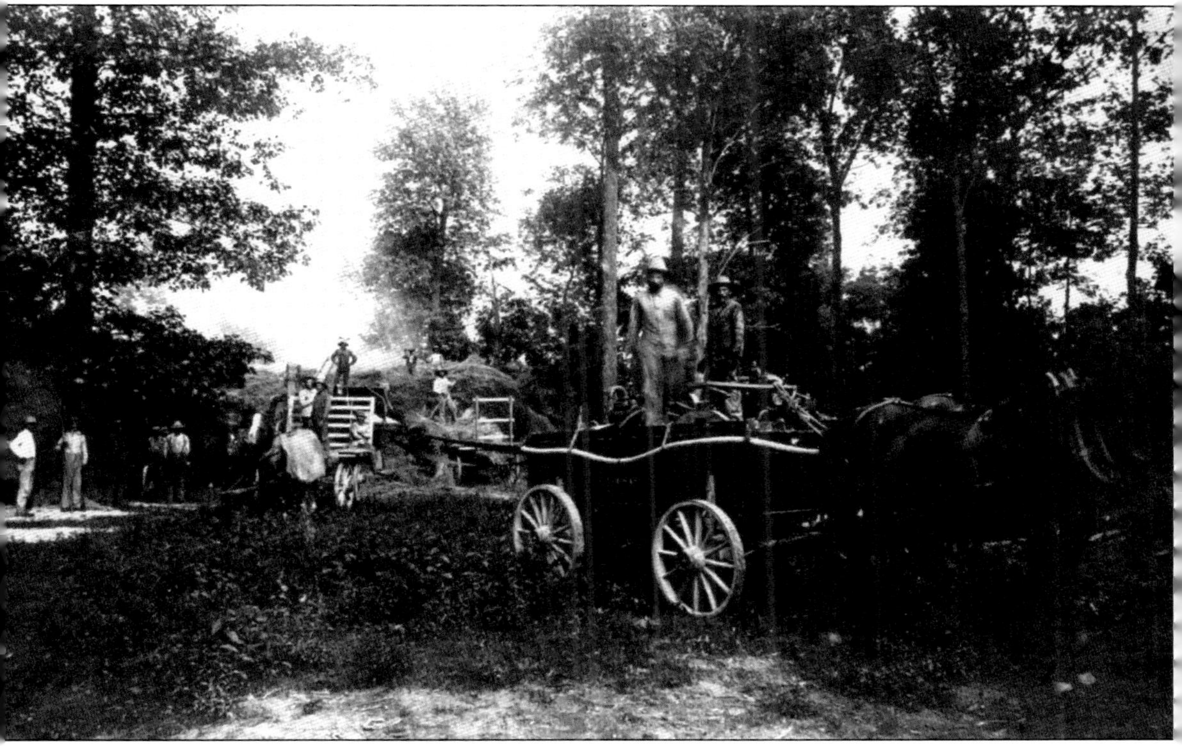

Horses provided the pulling power for work on the farm, too. This is a picture of a threshing ring in the fields of Hendricks County in the early 1900s. The belt between the wagon in front that goes toward the back is probably connected to steam-powered equipment. (Owen and Lucille Stamper.)

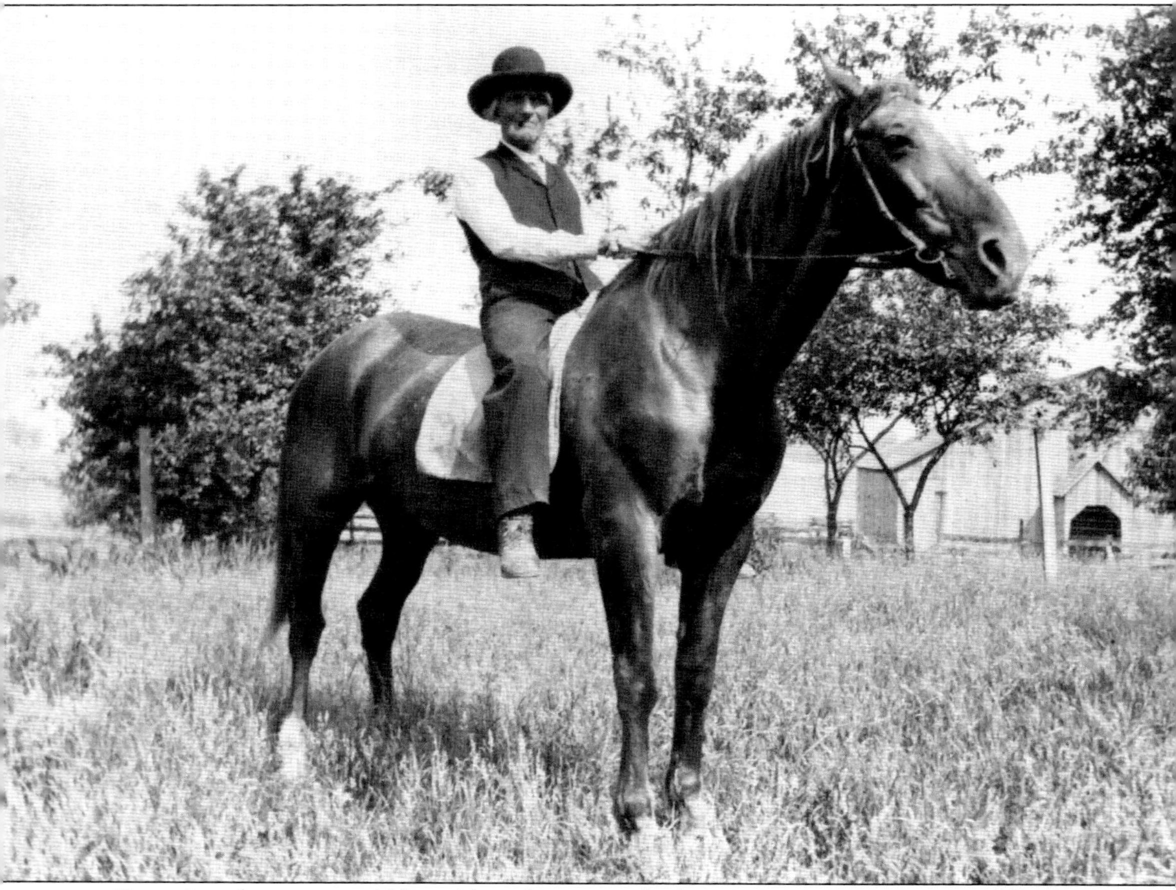

Sometimes horses were ridden without being attached to any equipment—even a saddle. Pictured is Michael "Uncle Mike" Higgins, who was born in September 1820 and moved to Hendricks County when he was only six months old. As an early pioneer of Hendricks County it is said that he was one of the few men (or women) to see all four of the courthouses that have stood in Hendricks County. Astride Ol' Jennie he is said to have led many great parades in Danville, including the one that was held for the dedication of the current courthouse on Wednesday, September 8, 1915. (Robert and Gloria Higgins.)

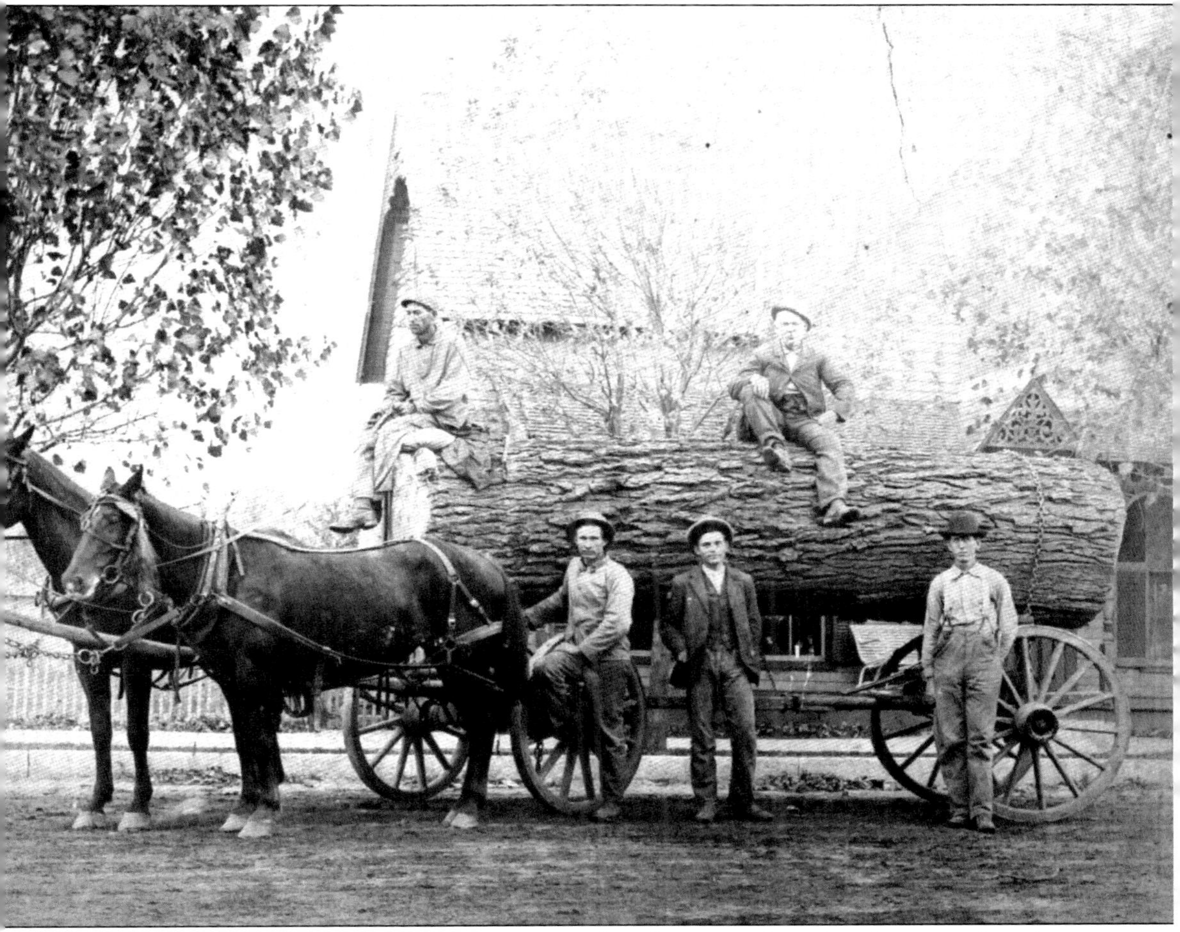

Hendricks County is not normally logging country, but this is one huge log that is ready to be rolled away by this team of horses. Other than Mont Miles (farthest left), neither the workmen nor place is identified, but it is believed to be in the Danville area. Virgin forests that had never been cut reportedly had many trees within them that were this size. This photograph is believed to have been taken between 1900 and 1920. (Judy Pingel.)

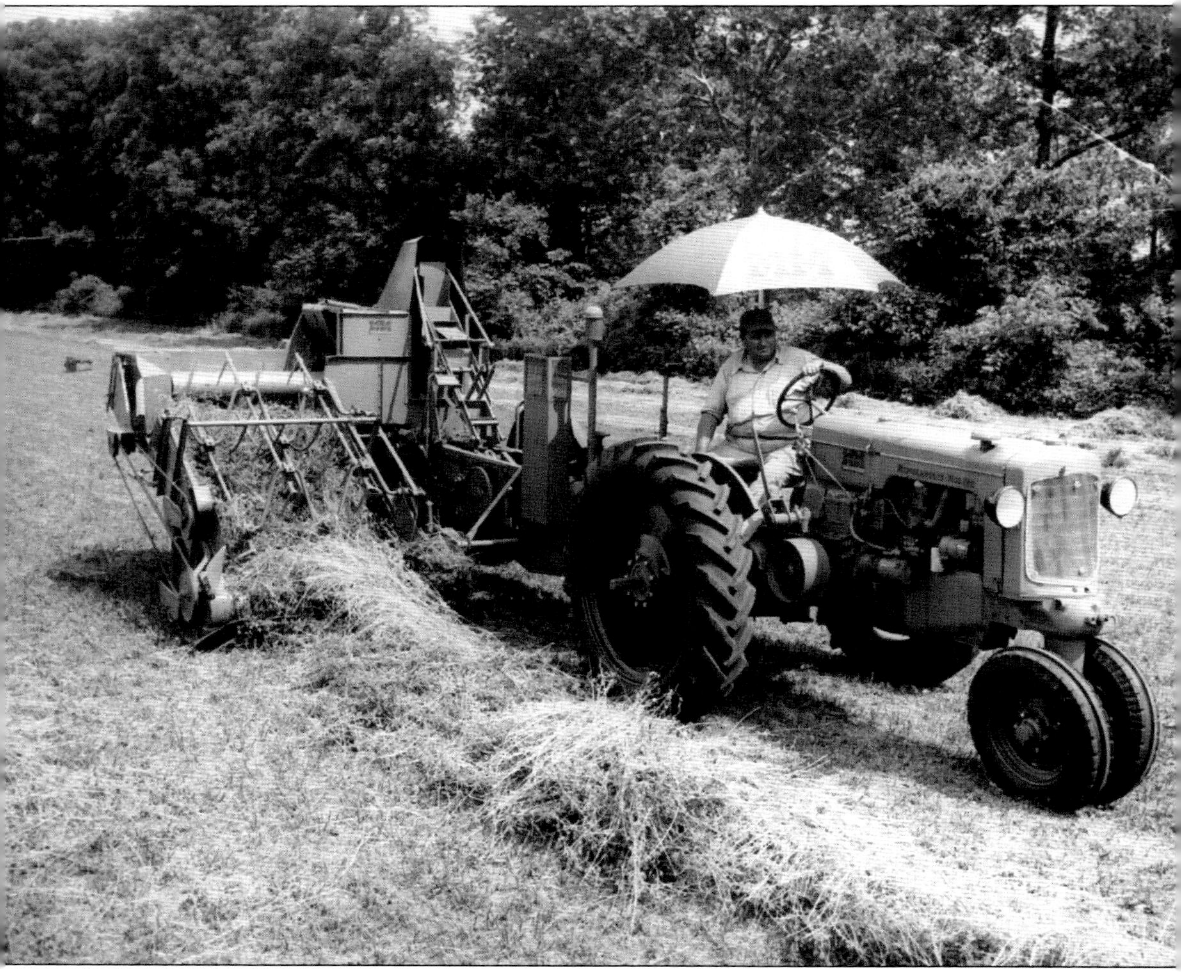

Gradually horsepower gave way to tractors with multiples of horsepower. In this photograph Chester Martin is shown baling hay on the property that eventually became the site of Danville North Elementary School. (Judy Pingel.)

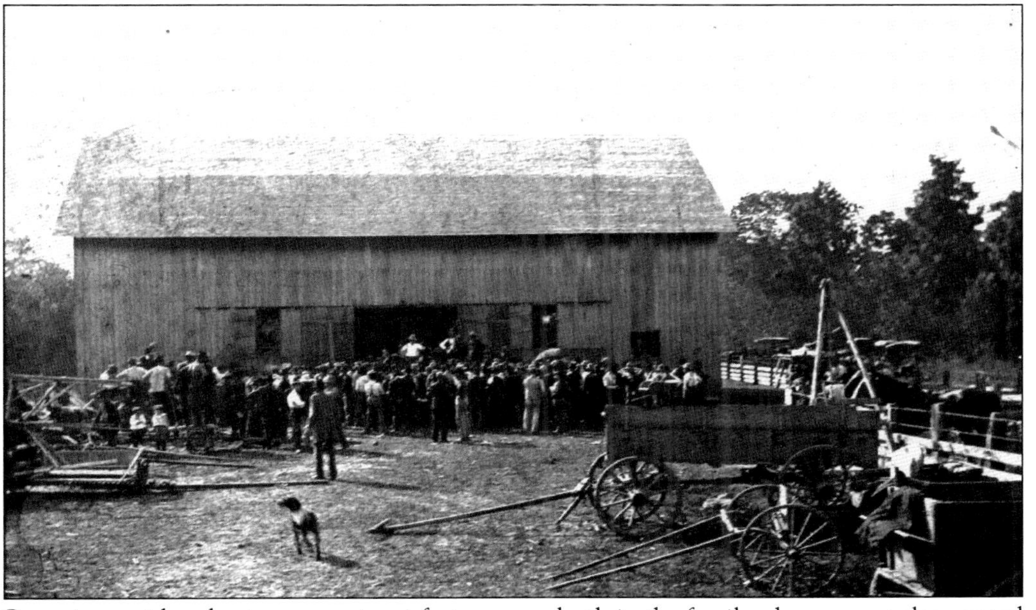

Sometimes, either due to economic misfortune or a death in the family when no one else wanted to pursue farming, the accumulated tools, equipment, and livestock of the farmer were liquidated by an auction. It is not known exactly when or where the auction took place. The large crowd is on hand, ready to equip themselves for better farming or maybe just to find a bargain. (Judy Pingel.)

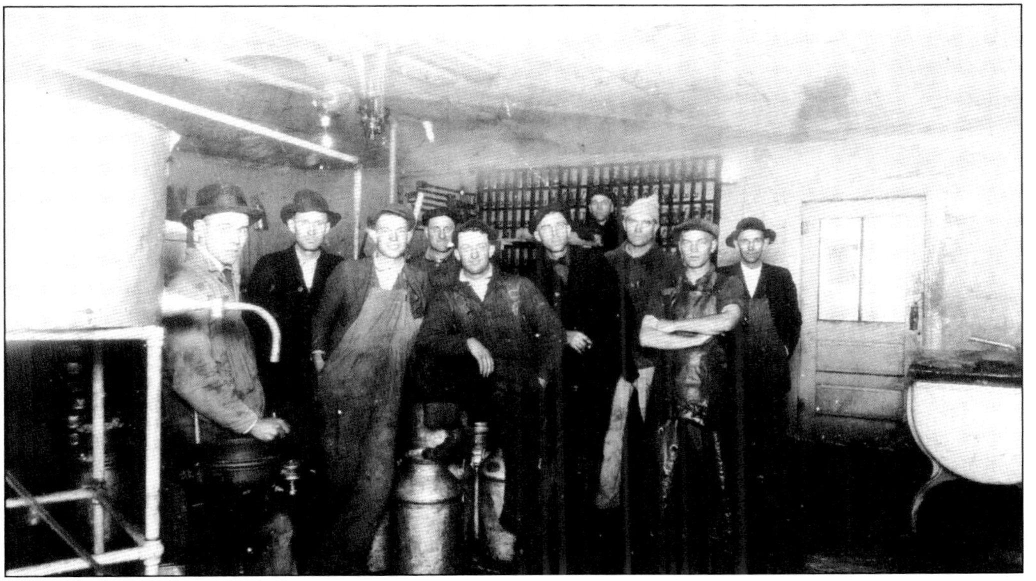

Gradually the farm life intersected with town life. Farmers began collecting so much milk from their cows that they had milk to sell. People in town found it too troublesome to keep a cow for milk, so they bought their milk from the surplus of the farmers. This picture is inside the Ballard Creamery, probably on Klondike Street (now Lincoln Street) on the south side of Danville. These are the route drivers who take trucks out to the farms around Danville and collect the milk that is to be sold. Mont Miles is in back. (Judy Pingel.)

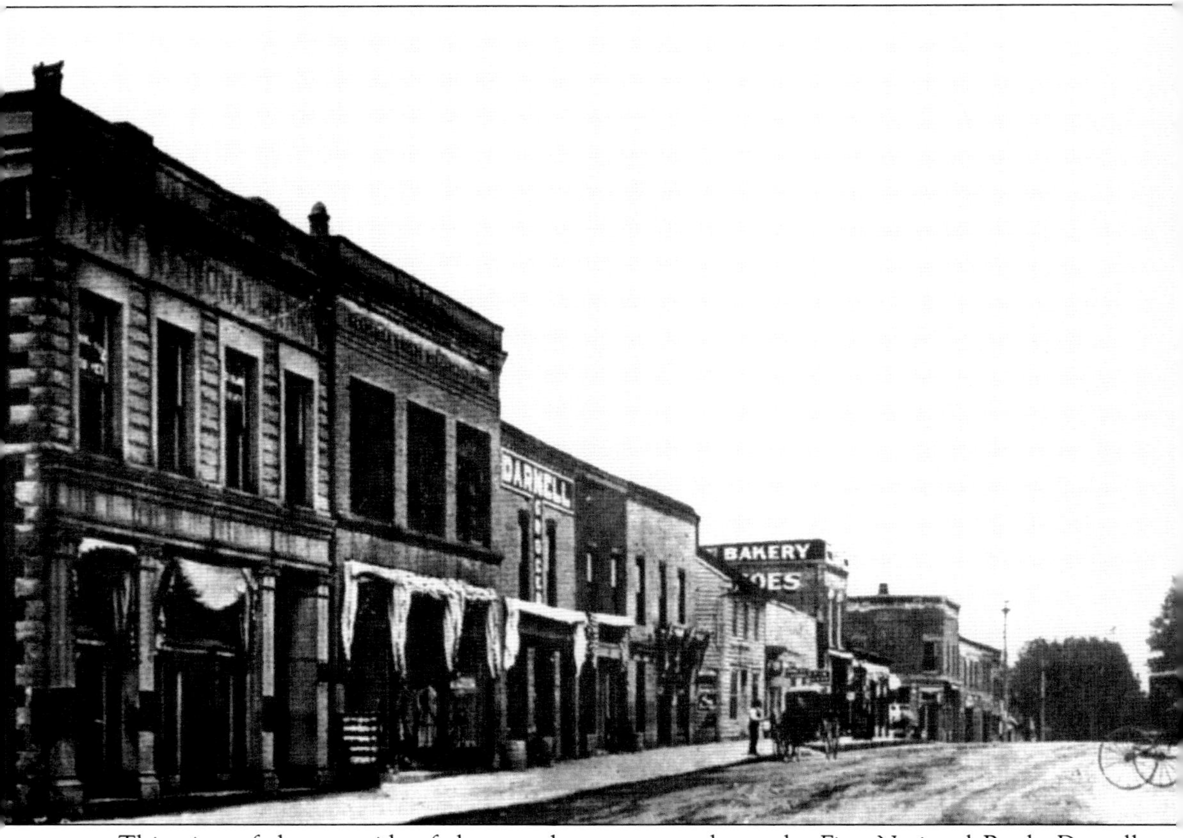

This view of the east side of the courthouse square shows the First National Bank, Darnell Grocery, a bakery, a peek at the southeast corner of the square, and several buggies. Up near the tops of the buildings at the farthest part of the street that is seen are streetlamps. It appears that Washington Street is just a dirt road. (Hendricks County Museum.)

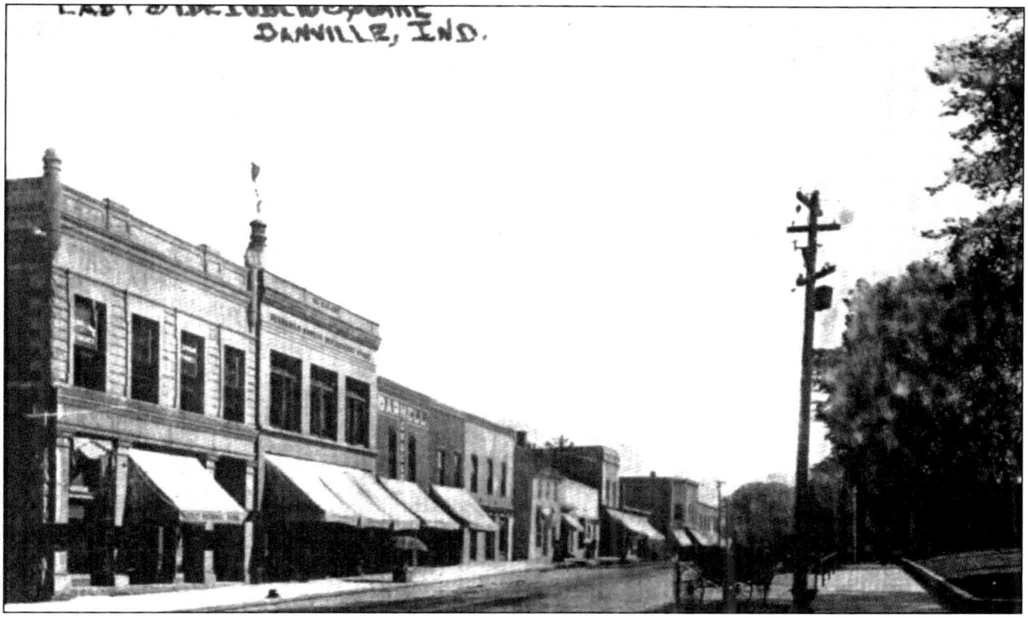

This picture of the east side of the courthouse square is from about 1910. Notice that the awnings are extended. This picture is taken from a bit farther to the west than the previous picture, and it allows one to see the hitching posts for the horses. Several of the businesses are the same as in the previous picture. (Hendricks County Museum.)

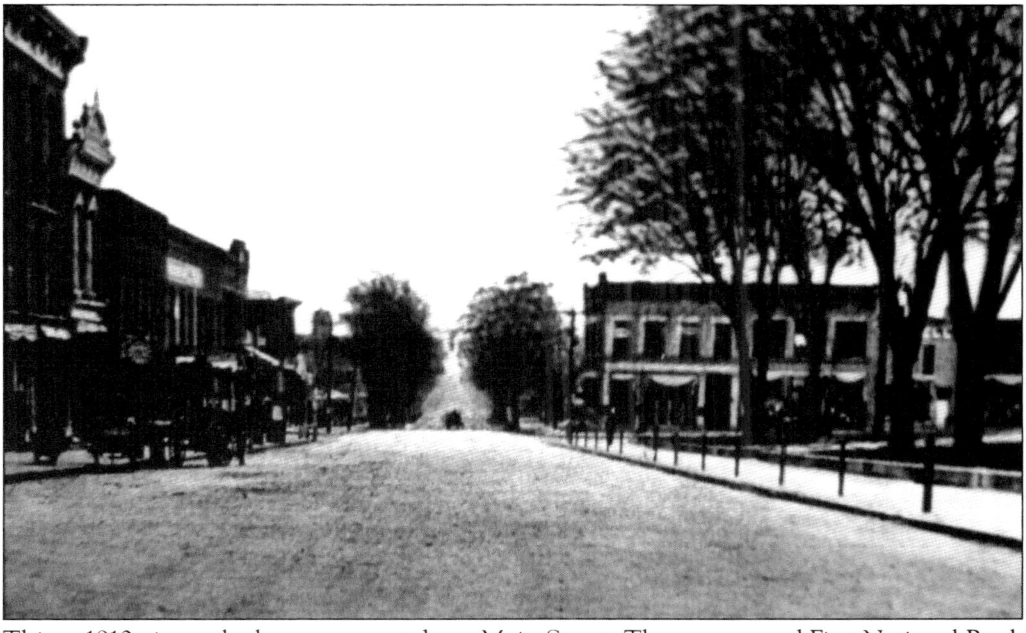

This c. 1910 picture looks west to east down Main Street. The area around First National Bank looks similar to the last picture. However, down the street to the left of the tree the tower from the recitation building at the college is apparent. Note the clock on the building on the north side of the square. The slope in Main Street from the square down toward "College Hill" is very pronounced in this view. (Hendricks County Museum.)

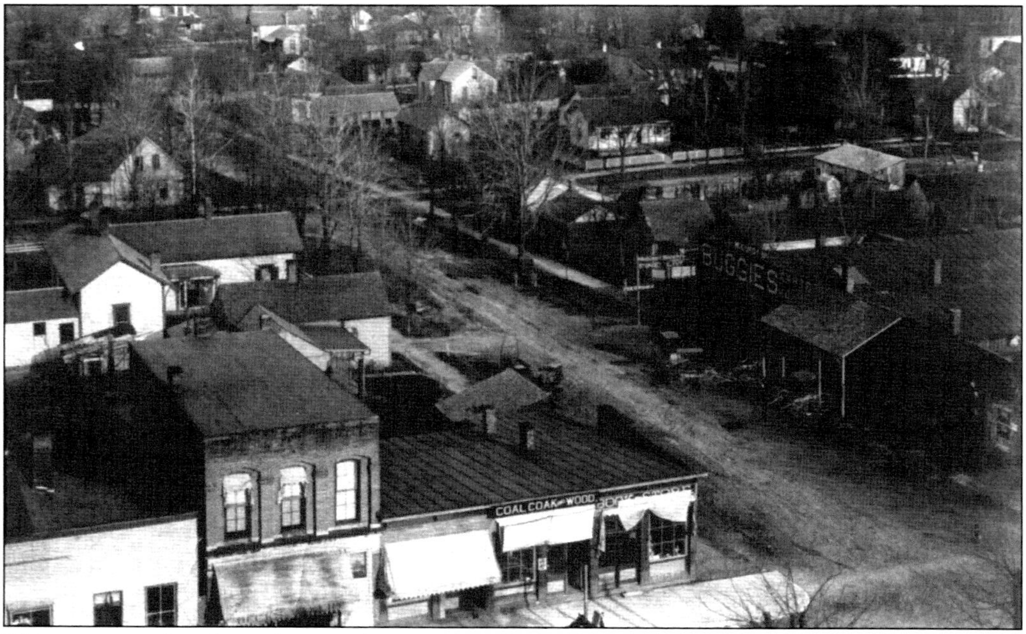

This picture, taken from the courthouse tower, shows the southeast part of the courthouse square on to the southeast part of Danville. It shows where the coal and wood seller was, as well as the livery stable where buggies are advertised in huge letters. Looking on, one can see houses in the southeast part of town, perhaps as far as East Broadway Street. (Hendricks County Museum.)

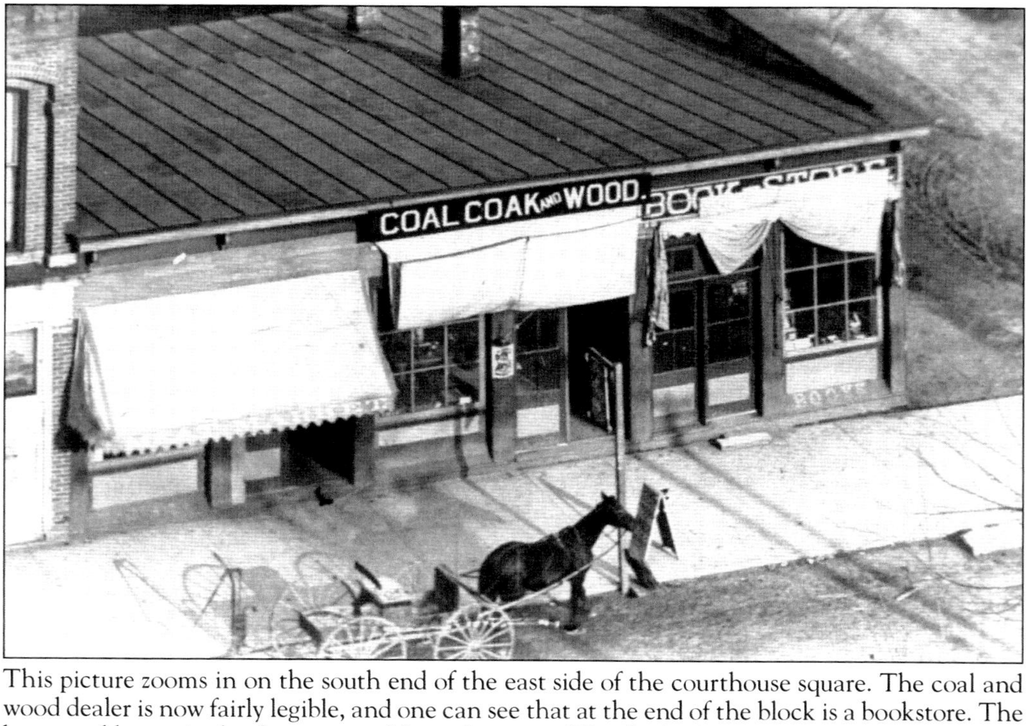

This picture zooms in on the south end of the east side of the courthouse square. The coal and wood dealer is now fairly legible, and one can see that at the end of the block is a bookstore. The horse and buggy is also far more visible in this view. (Hendricks County Museum.)

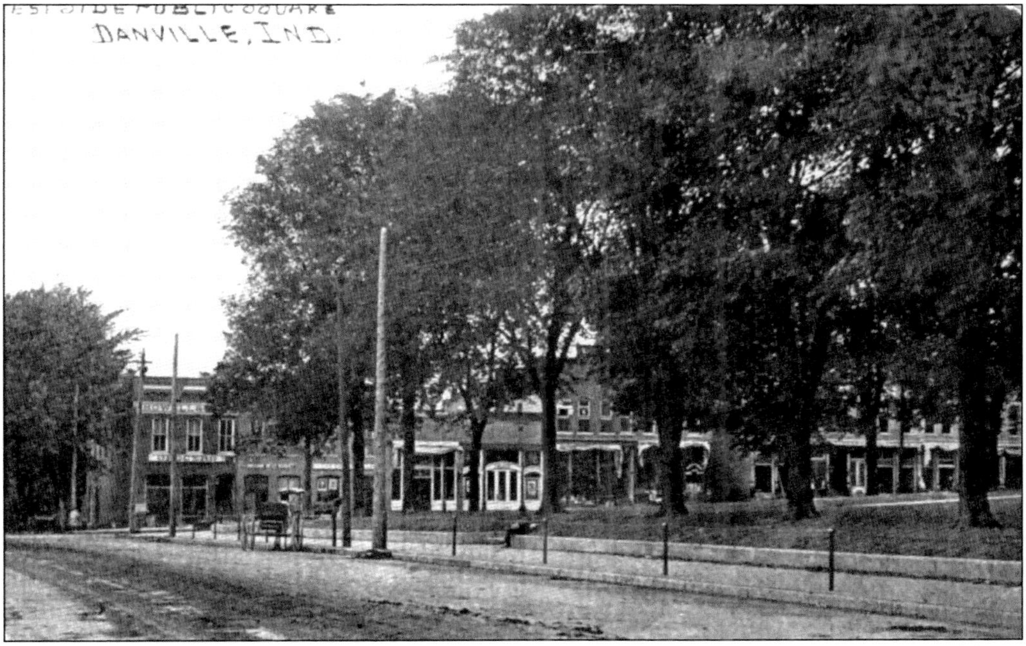

This view shows the west side of the public square from the south. On the south end of buildings there is what looks to be a grocery and next to that is a meat market. Note the tops of the facades of the buildings here as compared to other views of the west side of the square. (Hendricks County Museum.)

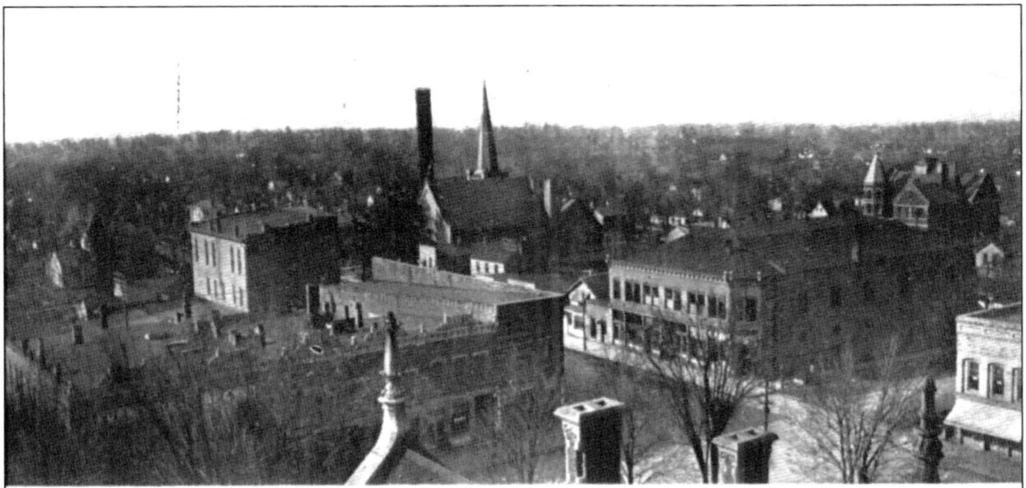

BIRDSEYE VIEW OF DANVILLE, INDIANA, LOOKING NORTHWEST FROM COURT HOUSE TOWER

This view of Danville looks northwest from the courthouse tower. At far right is the intersection of Jefferson Street and Main Street. To the left (west) is the County Fair Building, named for its size. For many years this building was home to Danner's five-and-dime store, which supplied toys, craft materials, and more. Farther left is the spire of the Danville Christian Church, and to the left of the spire is the Danville standpipe (water tower), built in 1892. Behind the County Fair Building, the building with a pointed tower is Danville High School, which stood at the corner of Cross and Clinton Streets from 1900 to 1928. (Hendricks County Museum.)

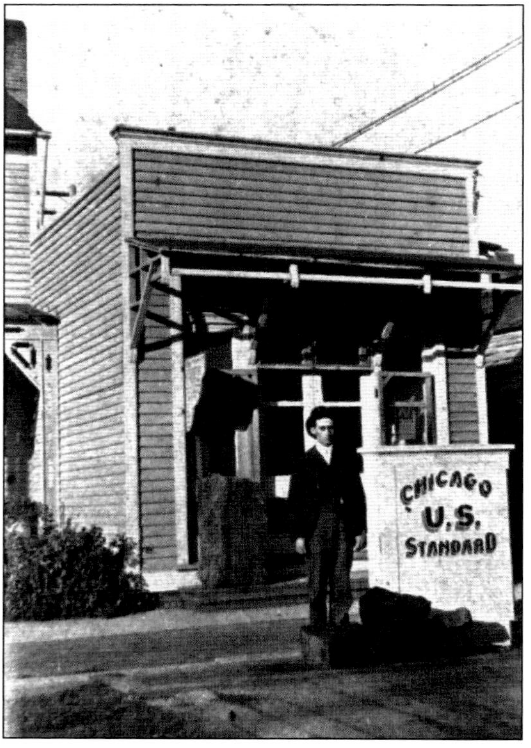

Pictured here is businessman Ira Martin at his business just west of the County Fair Building in the previous photograph as it fronts on Main Street. Later these little buildings were subsumed by expansions of the County Fair Building west to the alley so that it bordered the Danville Christian Church. (Guilford Township Historical Collection, Plainfield-Guilford Township Public Library.)

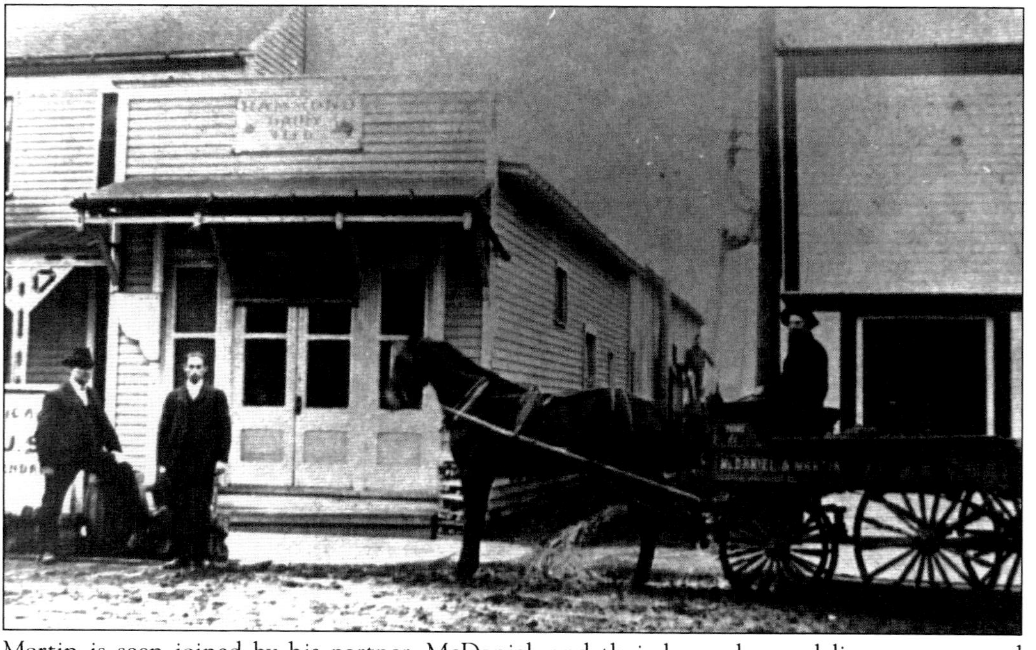

Martin is seen joined by his partner, McDaniel, and their horse-drawn delivery wagon and accompanying driver. Note that Main Street appears to have no kind of paving or covering of any kind. A fellow, somehow elevated in the alley, also unexpectedly got into the picture. (Guilford Township Historical Collection, Plainfield-Guilford Township Public Library.)

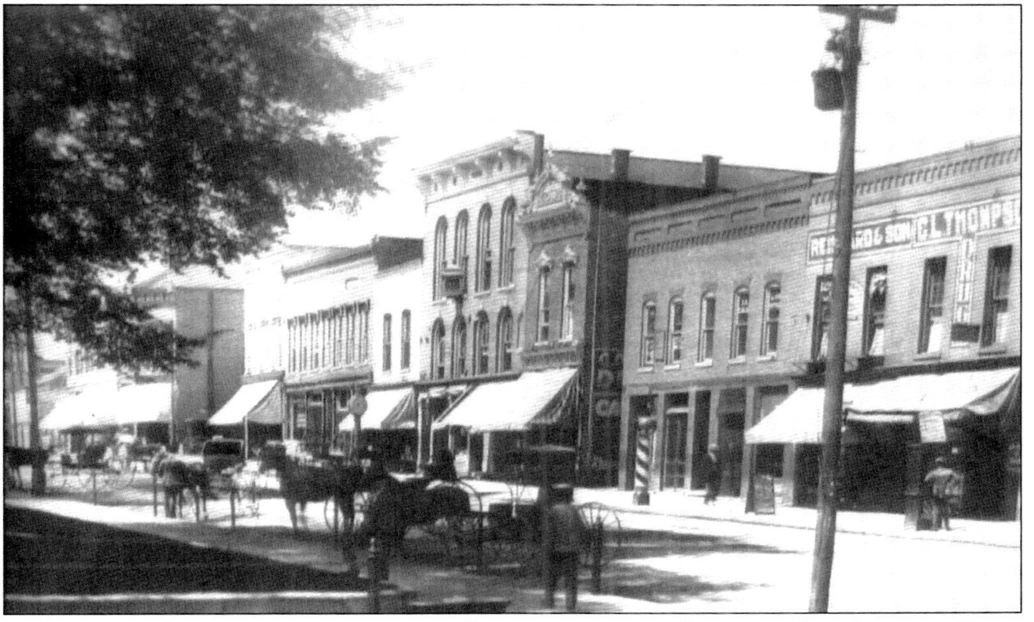

This picture and the following show Danville Square's north side. Notice the Thompson Drugs sign. Thompson Drugs ceased operation in the 1990s. Also note the streetlamps in use at the time. At left in the picture is the County Fair Building, which housed Hendricks County's largest department store. (Author's collection.)

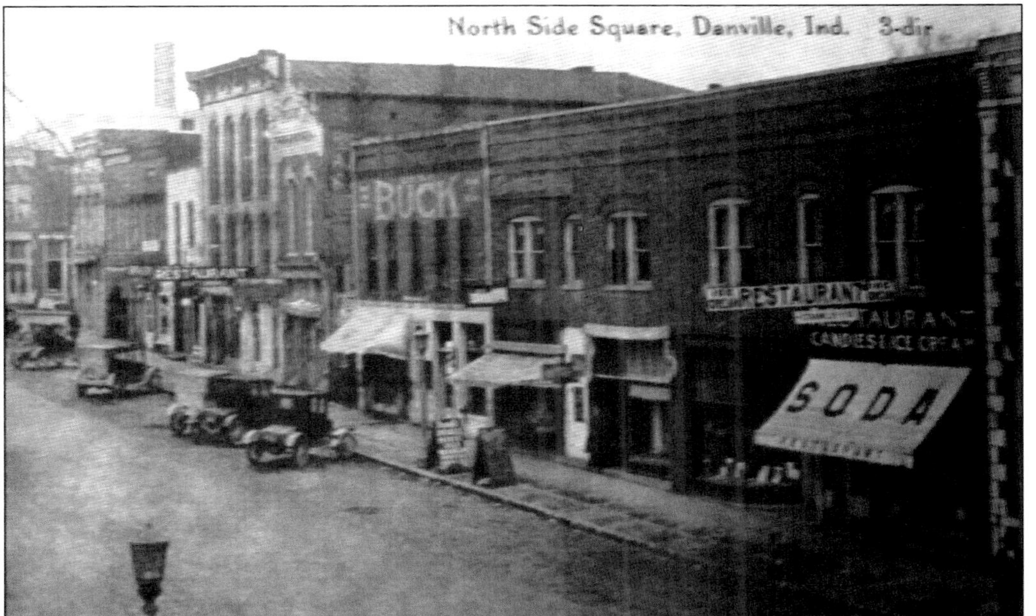

Looming over the County Fair Building in the left quarter of this photograph is a large tower. This is to be the water company standpipe, built in 1892 and still in use in providing Danville's municipal water supply in 2009. The texture of Main Street is much changed from earlier photographs—and all the hitching posts are gone. (Author's collection.)

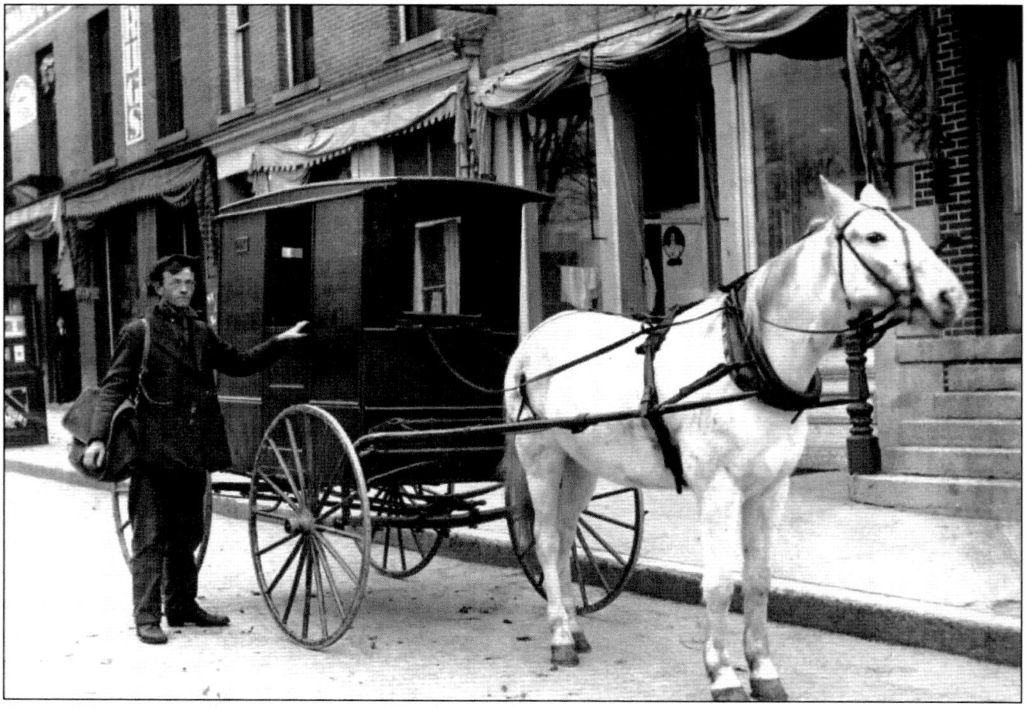

Amos Harvey stands next to a mail hack on what appears to be the north side of Main Street in front of the Thompson Drug Company. Harvey's mailbag hangs from his shoulder. An unidentified businessman stands in the background. (Guilford Township Historical Collection, Plainfield-Guilford Township Public Library.)

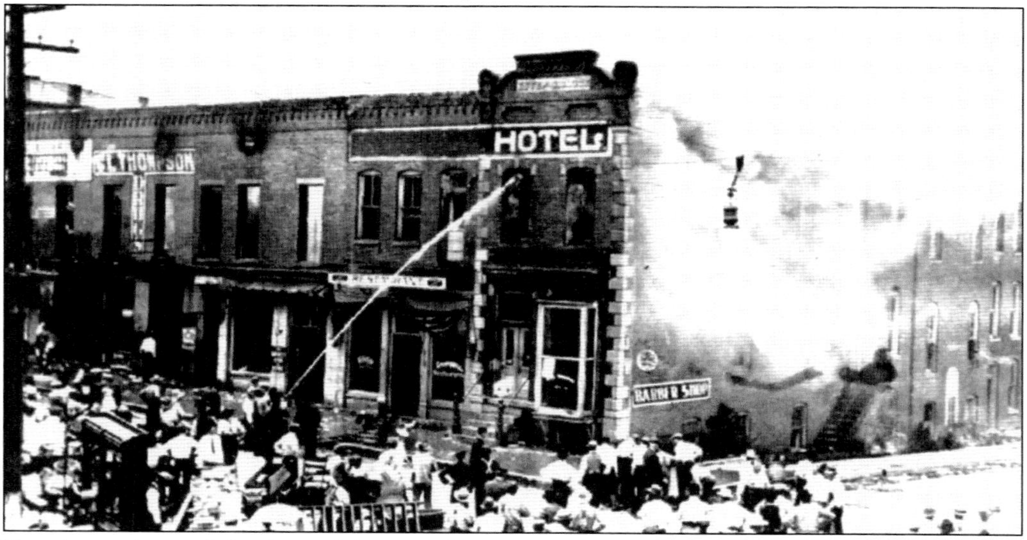

Fires have changed the face of the courthouse square many times. Firemen aim their hose at the hotel on the north side of the square at Main and Washington Streets. Buildings east of the alley were damaged by this blaze. Note the sign for the barbershop on the right side of the hotel. The shop was located down the outside set of stairs in the building basement. This building still stands on the square. (Danville Republican.)

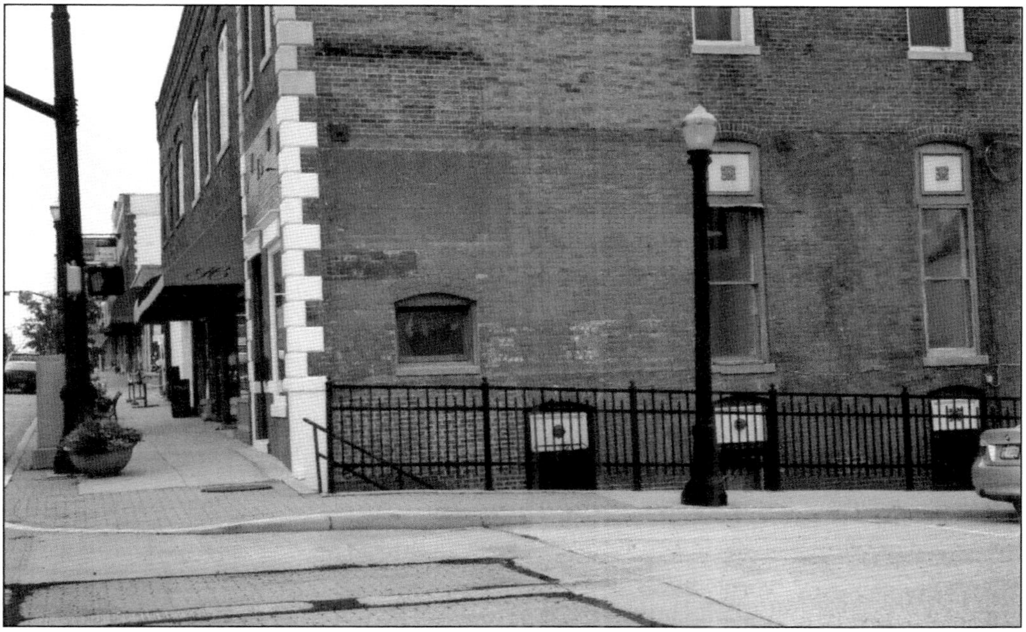

The Three Johns Barber Shop was located in the basement of the hotel on the northwest corner of Washington and Main Streets. The three barbers were black men, all named John. Many of the influential men in town got their hair cut at this barbershop, and the barbers were popular throughout the community. (Author's collection.)

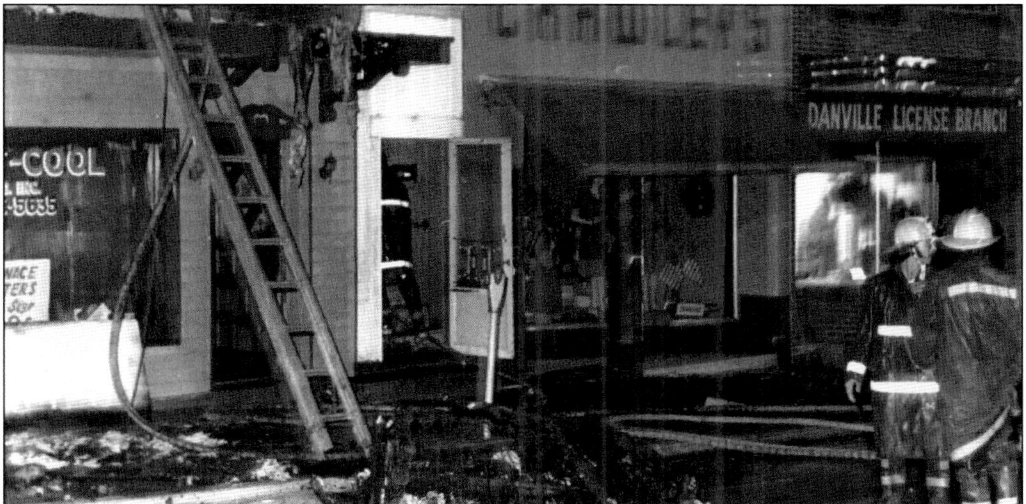

A fire occurred on the north side of the square in 1976 in the building occupied by Heat and Cool, next to the Crabb and Parker building. The fire is suspected to have started in an apartment over the store; damage was limited to adjacent stores. At the time, a fire whistle was used to call volunteers and a radio broadcast identified the nature and location of the fire. Spectators often gathered to watch the firemen work. During this fire, the author's father watched and waited to discover whether the author—in his apartment over the square—was safe and sound. (Guilford Township Historical Collection, Plainfield-Guilford Township Public Library.)

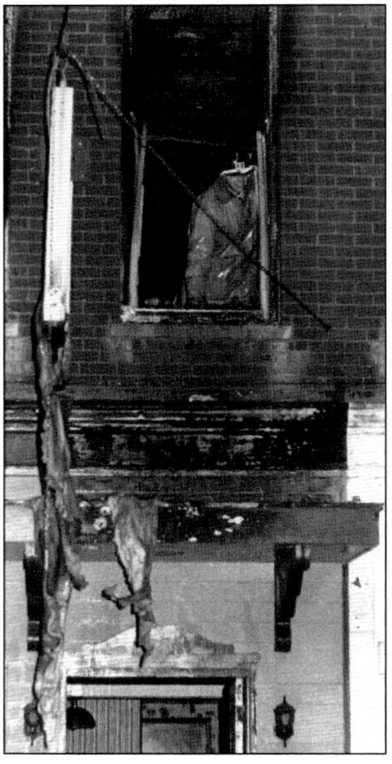

An unidentified volunteer fireman communicates with men on the ground. Danville has been served well by its volunteer fire department. For many years, at the sound of the fire siren men ran from their homes and businesses to fight a burning fire. As increasing numbers commuted to Indianapolis for work, the fire department now relies on a paid corps. (Guilford Township Historical Collection, Plainfield-Guilford Township Public Library.)

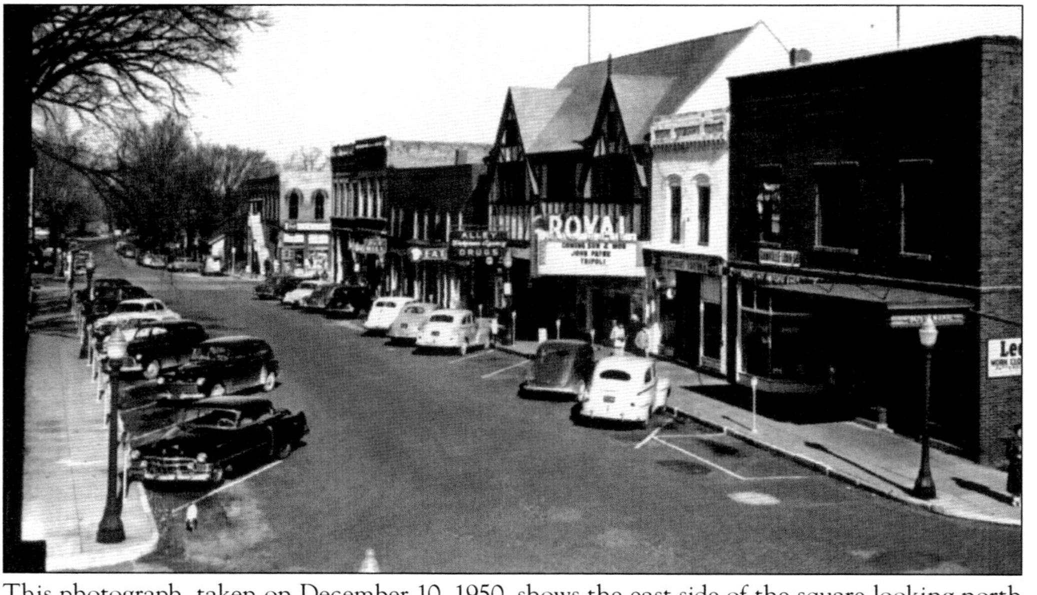

This photograph, taken on December 10, 1950, shows the east side of the square looking north toward Main Street. Notice cars parked in both directions—the square was made one way some years later. The Basket Shop can be seen at the end of the street. The first building on the near side of Main Street is the First National Bank building. The next building, which no longer exists, housed the B&W Grill. The other buildings on the block are still extant. (Hendricks County Museum.)

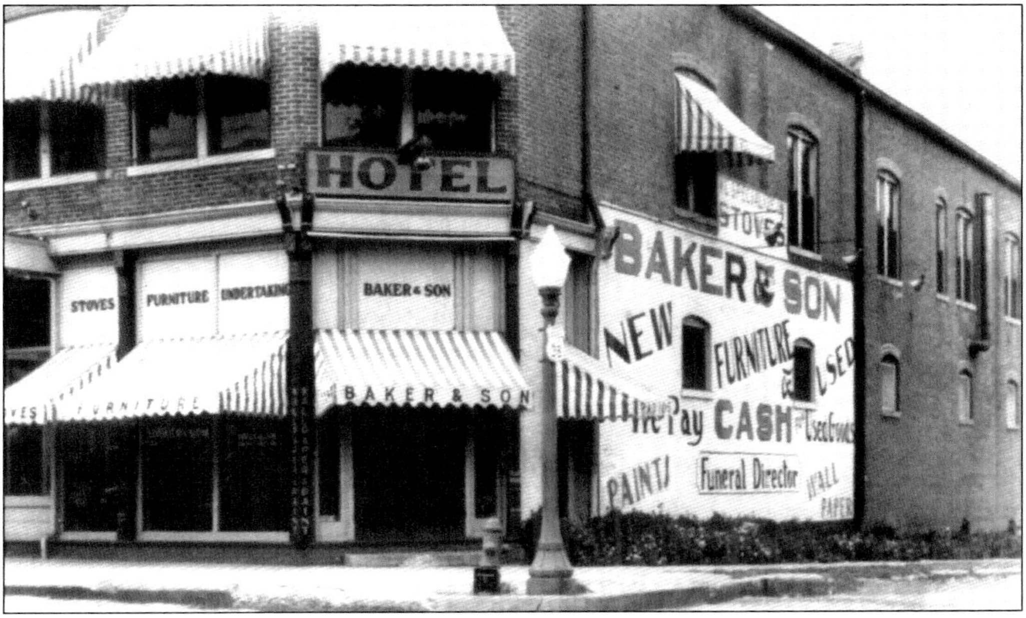

Looking in the opposite direction, toward the southeast corner of the square, the Baker and Son building can be seen. Charles E. Baker came to Danville in 1906 from Crawford County, Illinois, as a door-to-door sales agent for the W. T. Rawleigh Company. Seeing that his business would end with the advent of the automobile, Baker moved into stoves, furniture, hardware, and funerals. (Hendricks County Museum.)

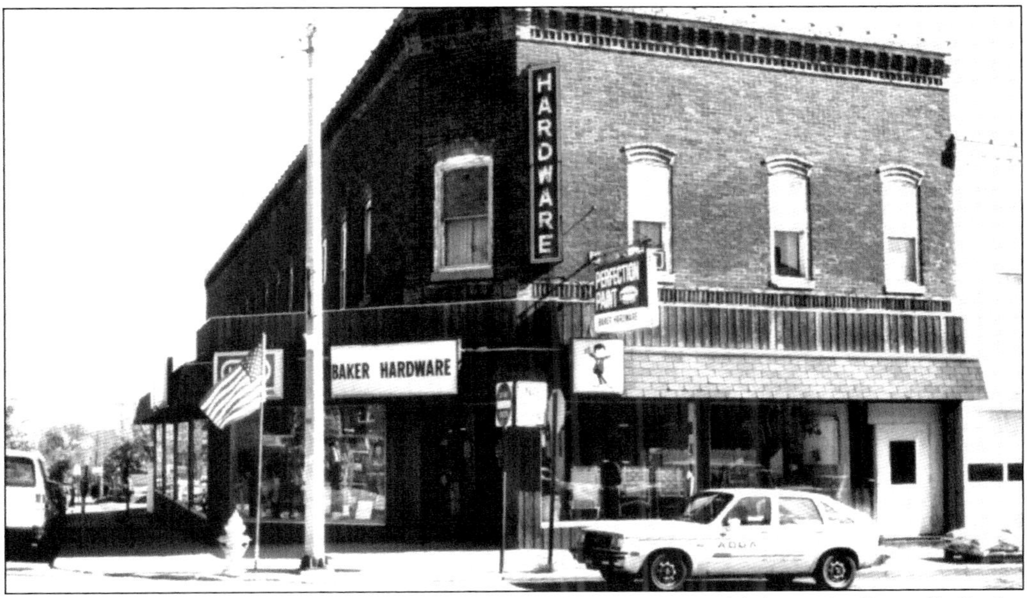

Rawleigh Baker, son of Charles, added to the family businesses, establishing the Danville Radio and Record Shop on the town square in 1946. Later he took the hardware and funeral businesses over from his father. Eventually the family focused exclusively on the hardware and funeral businesses. Baker Hardware remained housed at the same location. This building now houses the Danville Florist. (Hendricks County Museum.)

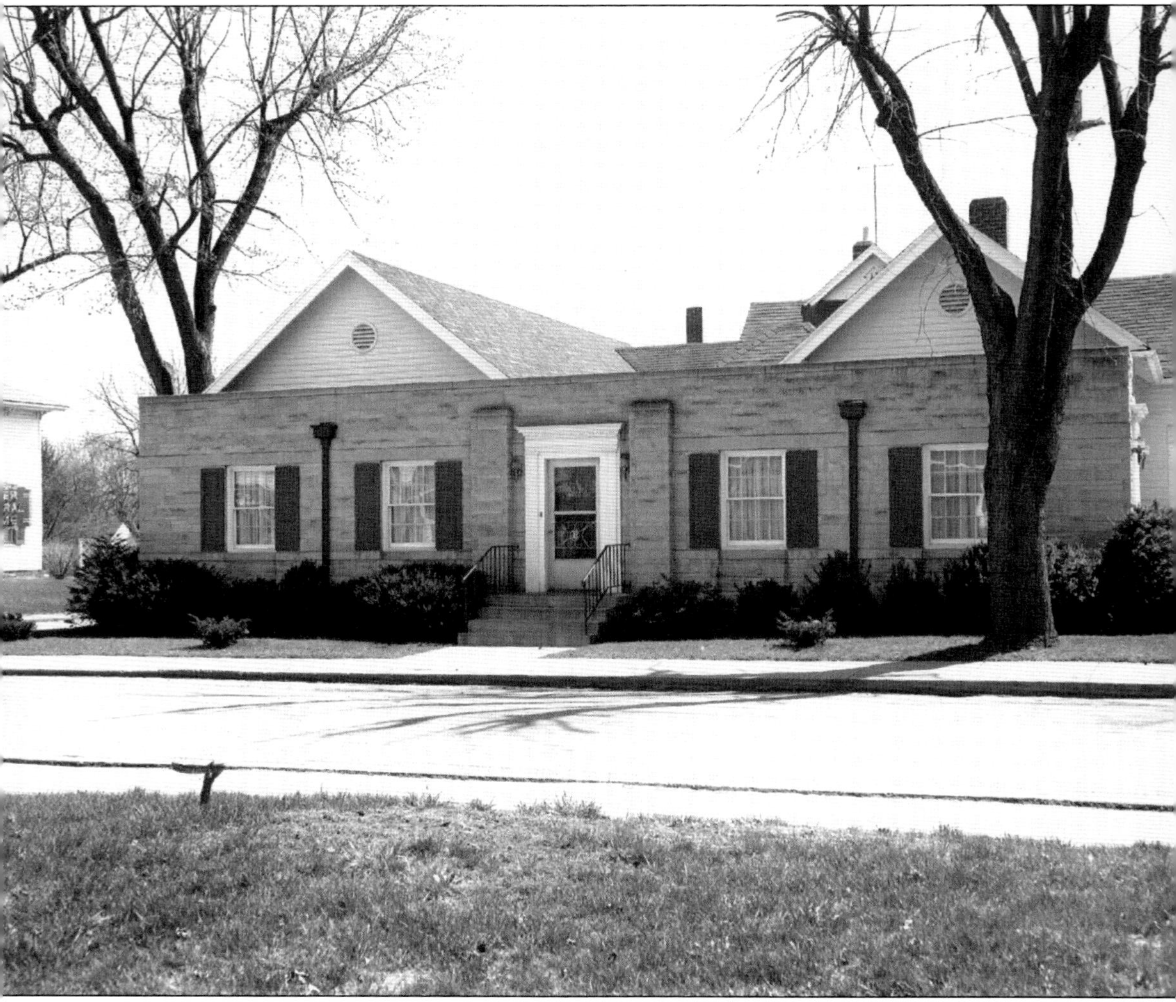

In 1923, Charles E. Baker purchased the property at 387 East Broadway, pictured above, to house the Baker and Son Funeral Home. J. Bruce Baker, a son of Rawleigh, now oversees the day-to-day activities of this long-running family business. (Indiana Room, Danville-Center Township Public Library.)

This photograph looks at the northeast corner of the square, showing the Basket Shop, Danville Republican, Danville Gazette, and the Masonic temple. The *Danville Republican* is the oldest newspaper in Hendricks County, dating its inception to 1847. Betty Weesner and Barbara Robertson ran the paper after Betty received it from her father, "Pug" Weesner, in 1974. Betty is now assisted by Lynda Morgan and Betty Bartley. (Judy Pingel.)

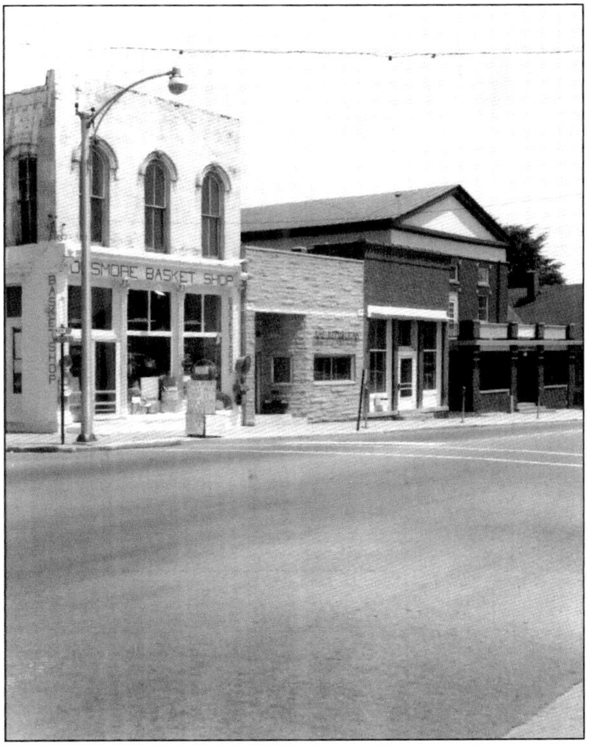

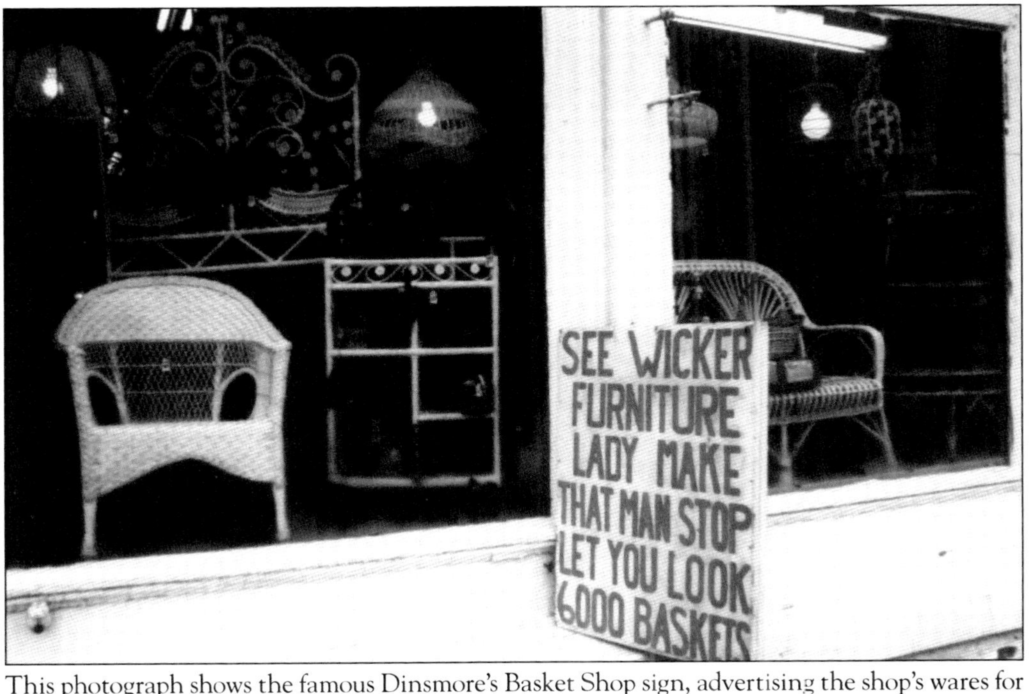

This photograph shows the famous Dinsmore's Basket Shop sign, advertising the shop's wares for many years and now in the collection of the Hendricks County Museum. Baskets hang on the outside of the building that houses Dinsmore's Basket Shop. (Hendricks County Museum.)

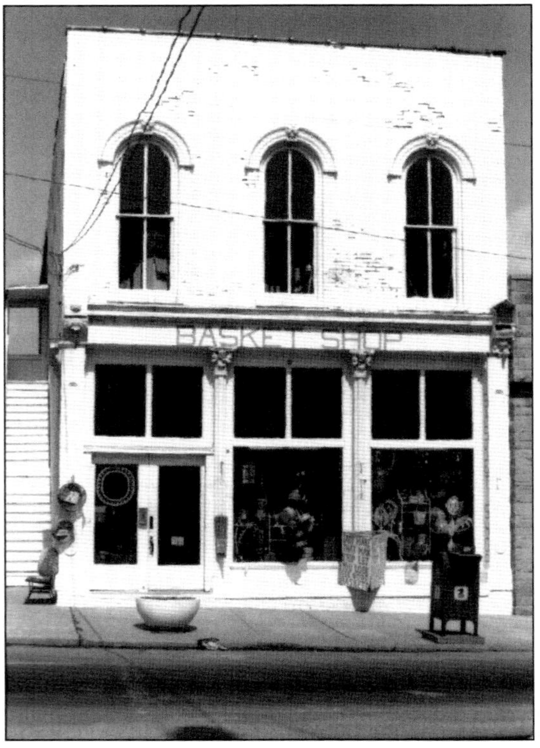

A step through the heavy old door and the smell of wicker baskets fills one's nostrils with a unique smell. Proprietors Noble Dinsmore and his wife Emaline Dinsmore send hungry customers back to the meat counter where their son, Earl, can slice off bologna, pickle loaf, or a variety of other traditional deli meats. Earl's wife, Carolyn, assists customers with other groceries, also located in the back of the store. (Guilford Township Historical Collection, Plainfield-Guilford Township Public Library.)

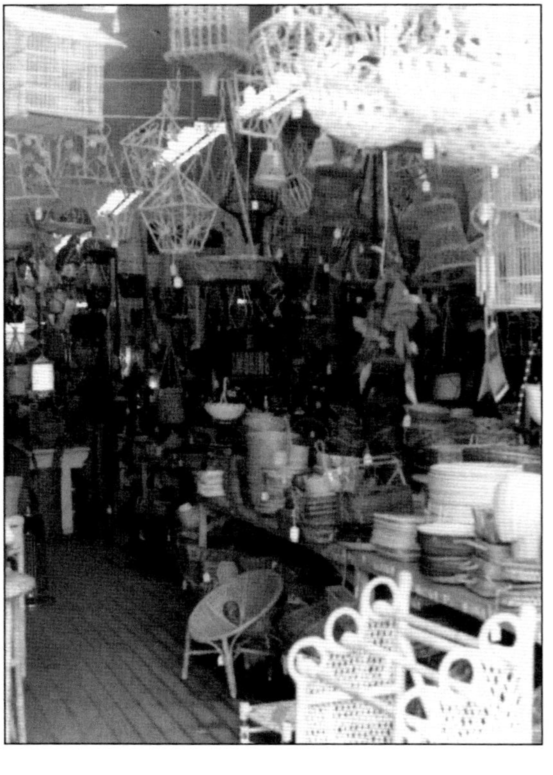

The old-fashioned counter in Dinsmore's Basket Shop is kid-sized so that young purchasers can see the candy, gum, and small toys on the shelves behind the counter. The antique cash register has handled the shop's business transactions for many years. (Guilford Township Historical Collection, Plainfield-Guilford Township Public Library.)

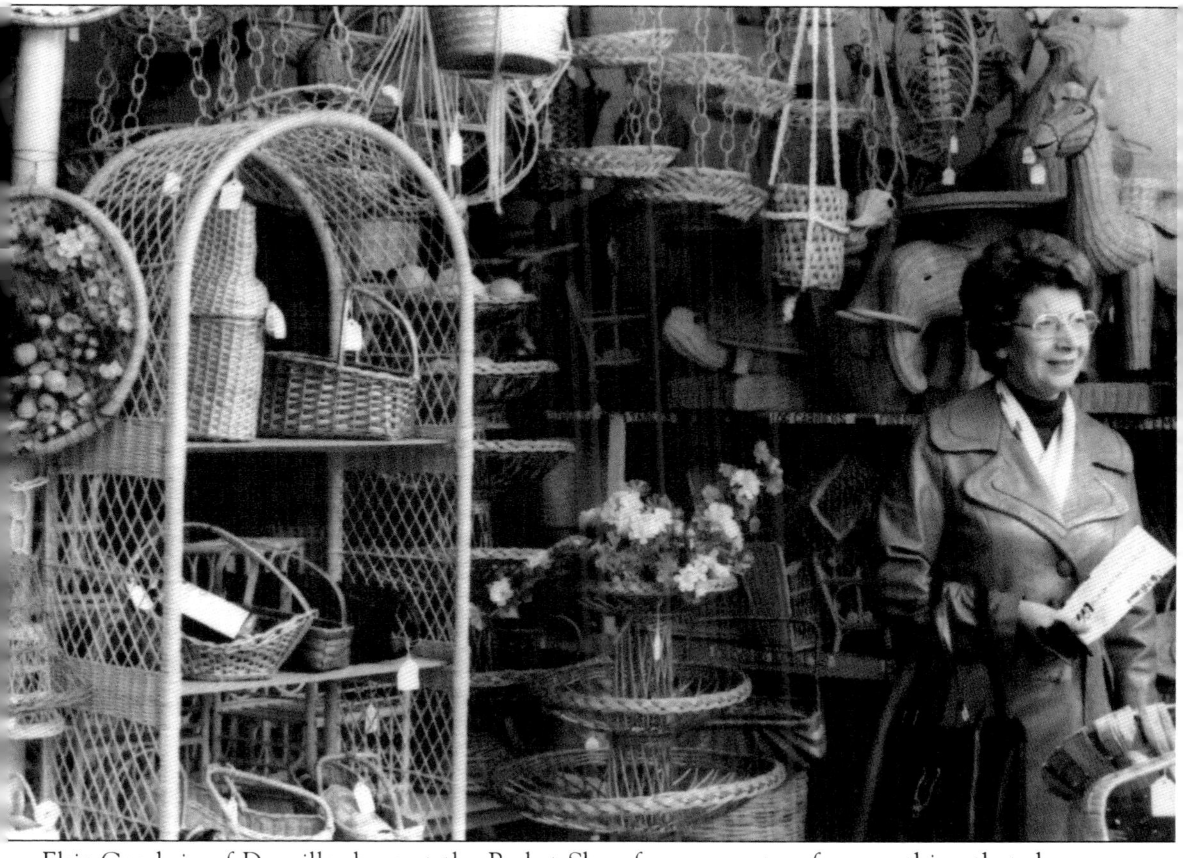

Elsie Goodwin of Danville shops at the Basket Shop for a present or for something that she needs at home. She may be shopping on her lunch hour or perhaps it is a Saturday or Sunday. The Dinsmore family has their store open seven days a week. Shoppers visit with the Dinsmores and talk about family or church or whatever is going on in town. Noble Dinsmore has been a leader in promoting Danville and its business community. He has the greatest laugh that one would ever want to hear, and he always has a smile on his face. (Guilford Township Historical Collection, Plainfield-Guilford Township Public Library.)

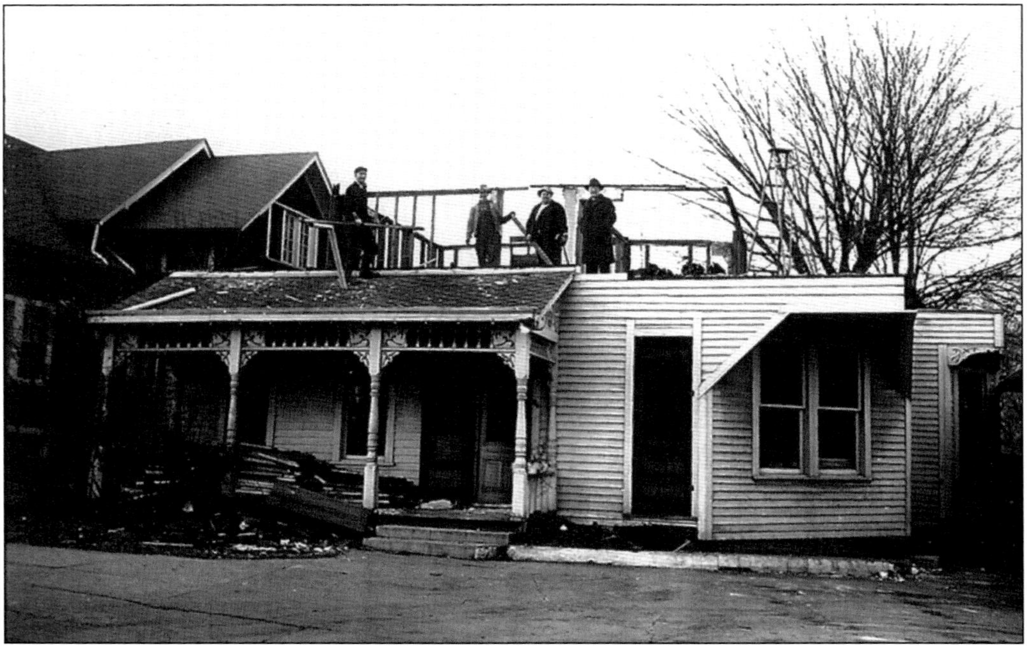

East of the Basket Shop was a large white home at the corner of Indiana and Main Streets. This property was purchased by the Shell Oil Company, and the house was given to the founders of the Danville Conservation Club if they would tear it down and move it off the property. Pictured above, from left to right, are Milford Hadley, Poe Gibson, Russell Beagley, and Charley Walls. The house was disassembled piece by piece, and the lumber was used for the building of the clubhouse at the Danville Conservation Club. (Danville Conservation Club.)

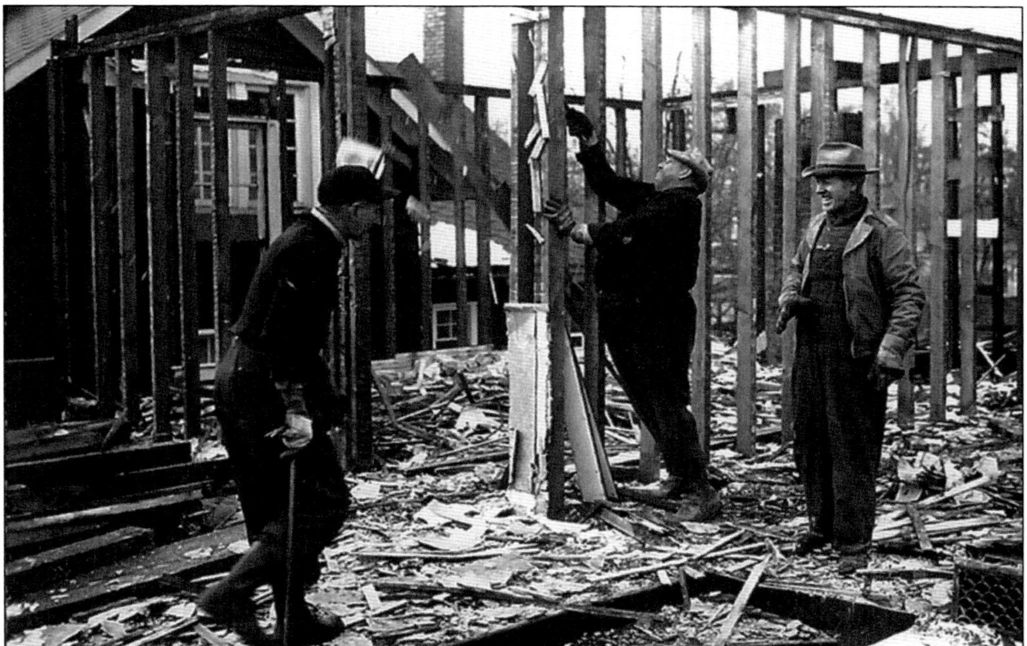

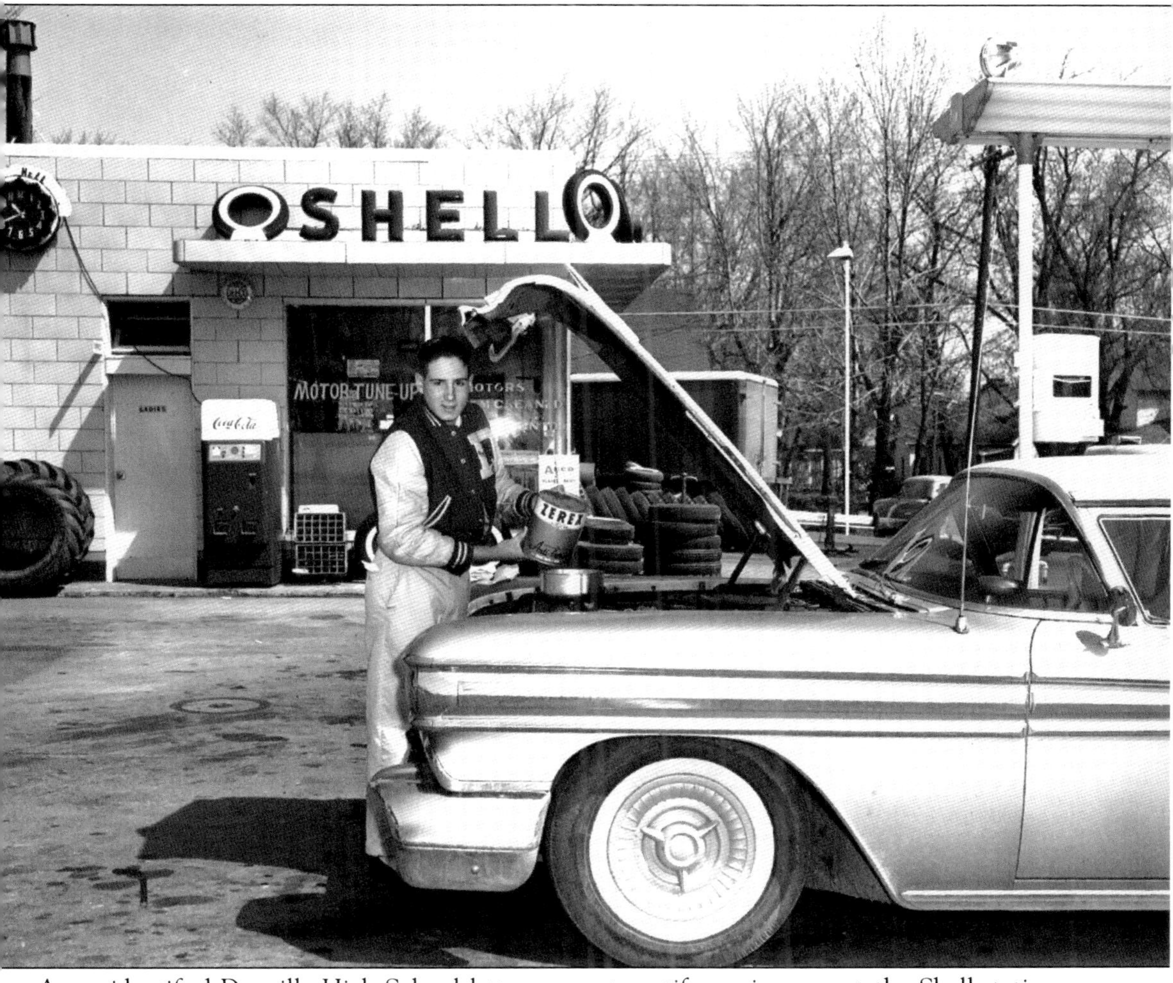

An unidentified Danville High School letterman puts antifreeze in a car at the Shell station located at Main Street and Indiana Street. Full service included filling a car with gas, cleaning the windshield, and checking and filling the fluids under the hood. Notice the pop machine in the background. It dispensed beverages in eight-ounce bottles. This site is now occupied by a small shopping center that houses a sandwich shop, a Chinese restaurant, and several other shops. (Indiana Room, at Danville-Center Township Public Library.)

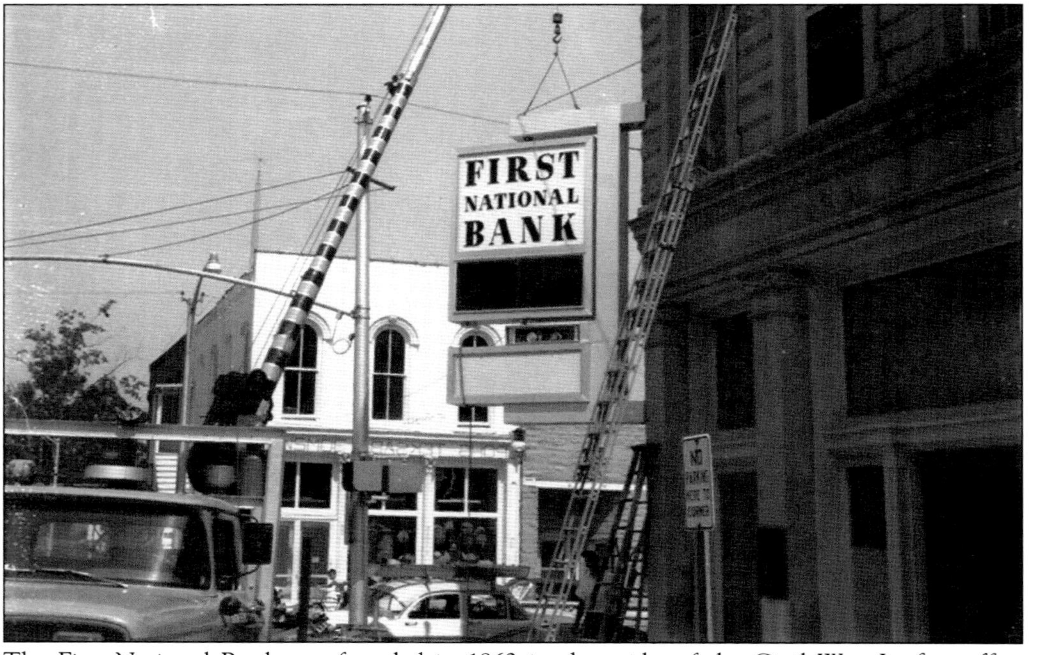

The First National Bank was founded in 1863 in the midst of the Civil War. Its first office was on the east side of the square, and in 1887, it moved to its corner location at the corner of Washington Street and Main Street. Its prominence was increased when this rotating time and temperature sign was added. It made the bank the talk of the town. (Indiana Room, Danville-Center Township Public Library.)

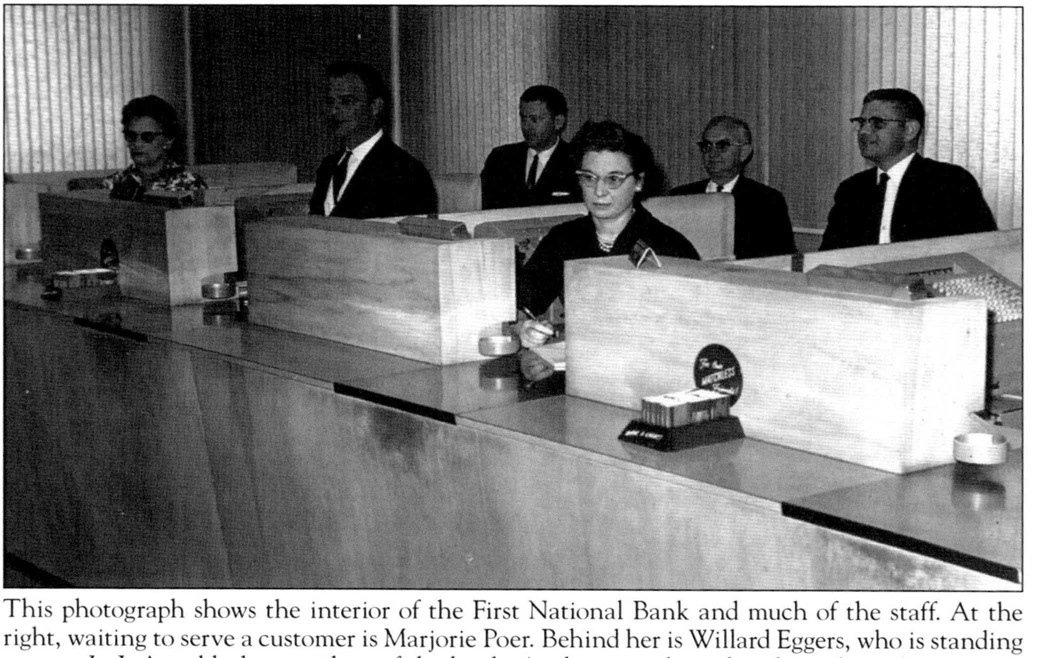

This photograph shows the interior of the First National Bank and much of the staff. At the right, waiting to serve a customer is Marjorie Poer. Behind her is Willard Eggers, who is standing next to L. J. Arnold, the president of the bank. At the second window from the right is Henry Clark. (Indiana Room at Danville-Center Township Public Library.)

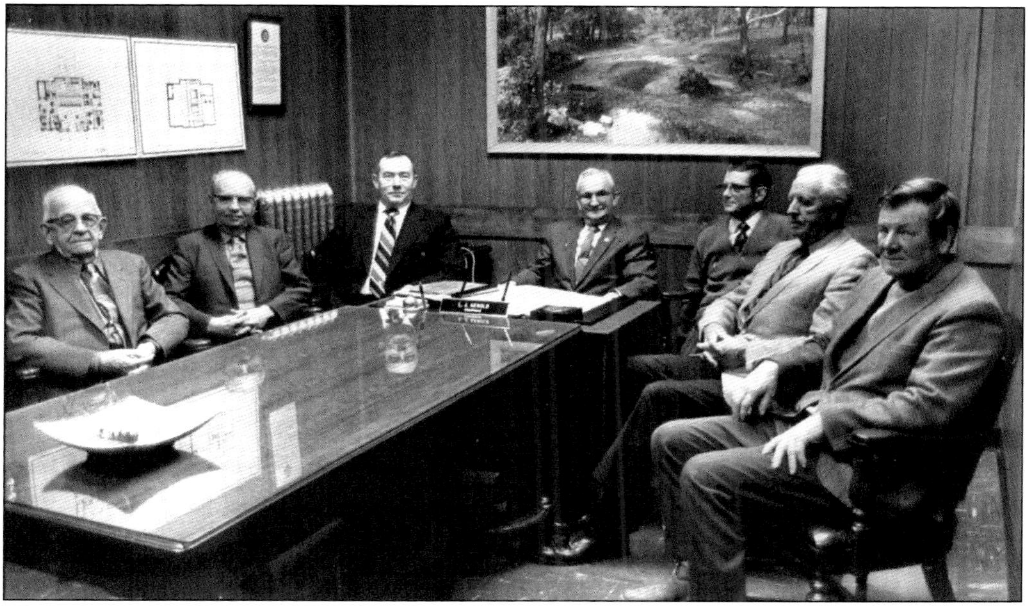

The First National Bank sat on the corner of the courthouse square from 1887 until July 1972, when it moved to a new building at 108 East Main Street. This photograph shows the board of directors of the bank with the drawing of the new bank building on the wall. Pictured clockwise around the table from the left are Amos Harvey, Rawleigh Baker, Joe Stevenson, L. J. Arnold, Willard Eggers, Charles Miles, and George Harvey. (Indiana Room, Danville-Center Township Public Library.)

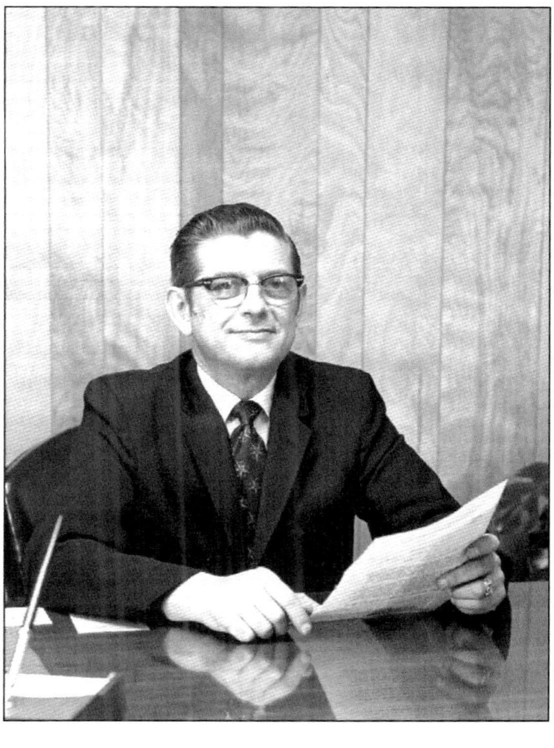

Willard Eggers started at the First National Bank of Danville at the bottom and worked his way up to be president. For years he entertained customers of the bank with his personality as he took care of their bank needs as a teller. He became a member of the Bear Down Euchre Club, a group of 12 men who play euchre once per month in a club that dates back to professors at the college (more about the college later). He created the Gavel, the prize for winning first place for the month in the euchre club. His wife, Bonnie, worked as a teacher for many years in the Danville school system. (Indiana Room, Danville-Center Township Public Library.)

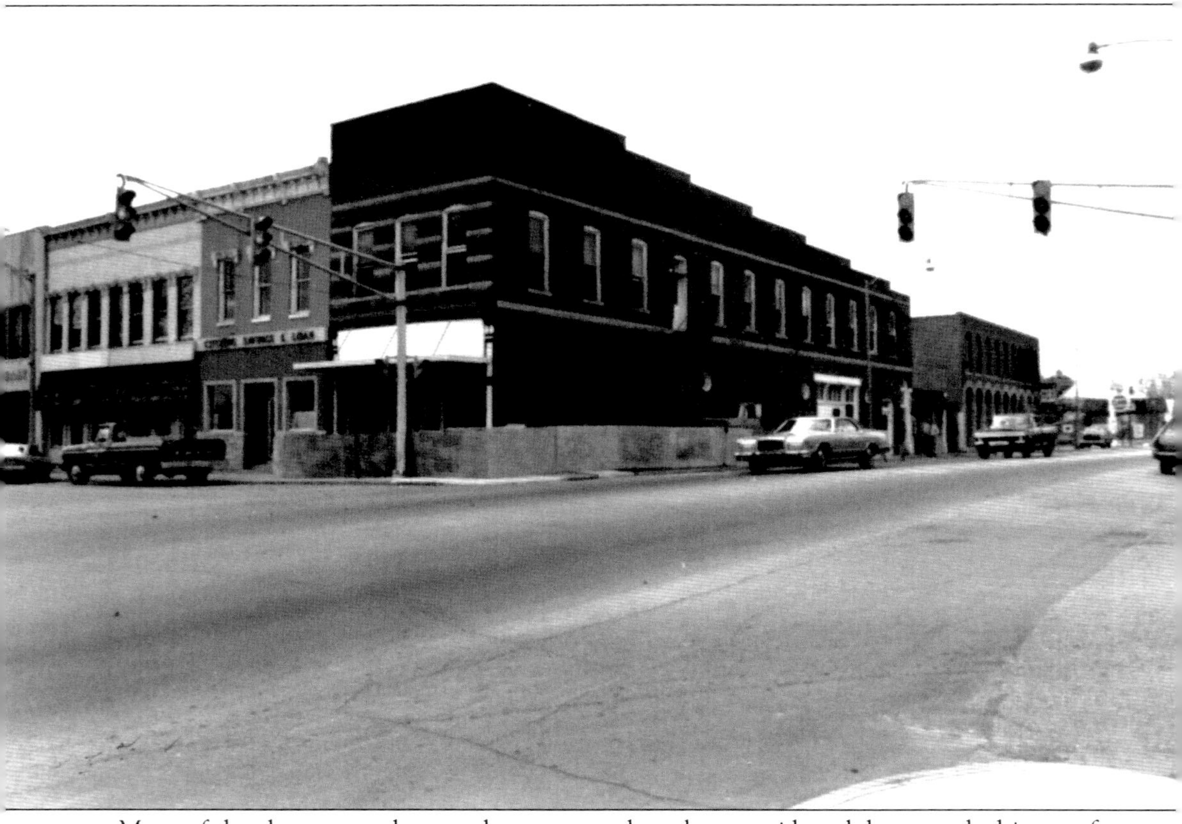

Many of the changes on the courthouse square have been accidental due to such things as fires. In this photograph taken on March 23, 1981, the building that last housed Danville Plumbing and Heating on the northwest corner of the square (Jefferson and Main Streets) is blocked off for pending demolition. (Hendricks County Museum.)

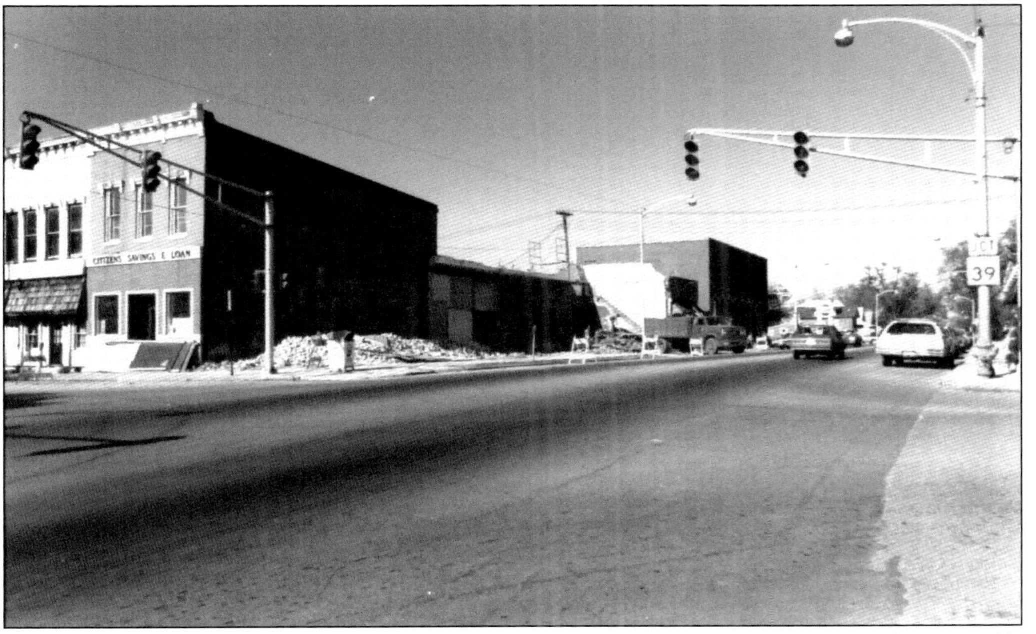

In this photograph taken later in March 1981, the rubble from the demolition of the Danville Plumbing and Heating building is being finished. Notice that what is left is the side of the Citizens Savings and Loan and beyond the truck with rubble is the building that housed the utilities serving Danville. (Hendricks County Museum.)

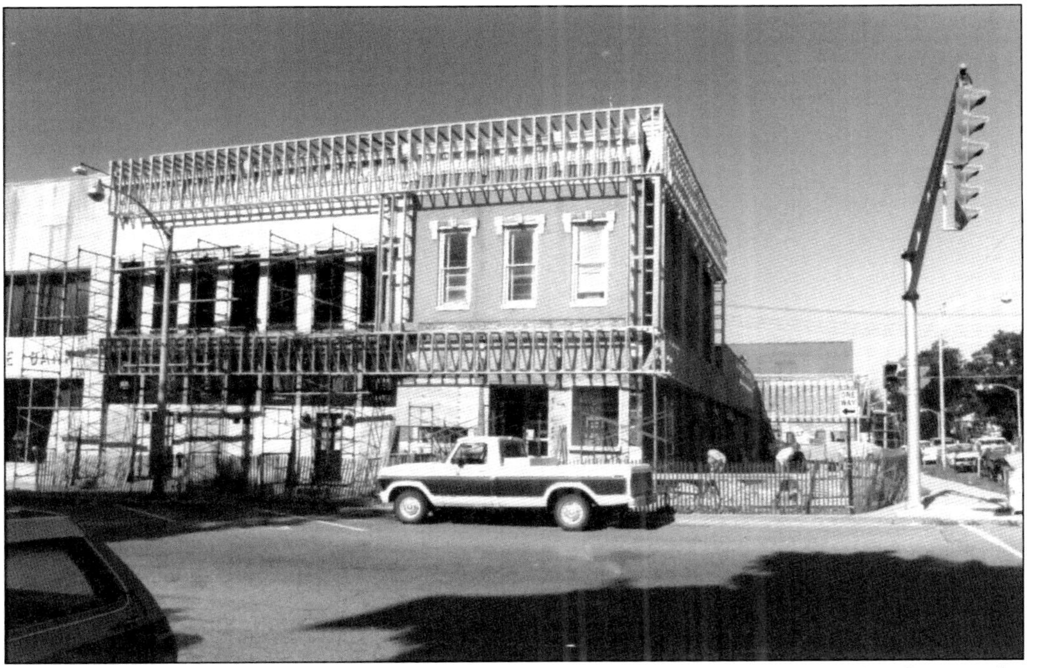

After the demolition was complete the Danville State Bank built a uniform facade over the remaining buildings as well as its building, which once housed the Kroger store on the Danville square. This facade remains to this day in 2009. (Hendricks County Museum.)

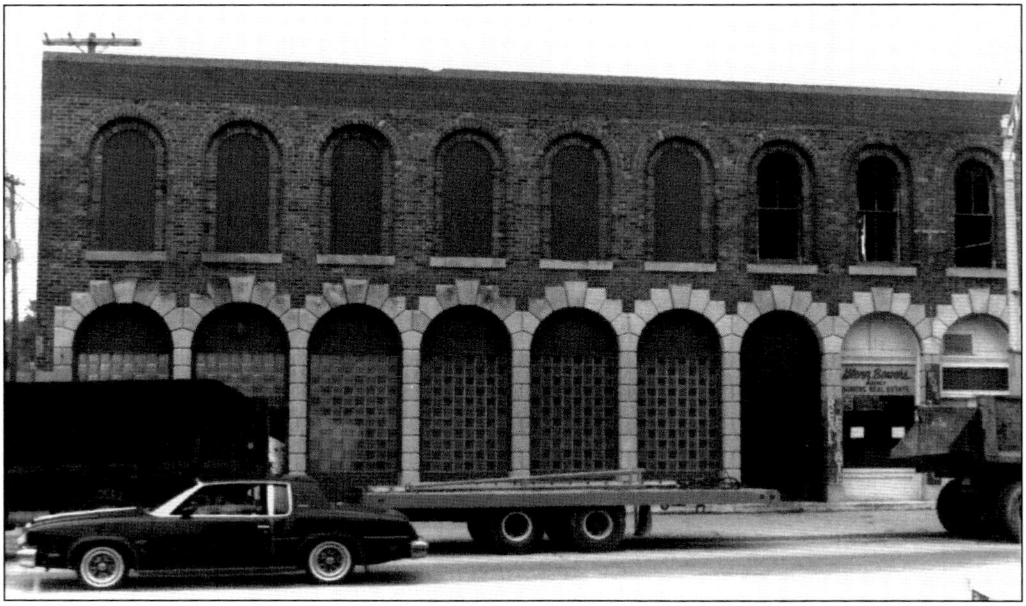

At the west end of the previous demolition pictures stood this building, which once housed the utilities serving the Danville area and which in 1981 housed Glenn Bowers's insurance and real estate office. Later in this book readers will see how this building fared with the tornado. This building, which stood on West Main Street, was torn down and now resembles a parking lot. (Hendricks County Museum.)

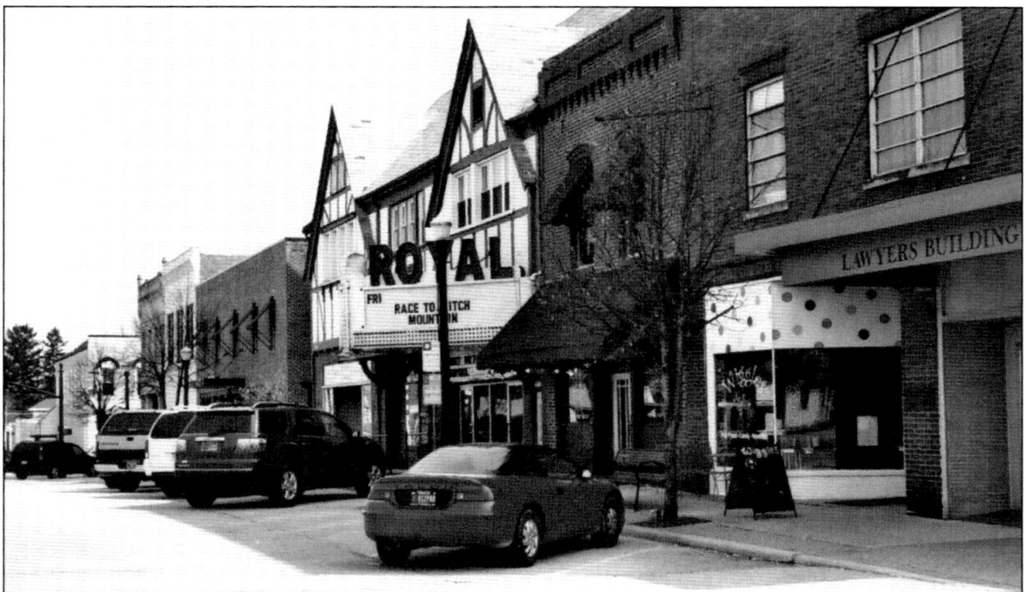

This photograph shows how the east side of the courthouse square looks today. Offices on each end of the block serve to highlight the three restaurants that are in between. Just north of the theater an art gallery is being prepared by the artisans of Hendricks County to showcase their wares. The courthouse square constantly reinvents itself. (Author's collection.)

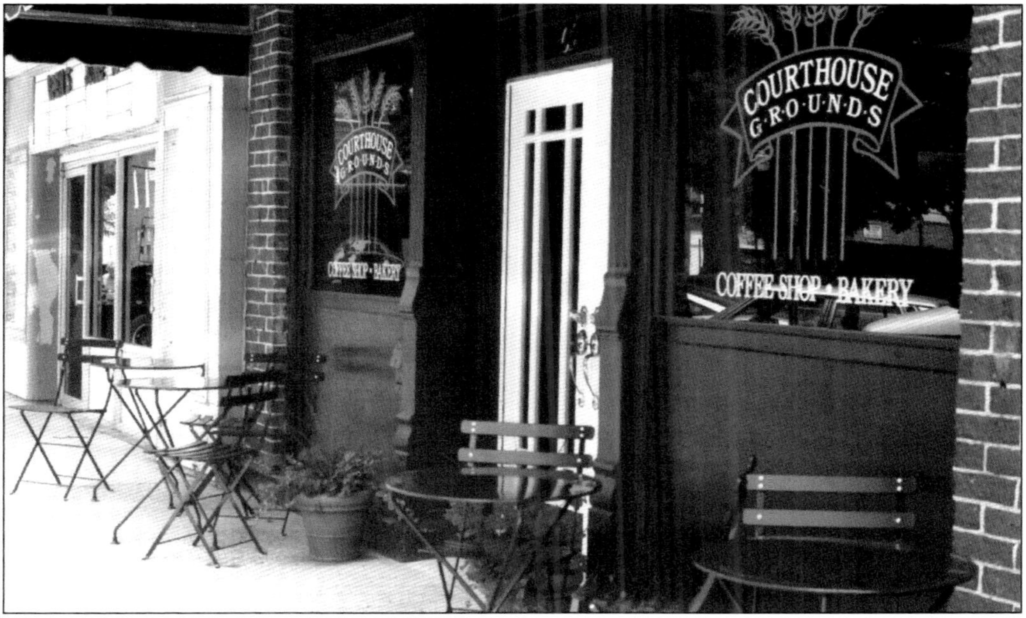

The Courthouse Grounds restaurant sits on the east side of the square at the location that formerly housed the Green Lantern Tavern. At the time of publication Courthouse Grounds was in its 10th year. Sidewalk seating augments the seating inside. (Hendricks County Museum.)

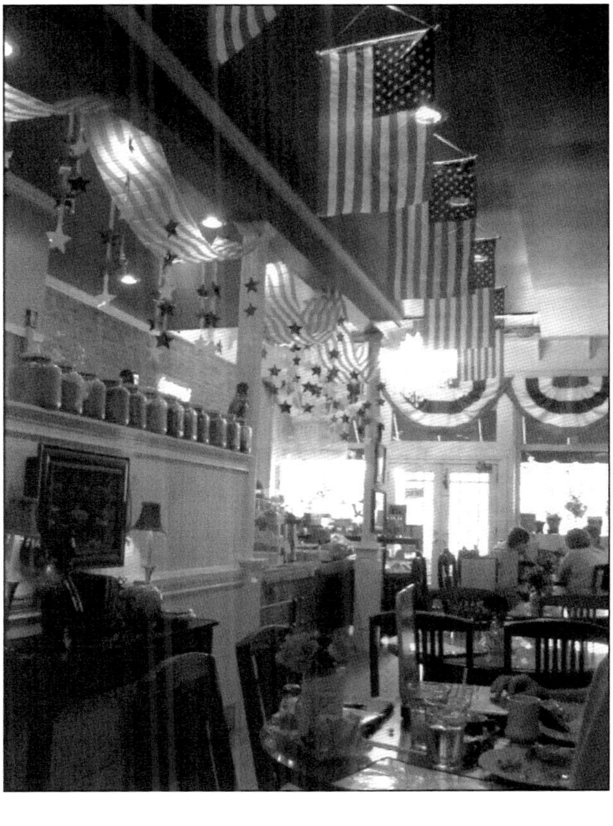

Many of the buildings on the square are long and narrow on the inside. This photograph, taken near the back of the Courthouse Grounds restaurant, looks toward the front windows on Washington Street. (Danville Republican.)

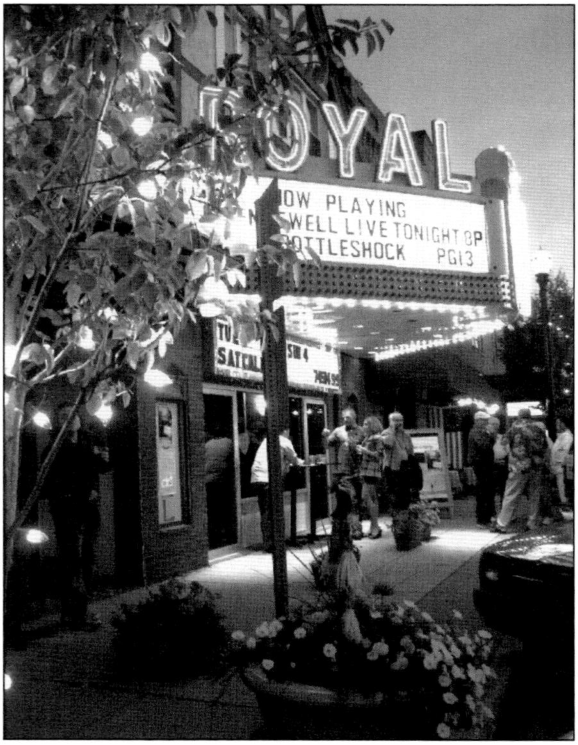

Built in 1927, the Royal Theater is the sole survivor among several theaters that once stood on the courthouse square. The first building in Danville constructed to be a theater, the Royal was extremely elaborate. (Danville Republican.)

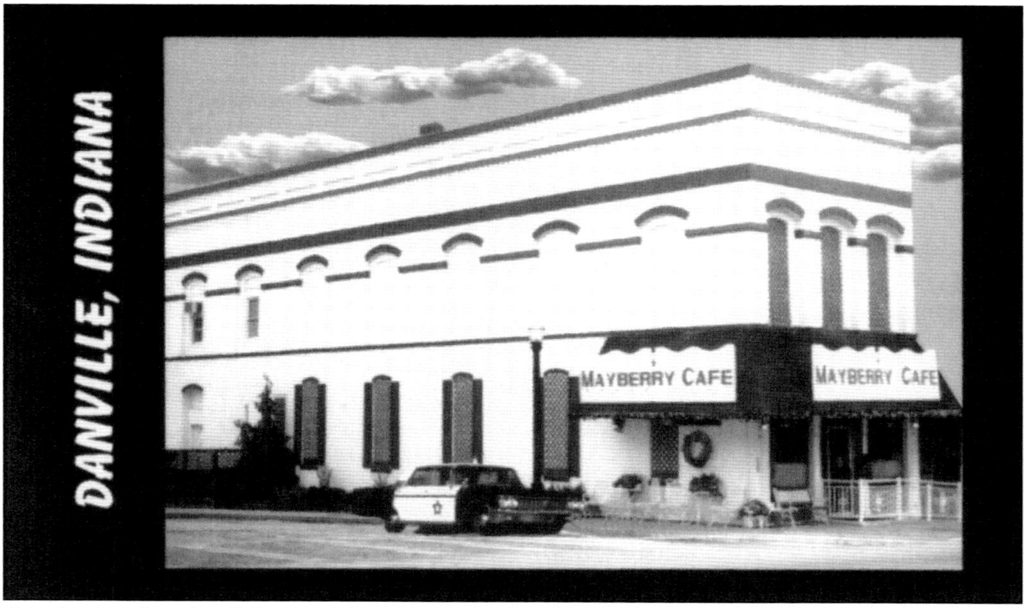

On the north side of the courthouse square, on the northeast corner of Jefferson and Main Streets, the building now occupied by the Mayberry Café once housed a Waffle House. Brad and Christine Born themed their restaurant around the *The Andy Griffith Show*, and today they are visited by tourists and tour buses from near and far—the sheriff's car usually sits nearby. (Hendricks County Museum.)

Over the years the courthouse square has reflected the lives and values of the residents. One such change is this flagpole and a fountain that was constructed at the northwest corner of the courthouse lawn. Pictured here, an unidentified troop of Boy Scouts conducts a flag ceremony. (Hendricks County Museum.)

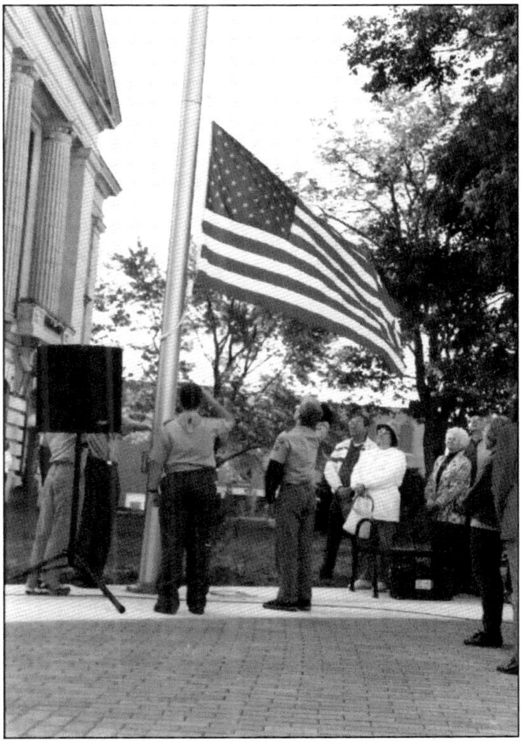

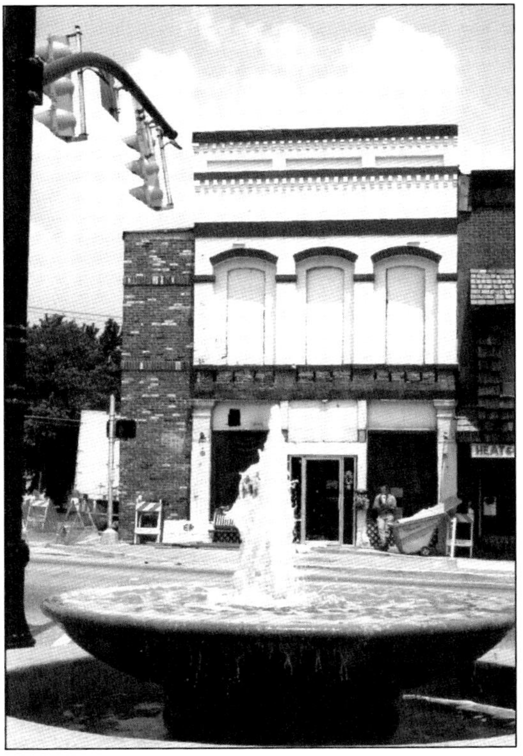

Near the flagpole is this fountain, which was constructed and is maintained by the Town of Danville. It gives a nice look and sound as one traverses by on the sidewalk. However, on windy days the person who walks by also stands a good chance of getting wet. A look across the street catches the Mayberry in the midst of its renovation, which widened the restaurant to put more seating along its west side. (Hendricks County Museum.)

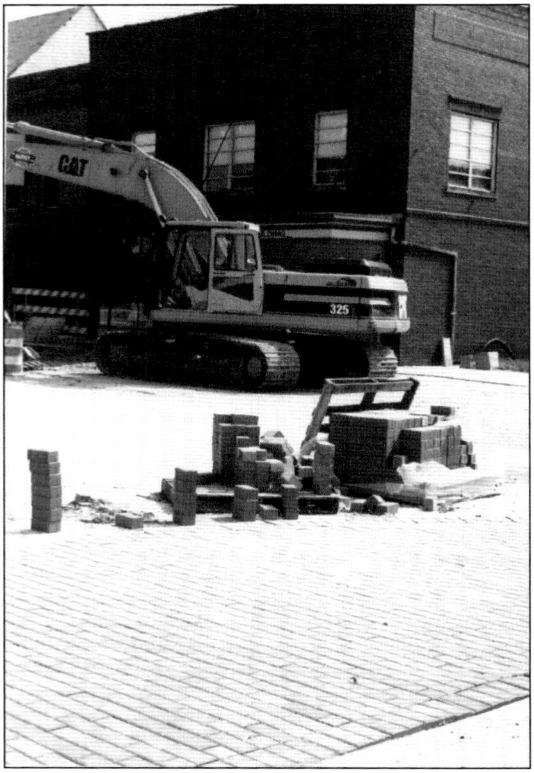

Early Danville's dirt streets were eventually bricked, and by the 1960s, Danville's brick streets were paved with asphalt or asphalt and stone. Later brick streets became desirable again for towns wishing to draw tourists interested in history. Danville laid bricks around three sides of the courthouse square, excluding Main Street. Work is pictured at Marion and Washington Streets on the southeast corner of the square. (Hendricks County Museum.)

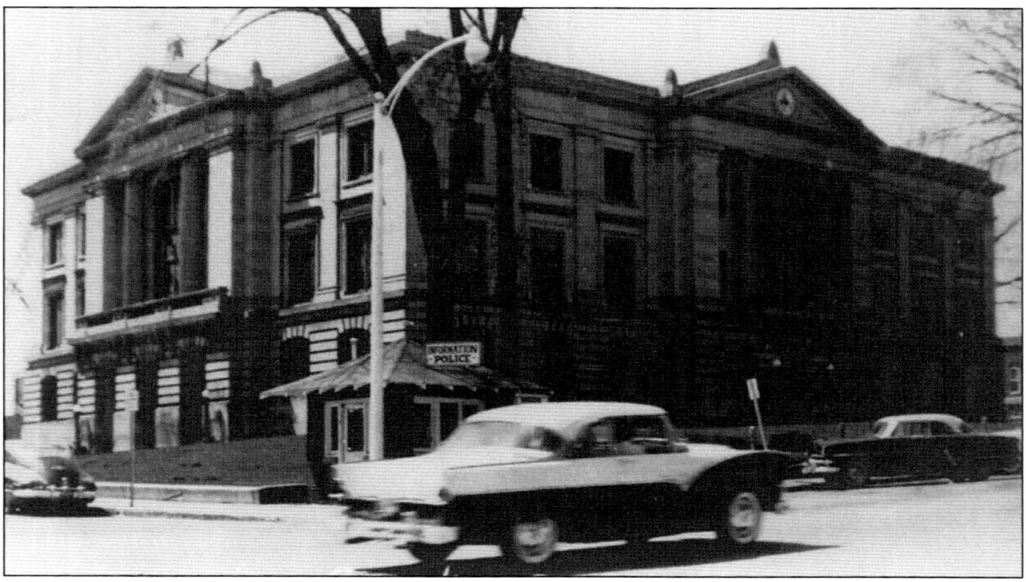

A car speeds west on Main Street past the police station located at the northeast corner of the courthouse yard. The police station, only big enough to hold a couple of people, served as the outpost of the Danville Police Department for many years. This was a time when residents did not lock their doors at night. However, the business community liked to have law enforcement nearby. (Indiana Room, Danville-Center Township Public Library.)

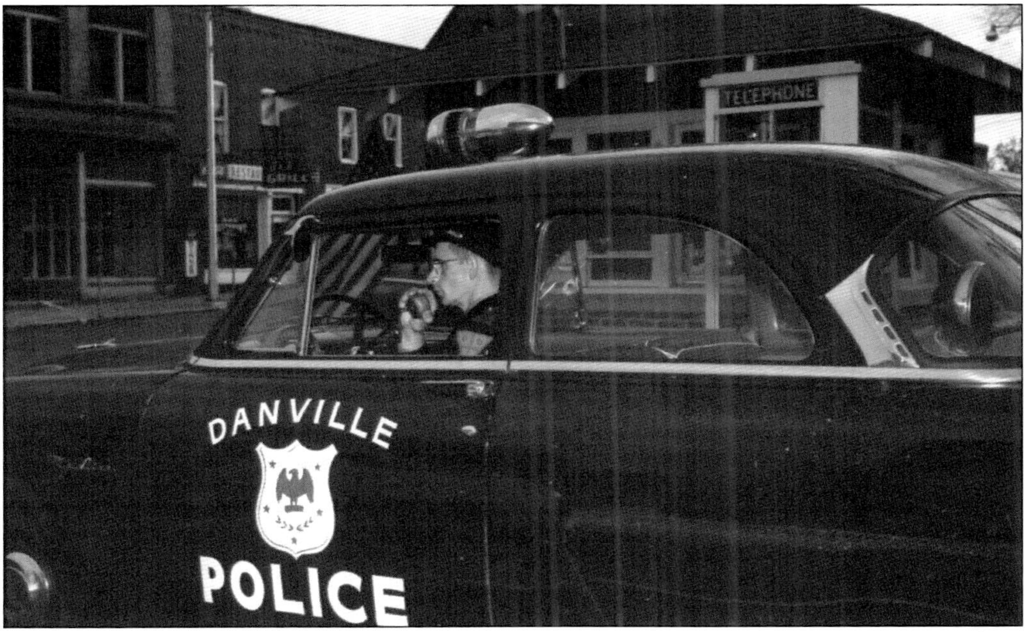

This older view shows the telephone booth, in frequent use by kids on their way home from school. Not pictured, but also in popular use, was the water fountain on the square. Across the street to the east is the B&W Grill—a local favorite. The police officer is unidentified. (Danville Republican.)

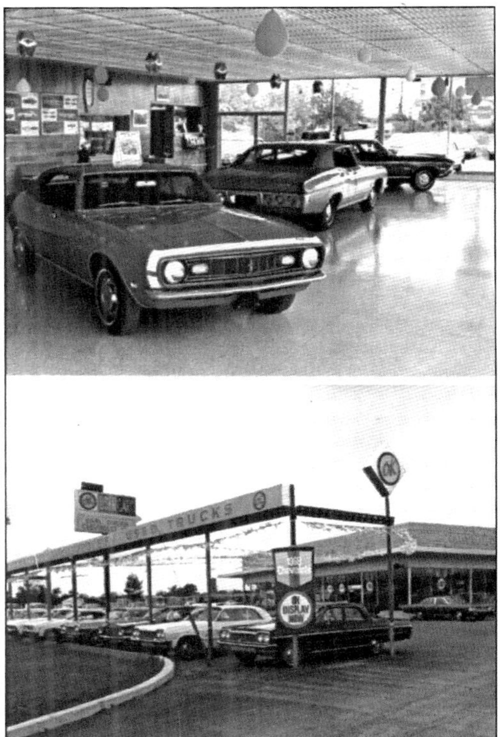

In the 1960s, some businesses began to migrate from the center of Danville to the east of the original town. The new Hendricks County Hospital, built on East Main Street in 1962, was an anchor in the new development area. Earl Dugan bought the former Rodney Chevrolet dealership on the second block of West Main Street and installed it in a new facility next to the hospital. This postcard celebrated "Hendricks County's Newest Chevrolet Dealer." (Hendricks County Museum.)

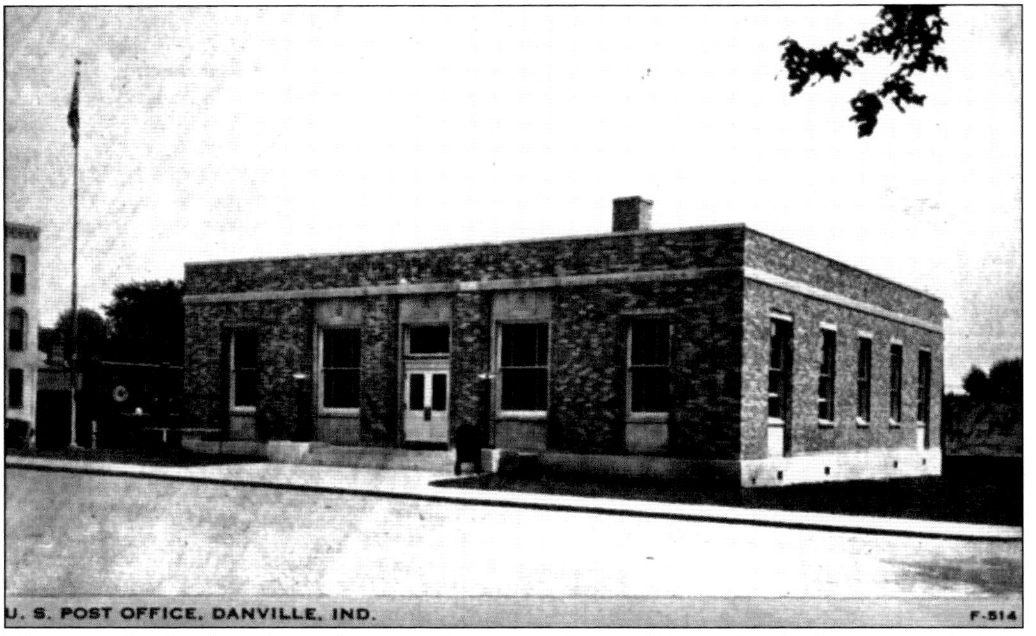

The post office has been housed at many locations, often within another businesses, particularly in instances in which the business owner was also the postmaster. For many years, the post office stood on Marion Street adjacent to the courthouse square. In the 1990s, the post office was also relocated to the east of Danville's downtown. (Hendricks County Museum.)

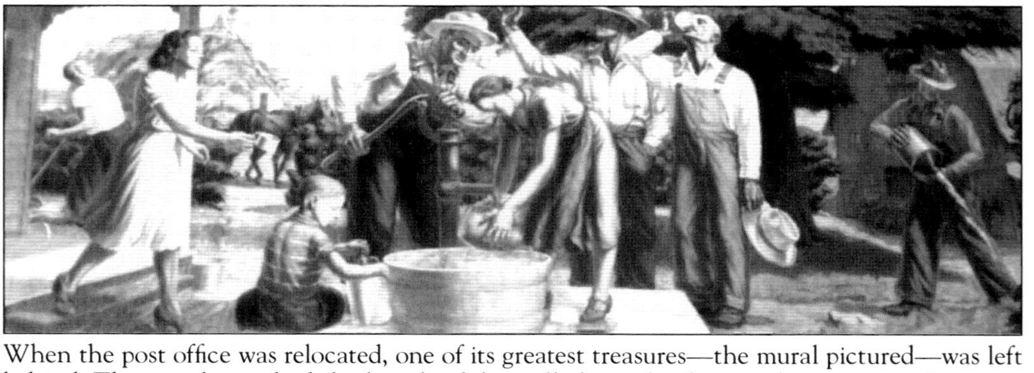

When the post office was relocated, one of its greatest treasures—the mural pictured—was left behind. The mural stretched the length of the wall above the door to the postmaster's private office. The mural, called *Filling the Water Jugs—Haymaking Time*, was painted with oil on canvas by artist Gail W. Martin in 1939. Although the post office building was conveyed to Hendricks County, the mural still belongs to the U.S. Postal Service. (Hendricks County Museum.)

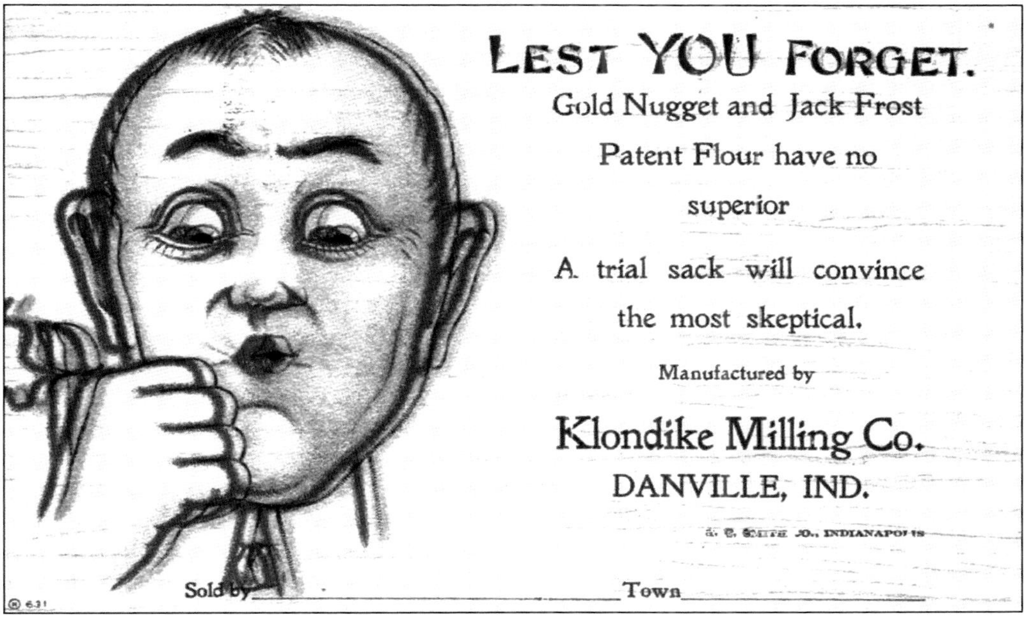

Not all business in Danville originated on the courthouse square. This advertisement for Gold Nugget and Jack Frost flour from the Klondike Milling Company emphasized a product that grew from Danville's agrarian roots. But the Klondike Milling Company was on Klondike Street (now Lincoln Street) in the southern outskirts of Danville and along the train track. This allowed for the transportation of Klondike's flours far from the kitchens of Danville to the world beyond. (Indiana Room, Danville-Center Township Public Library.)

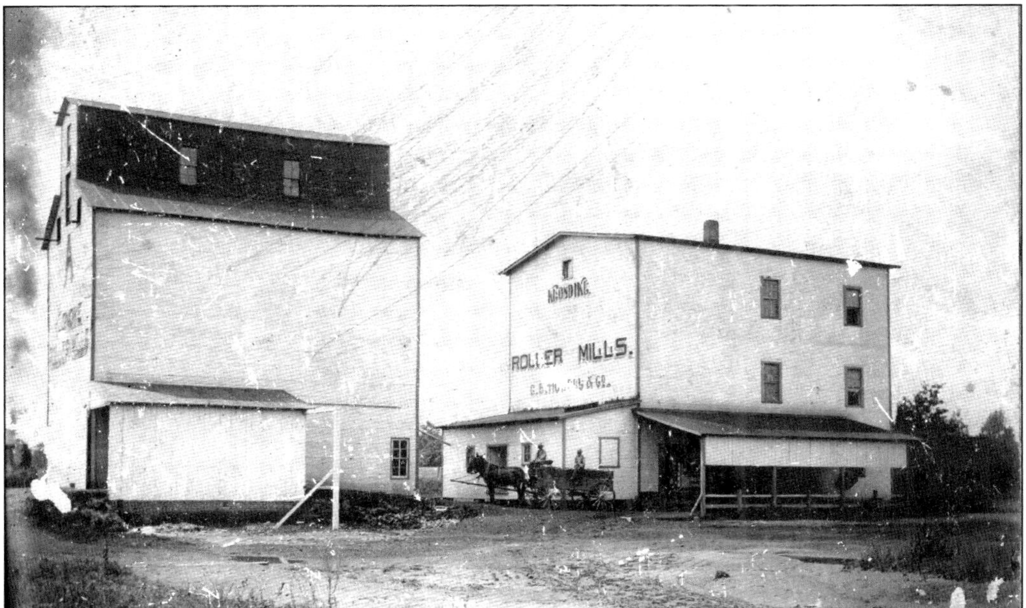

Having such a close market for their product enabled farmers such as these to prosper. Wheat could be brought to the Klondike Roller Miller to be milled into Jack Frost and Gold Nugget. (Guilford Township Historical Collection, Plainfield-Guilford Township Public Library.)

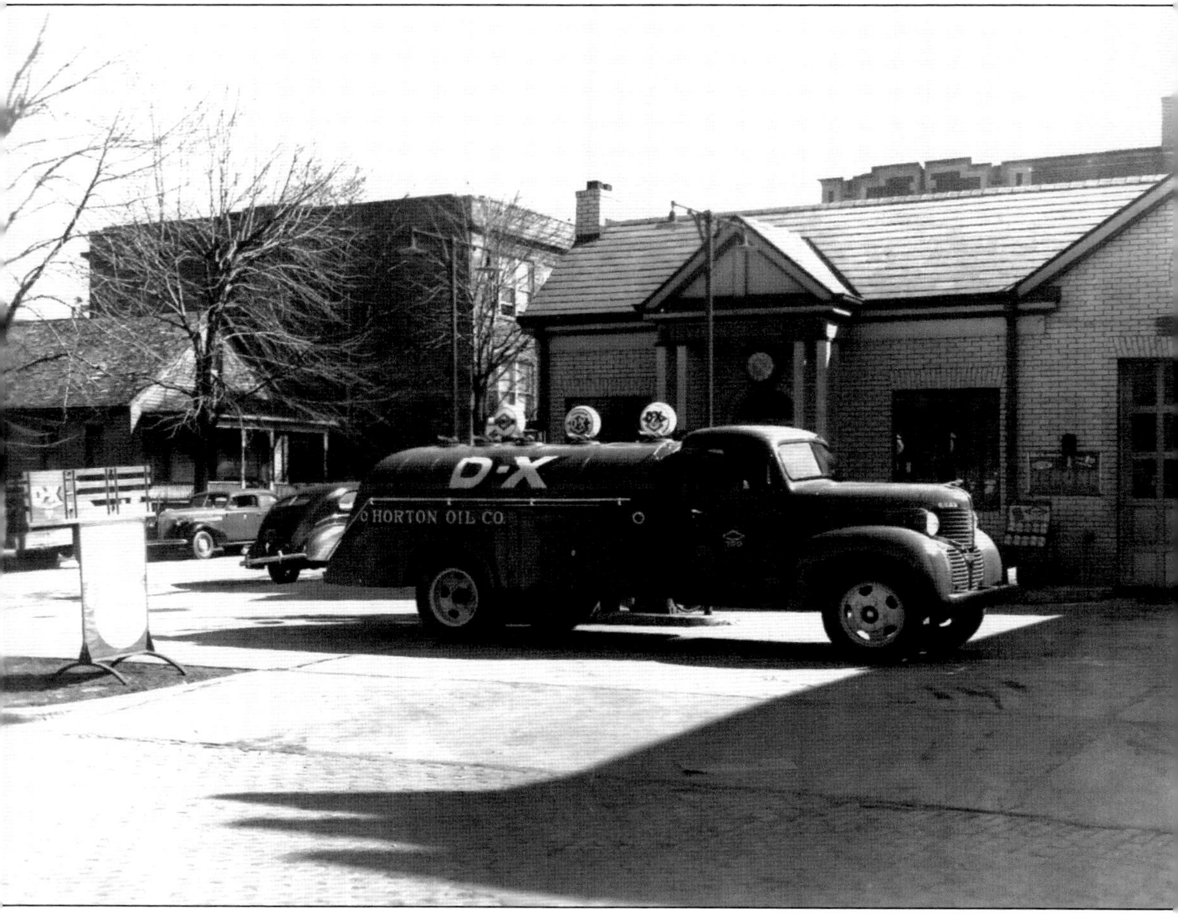

Businesses that served the automotive customer located conveniently on Main Street to serve their customers. This view from the southwest shows the Horton Oil Company (DX) with the Danville Christian Church in the background. Over the top of the service station is the utility building along Main Street. The house that is shown in the picture was torn down to build the bank drive-up window that is located at Main Street and Cross Street. (Judy Pingel.)

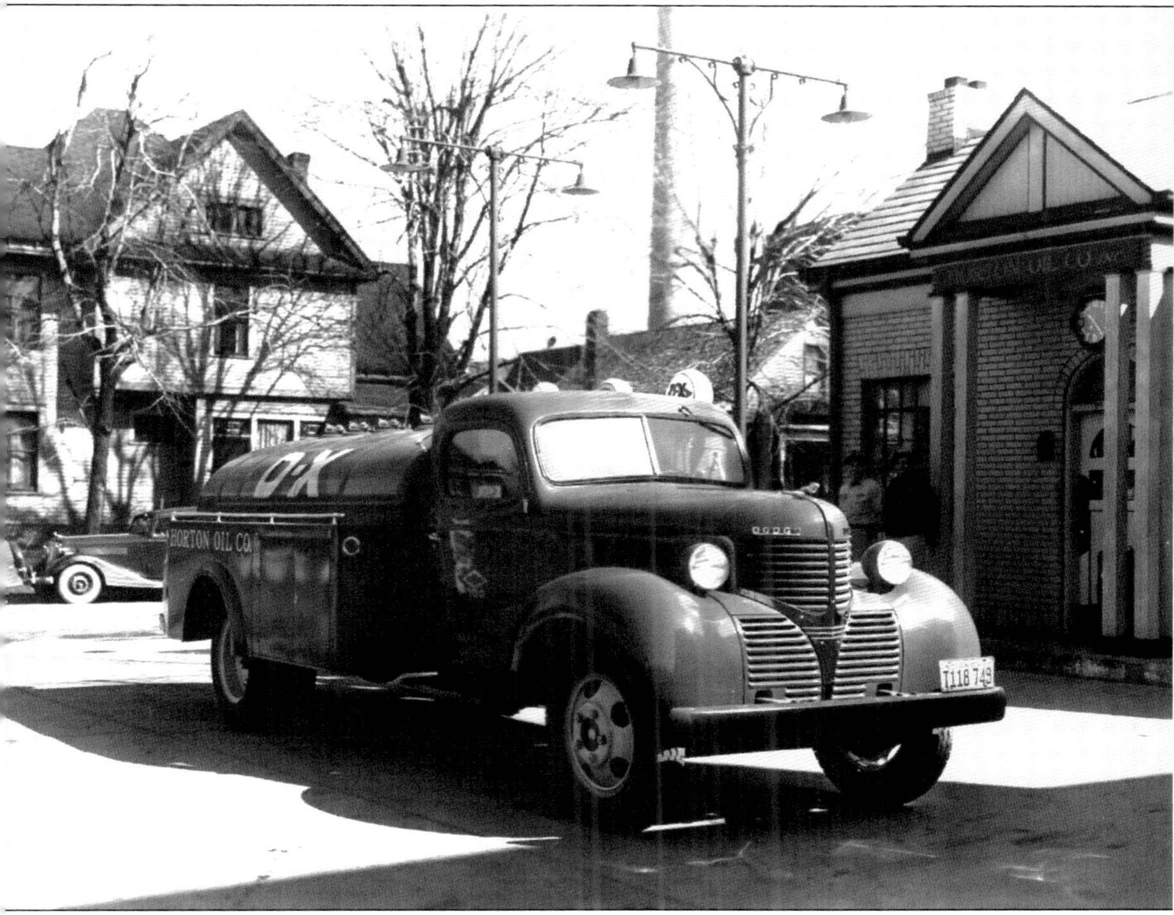

This view of the DX station is taken from the south and is located more to the east. This view shows the Danville Standpipe, which was built in 1892. This water tower, built in response to the 1891 fire that destroyed the entire west side of the courthouse square except for the building on the south end, is 100 feet tall, measures 12 feet in diameter, and holds 85,000 gallons of water. It is built on a foundation of Bedford limestone eight feet thick. (Judy Pingel.)

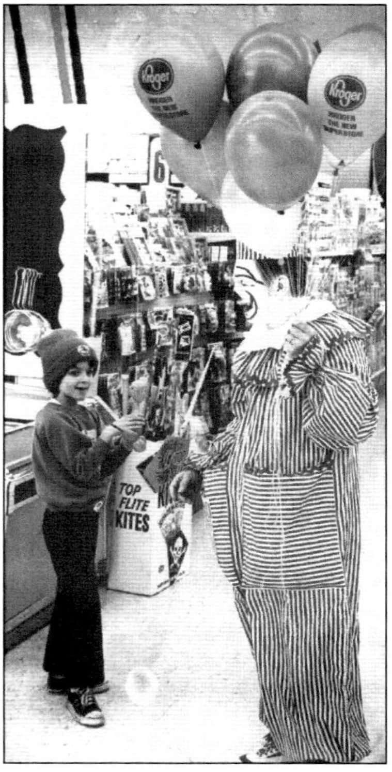

Until the early 1960s the Kroger store sat on the west side of the square in the building that now houses the Hendricks County Court's probation department. Eventually Kroger built a new store at the bottom of "College Hill." A clown promotes the new location. Kroger has moved twice in the years since. (Guilford Township Historical Collection, Plainfield-Guilford Township Public Library.)

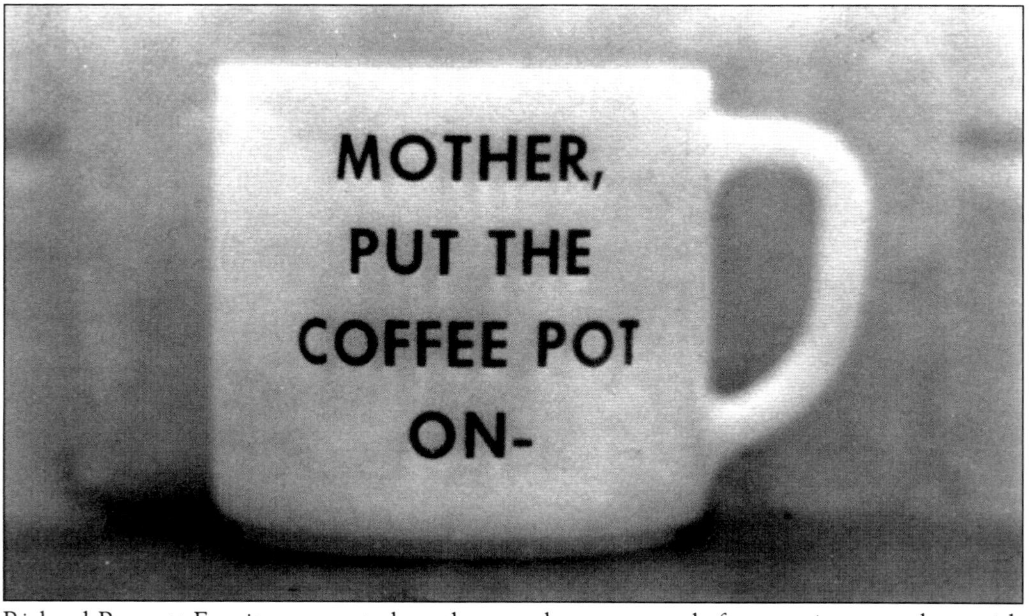

Richard Bennett Furniture operated on the courthouse square before moving east along with many other businesses. Richard Bennett Furniture distinguished itself among area businesses—the first thing it did when a customer walked through the door was to offer a cup of coffee. Richard Bennett's tagline was "Mother, put the coffee pot on." (Guilford Township Historical Collection, Plainfield-Guilford Township Public Library.)

Two

Government and Politics

Danville was established for the business of government. The purpose of establishing a county seat is to have a place for the county government to act. And the egalitarian agrarian believed that putting the county seat into the middle of a government unit made it equally available to all.

Of course, the need for government in a new area of settlement meant that tracts of lands and their ownership in the hands of new residents as buyers from the government meant that they had to have a way to keep track of who owned which piece of land. This, of course, was the township system from the Northwest Ordinance of 1787.

But this emphasis also meant that disputes would arise between citizens. Accordingly, law enforcement agents and courts were provided to resolve disputes and to enforce the criminal law in order that the frontier might fully develop and that law-abiding people would settle there.

The county prospered and grew, and the courthouse went from being a log cabin to a small brick structure and large and wonderful edifices that showed the wealth and power of Hendricks County.

Because of the geographic origins, the occupations, the relative wealth, and other factors that political scientists consider, Hendricks County has stood rather decidedly for the political party represented by the elephant for quite a long period of time.

Local citizens were fired up for William McKinley, and they were even more fired up for the visit of Pres. Ronald Reagan.

Danville, being the county seat, has always been the focus for these outpourings of the political spirit, and presumably it will continue to be so, no matter what the future leanings of the populace happen to be.

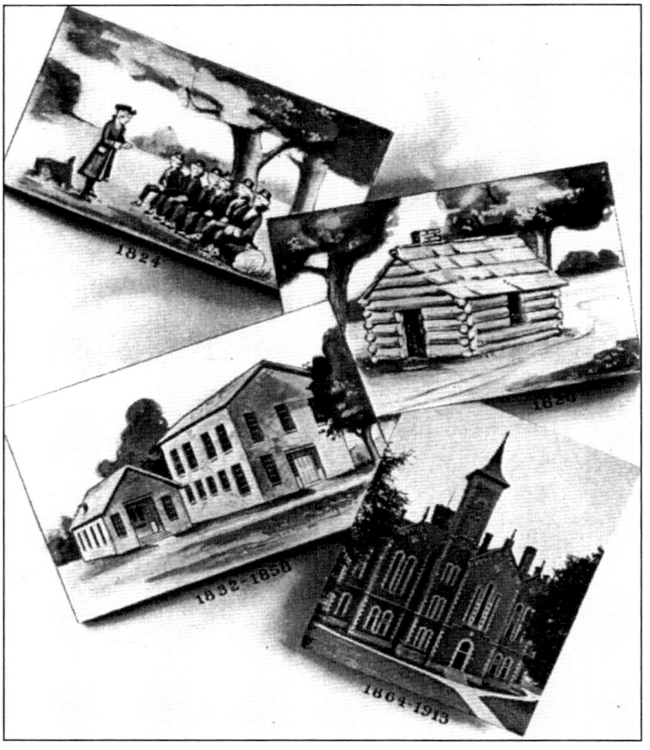

Danville was created in 1824 as the county seat of Hendricks County. Four courthouses have served the public, beginning with a log structure built about 1826. A brick Gothic Revival–style courthouse was constructed between 1859 and 1863 and demolished on January 9, 1912, after its roof collapsed. The current courthouse, constructed in 1912 and 1913, was designed in the neoclassical style and is considered to be fireproof. This photograph was used in the 1915 invitation to the dedication. (Author's collection.)

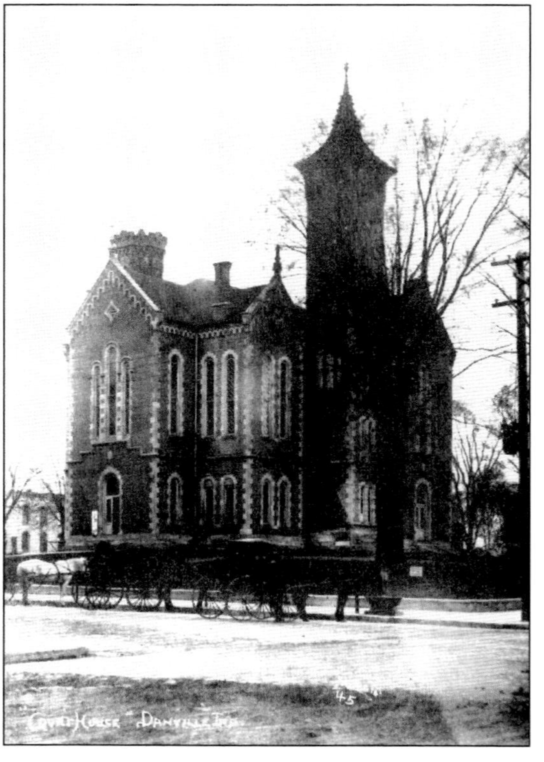

The third courthouse was constructed of brick in the Gothic Revival style between 1859 and 1863. It was built at a cost of $60,000. It was a grand structure, featuring both a bell tower and an observation tower. Because of these towers there are a few really marvelous pictures of post–Civil War Danville. (Author's collection.)

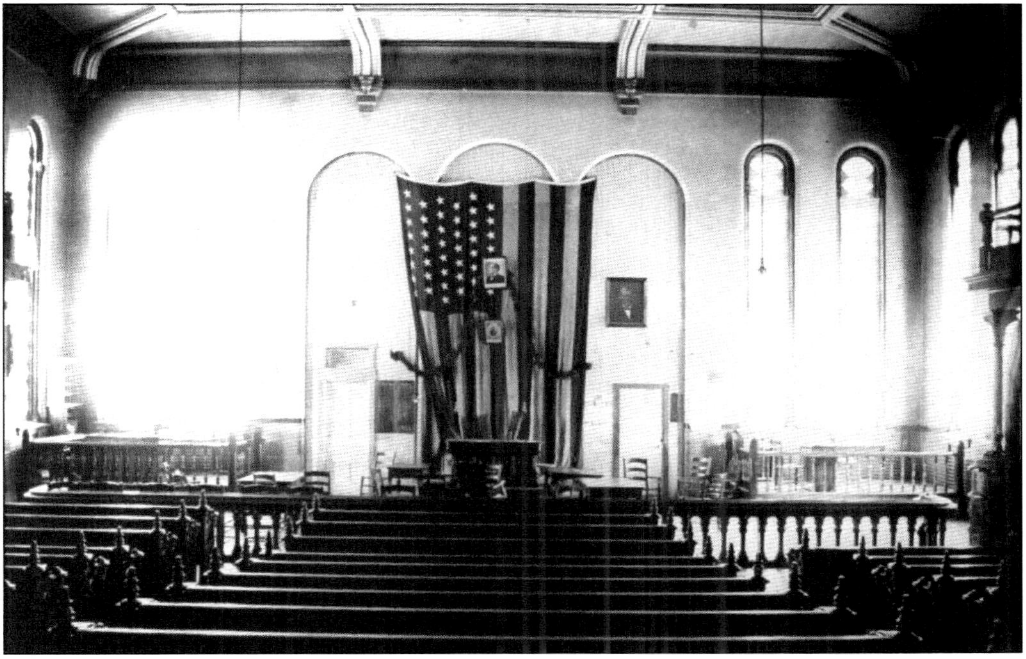

When the third courthouse was built, its court room was probably the largest room in Hendricks County. Located on the second floor, the room featured an extremely high ceiling. The judge's bench and chair are not ornate. Counsel tables are small and served by straight-back chairs. The lights, most visible where they attach to the ceiling, were powered by gas instead of electricity for most of the life of this courthouse. (Hendricks County Museum.)

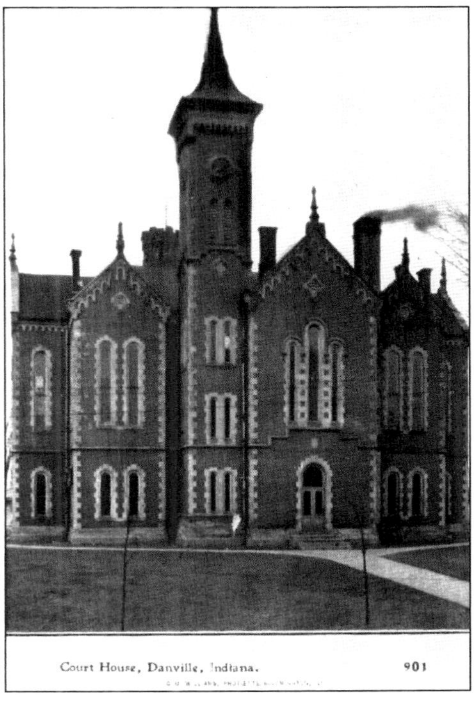

This postcard depicting the third courthouse shows the grand structure, featuring a bell tower and an observation tower. One January night in 1912, Danville residents heard a loud crash in the square. A heavy snow had collapsed the courthouse roof, ruining much of the third floor. Due to the cost required for repair, the building was razed and the present courthouse was built beginning in 1913 at a cost of $225,000. (Hendricks County Museum.)

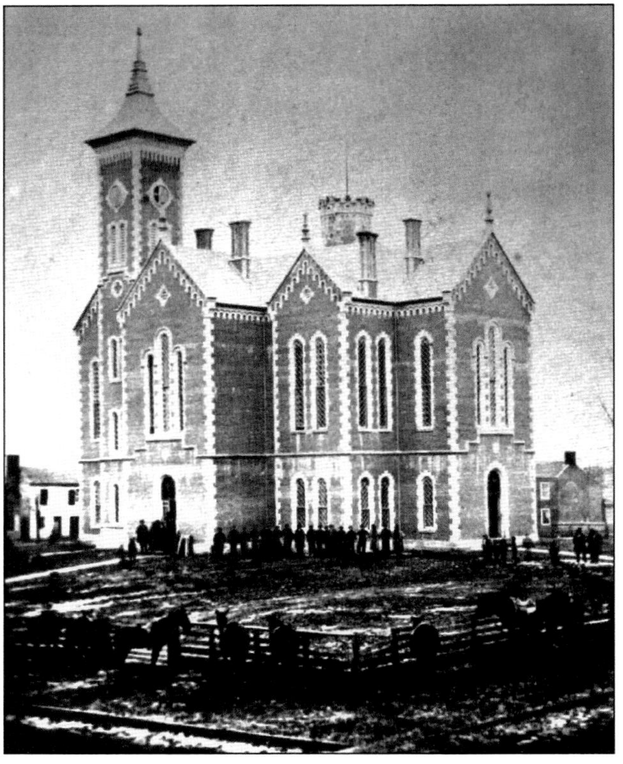

This view from a greater distance shows the fence around the courthouse and horses tied there. Although the courthouse was in the exact geographic center of the county, for some it was still a long ride by horseback to transact necessary business. (Guilford Township Historical Collection, Plainfield-Guilford Township Public Library.)

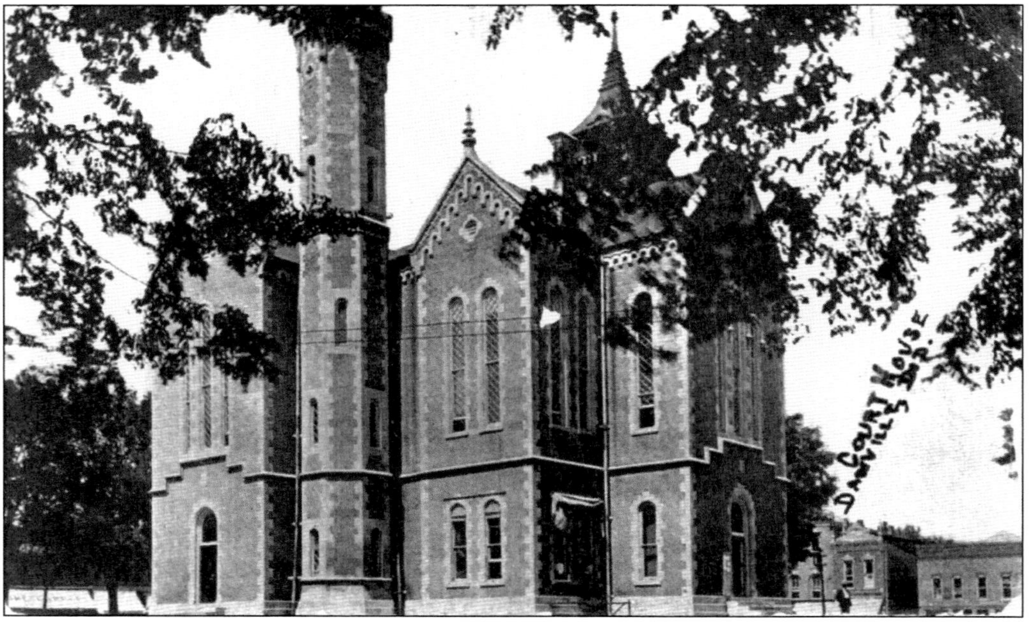

This photograph is unusual in that it is taken from the side of the courthouse with the round tower. Most of the pictures of this courthouse seem to have been taken from the side of the other tower. A brief view of the business buildings beyond can also be seen. The man standing outside the building is not identified. (Indiana Room, Danville-Center Township Public Library.)

The county courthouse has always been used for a location to discuss the political matters of the day. The event of this gathering was to hear speakers at a Republican rally in 1896. There is quite a crowd on the lawn, and the horses and carriages are lined up on the street. (Indiana Room at Danville-Center Township Public Library.)

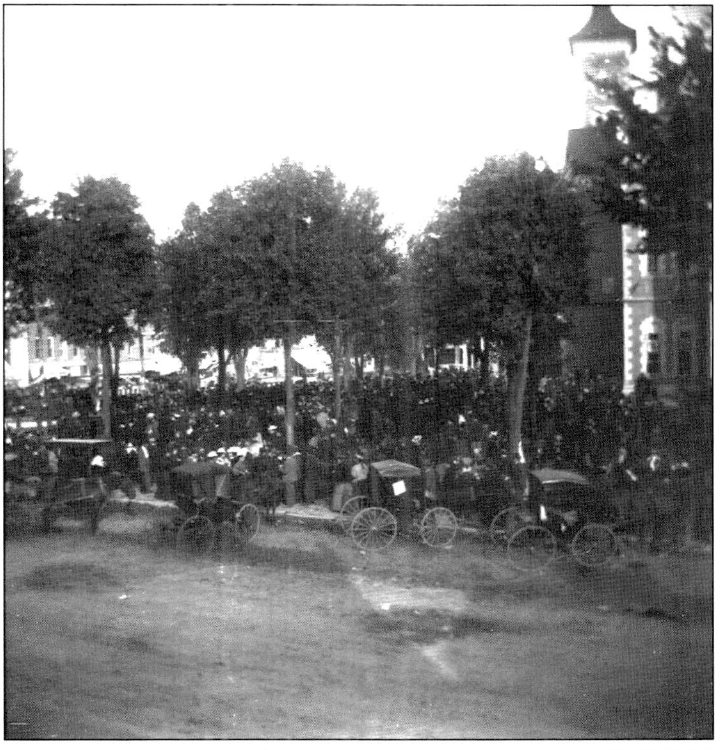

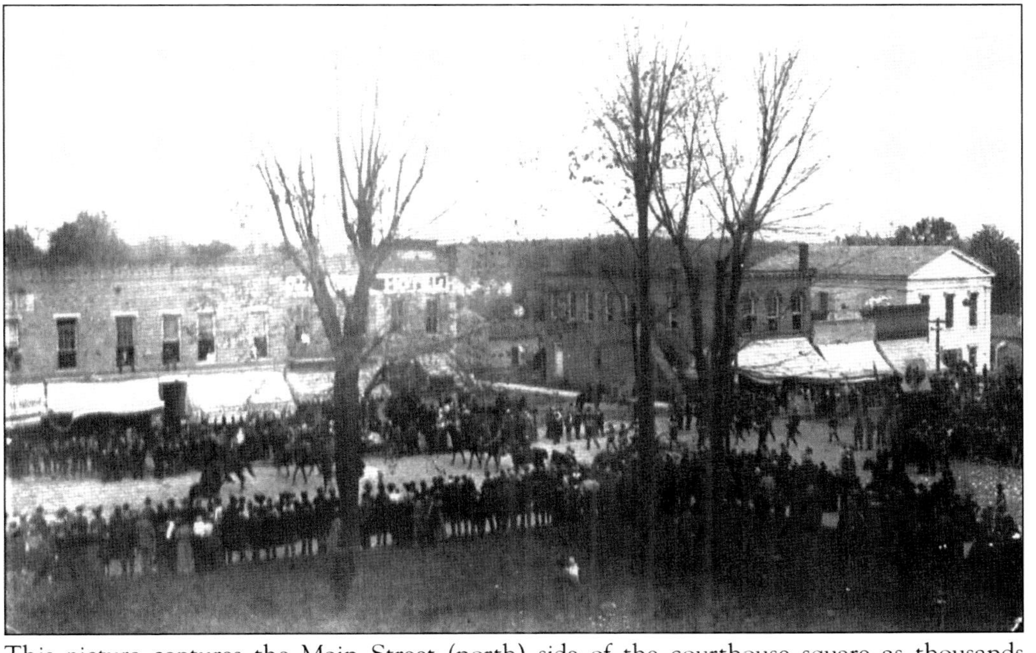

This picture captures the Main Street (north) side of the courthouse square as thousands participate in a parade estimated at four miles long in support of the candidacy of William McKinley for president of the United States. Note the people on top of the store building in the middle of the picture.

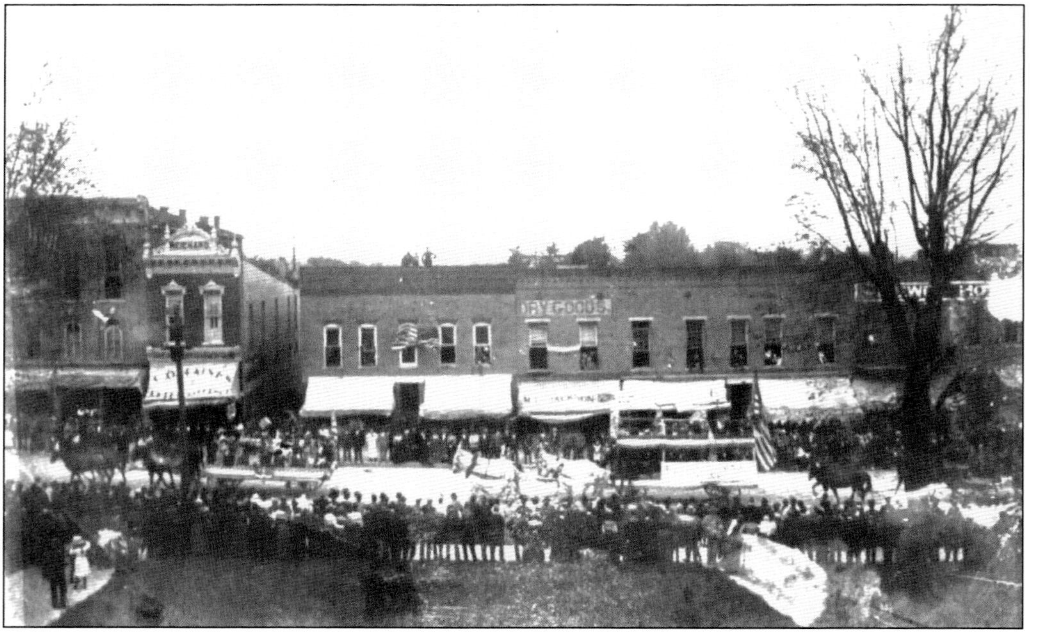

According to the *Danville Republican*, November 1, 1900: "It was a mighty demonstration. It was the tribute of Hendricks county people to the government at Washington. It was the homage paid to prosperity, to good times, to an honest dollar and a chance to earn it." Danville was full—estimates numbered the crowd watching the parade at 12,000 to 15,000. (Danville Chamber of Commerce.)

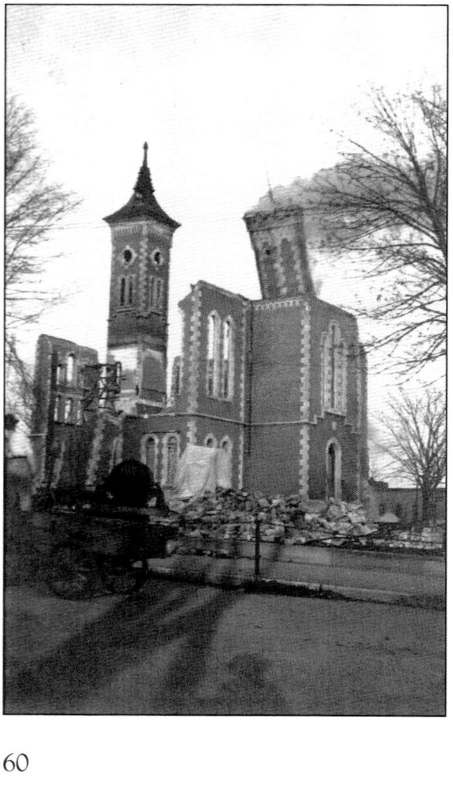

The tower falls during demolition of the third courthouse. The second, third, and current courthouses have all stood on the same site, across the street from the geographic center of Hendricks County. Today the courthouse is the center of the court system and the county uses the Old South Elementary School as the Hendricks County Government Center, housing other arms of county government there. (Indiana Room, Danville-Center Township Public Library.)

Watching the demolition must have been a popular pastime, for there is a large crowd watching as a substantial part of the courthouse has been torn down. This is one of a series of real-photo postcards that were made of the destruction of the courthouse that had been the home of Hendricks County government for just about 50 years. (Indiana Room, Danville-Center Township Public Library.)

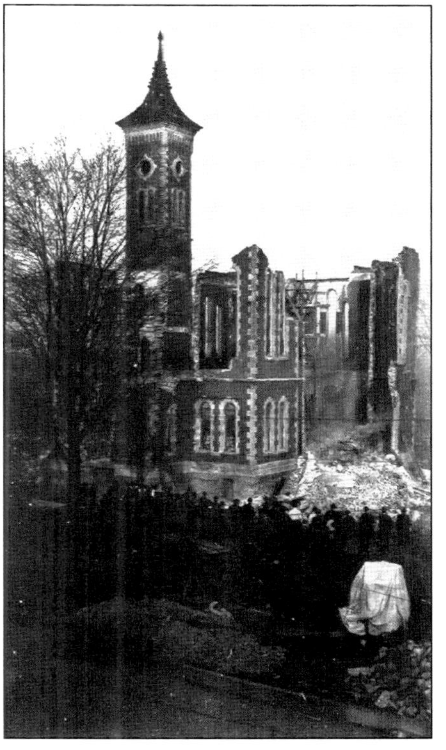

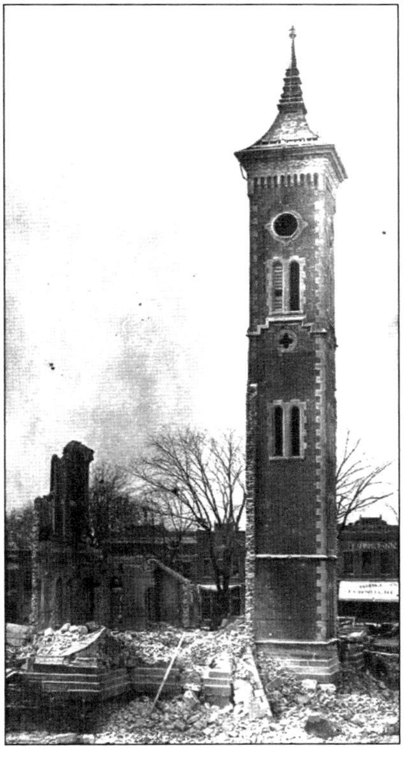

Early Danville residents must have considered this tower to be the signature feature of the third courthouse, for they left it standing until last in the demolition process. Or perhaps it was just postponing the inevitable, for it must have been a sad day to see this last vestige of beautiful architecture turn into dust. (Indiana Room, Danville-Center Township Public Library.)

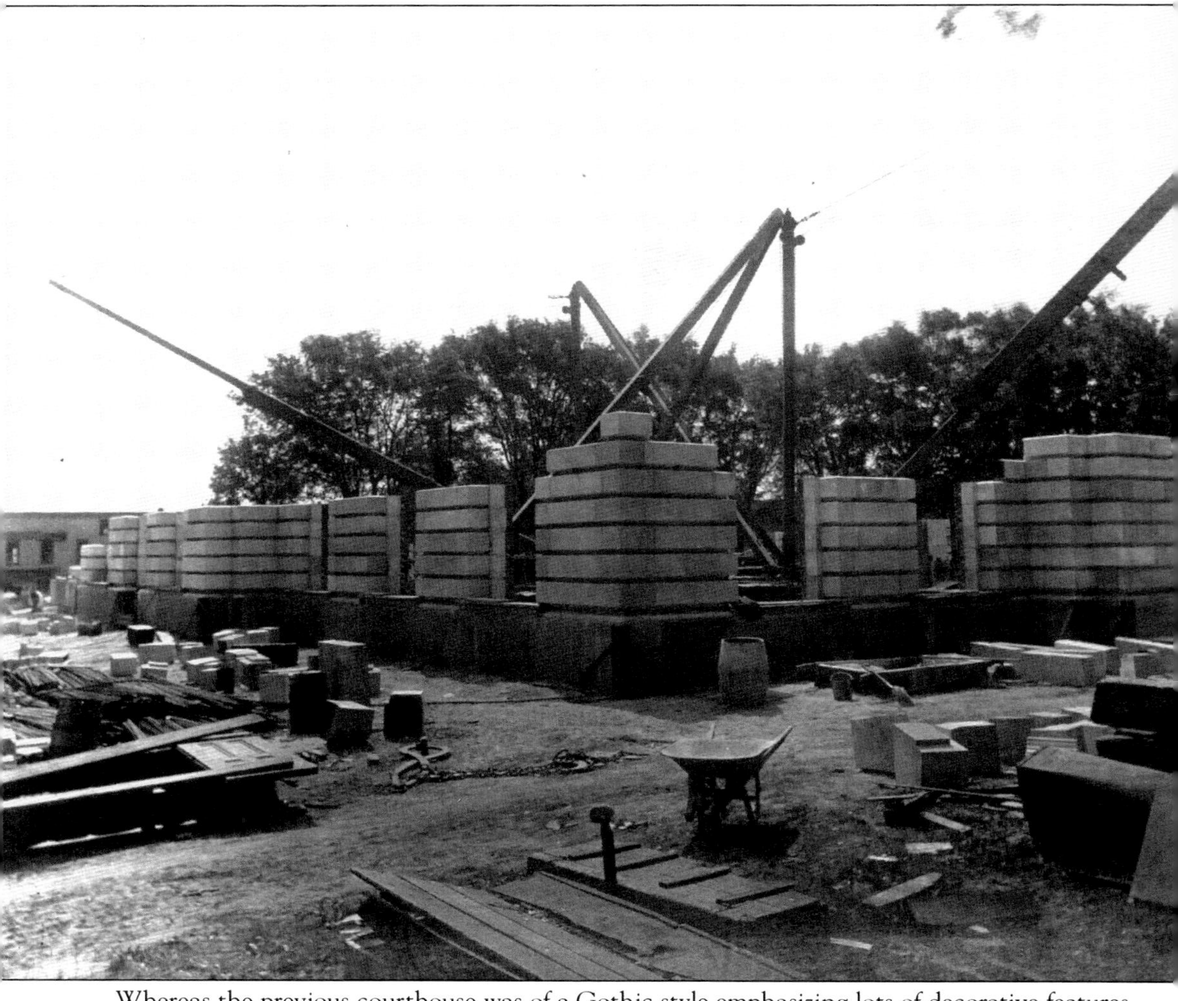

Whereas the previous courthouse was of a Gothic style emphasizing lots of decorative features, the new courthouse was designed to resemble a Roman temple utilizing Grecian Doric style and big slabs of Bedford Oolitic stone for the exterior. To support this building of monumental proportions, huge ribs of iron or steel were erected. (Judy Pingel.)

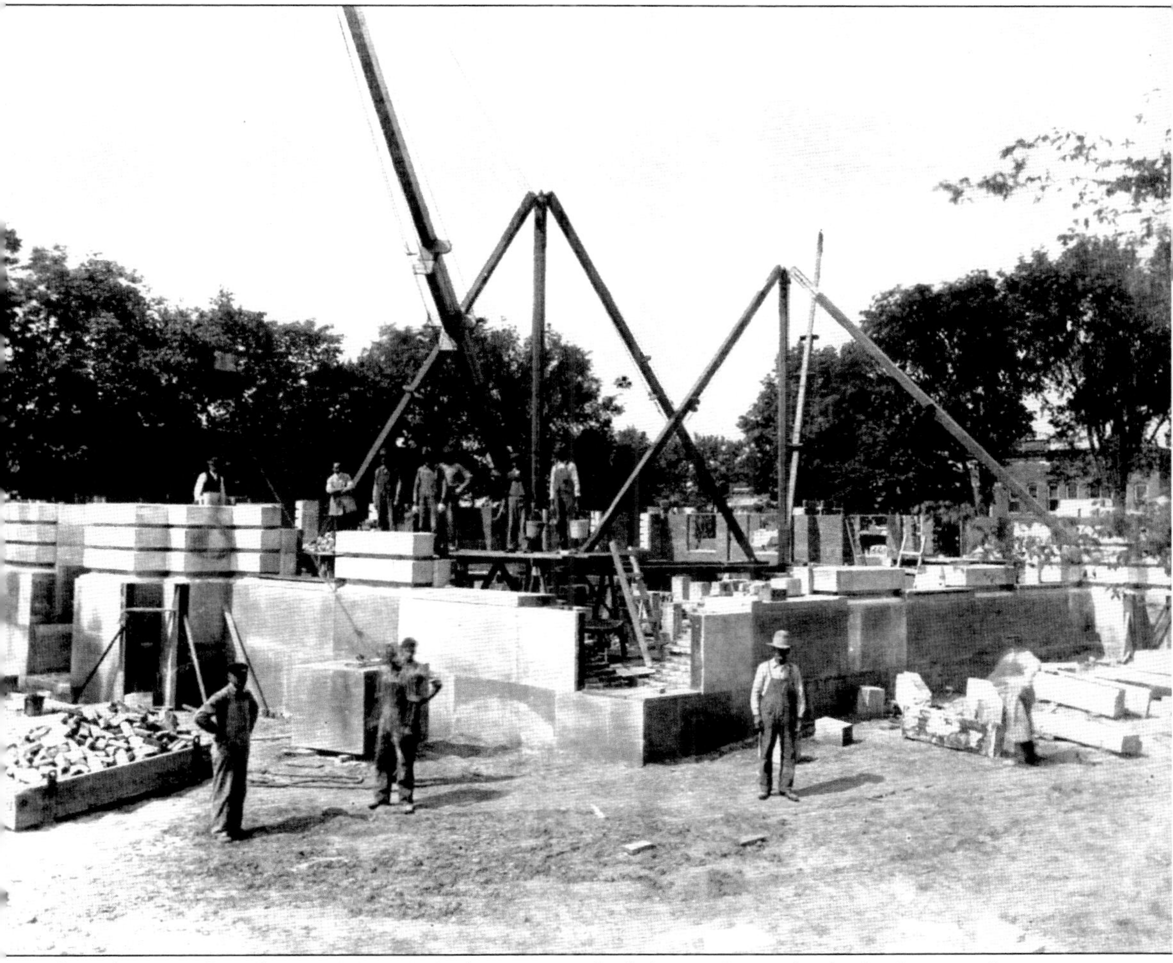

This photograph, taken in May 1913, shows several of the workers who built the courthouse. Many of them were local craftsmen and farmers who took great pride in being allowed to participate in the construction of this new edifice to serve as the home of county government. A story persists about one particular workman of color who was deathly afraid of snakes. Boys will be boys whether it is 2009 or 1913, and this particular workman was chased all over the construction site by his fellow workmen with a faux snake until a halt was finally called to the "fun." (Judy Pingel.)

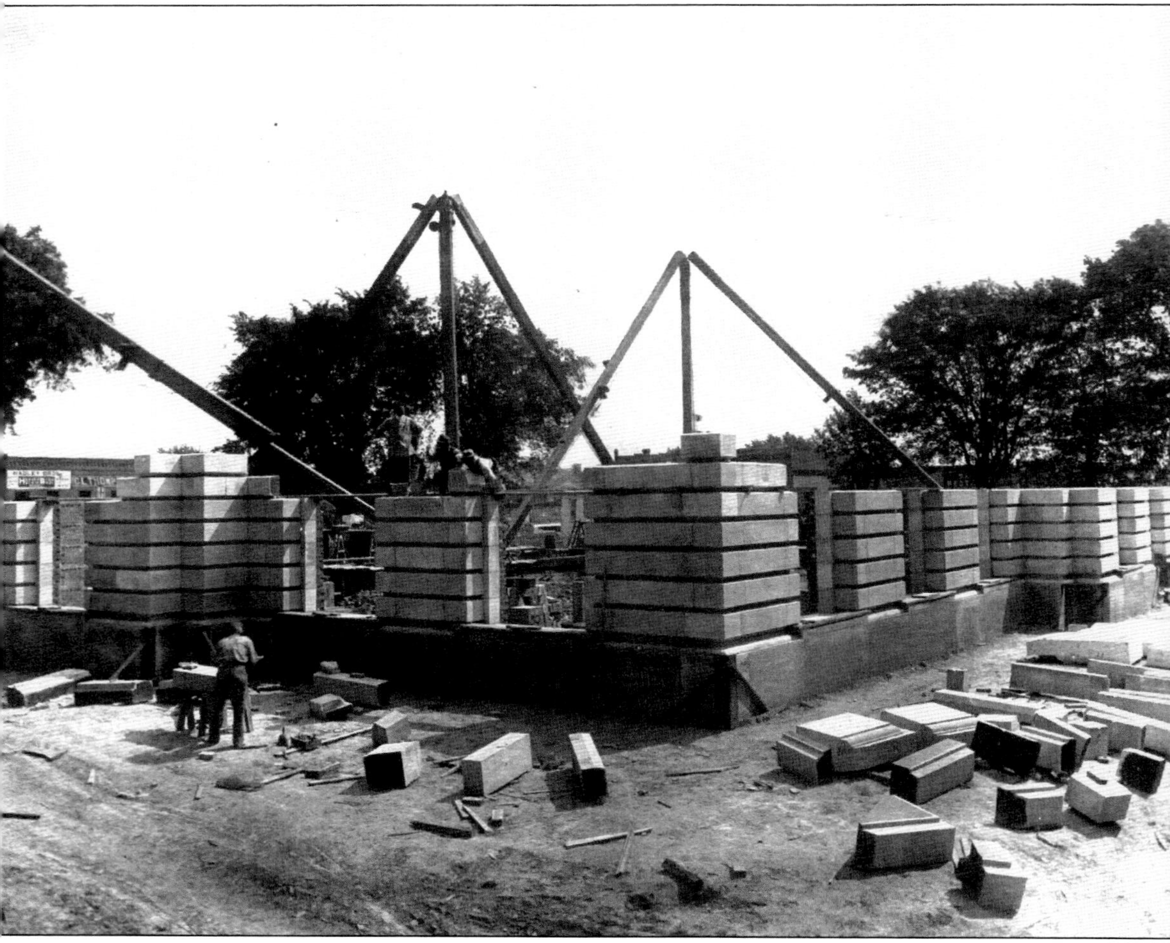

This photograph, taken in May 1913, shows construction on the west side of the courthouse. The workman on the ground appears to be cutting a stone for placement, while the workmen and an apparent supervisor atop the construction are fitting a stone into place. The Thompson Drug store building on Main Street can be seen over the top of the construction. (Judy Pingel.)

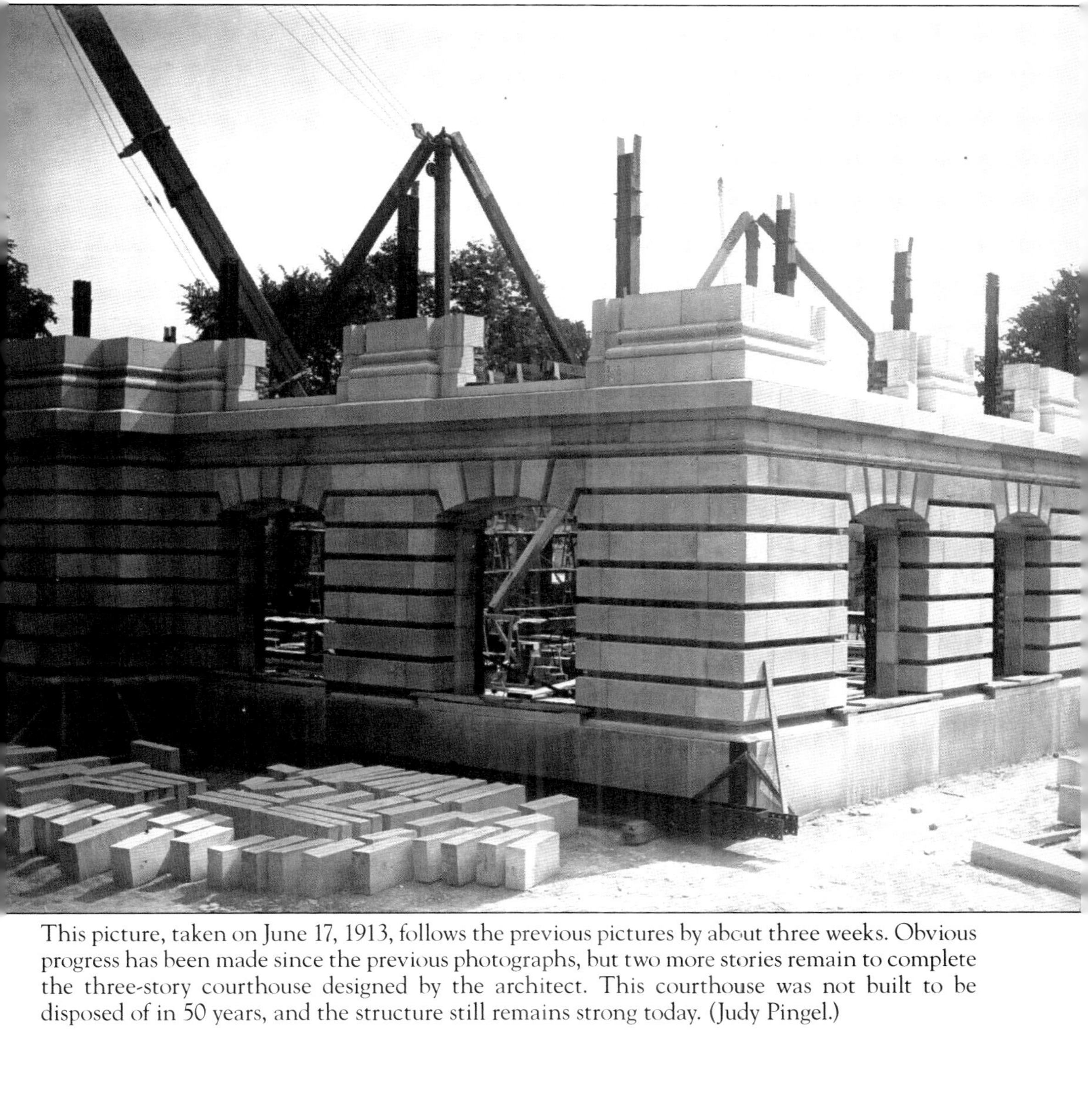

This picture, taken on June 17, 1913, follows the previous pictures by about three weeks. Obvious progress has been made since the previous photographs, but two more stories remain to complete the three-story courthouse designed by the architect. This courthouse was not built to be disposed of in 50 years, and the structure still remains strong today. (Judy Pingel.)

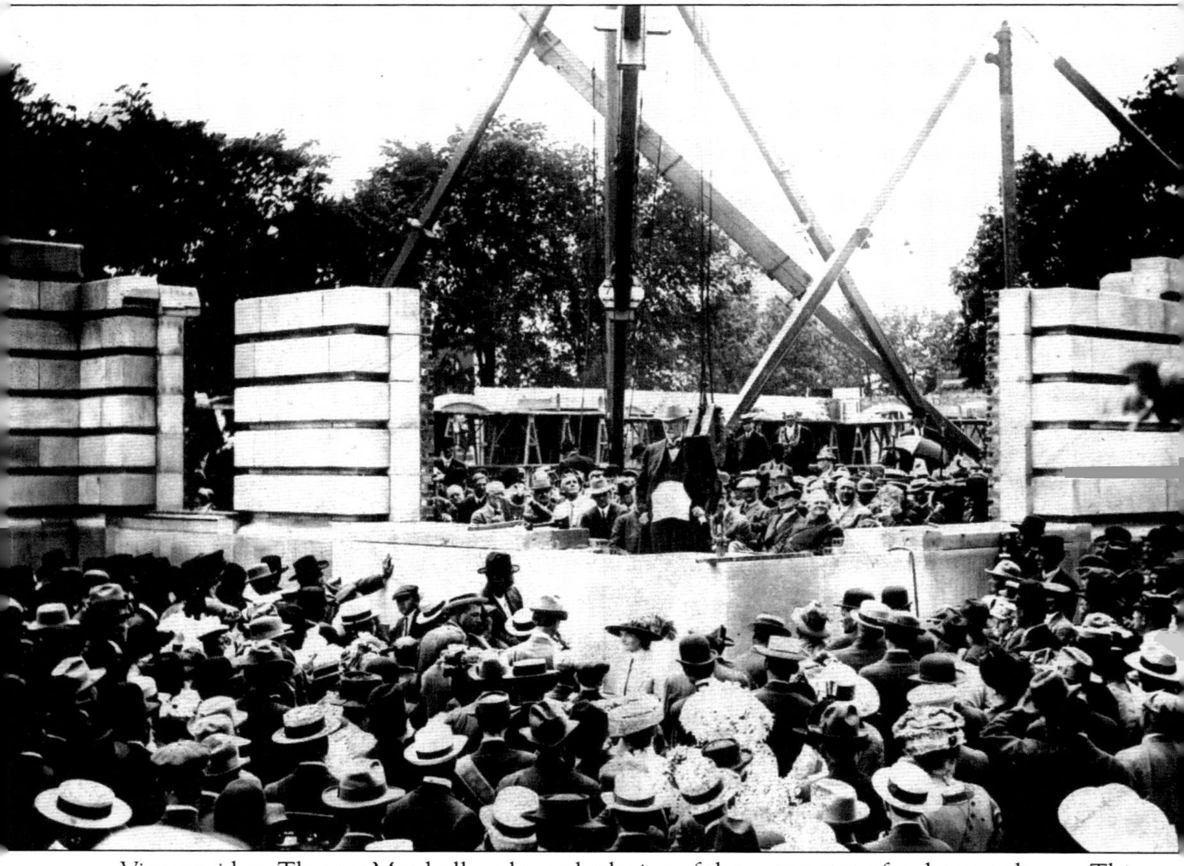

Vice president Thomas Marshall spoke at the laying of the cornerstone for the courthouse. This was unusual for several reasons. Since the Civil War, Hendricks County has voted for very few Democrats, let alone the Woodrow Wilson–Thomas Marshall ticket. However, he was the sitting vice president of the United States and history was devoid of such lofty visits to Danville. And secondly, he was a Hoosier having studied at Wabash College in nearby Crawfordsville. Notice the absence of any loudspeaker system other than the politician's lungs. Therefore, the crowd is huddled close to be able to hear all that was said. The laying of the cornerstone was a Masonic service as is revealed by Marshall's white apron. (Judy Pingel.)

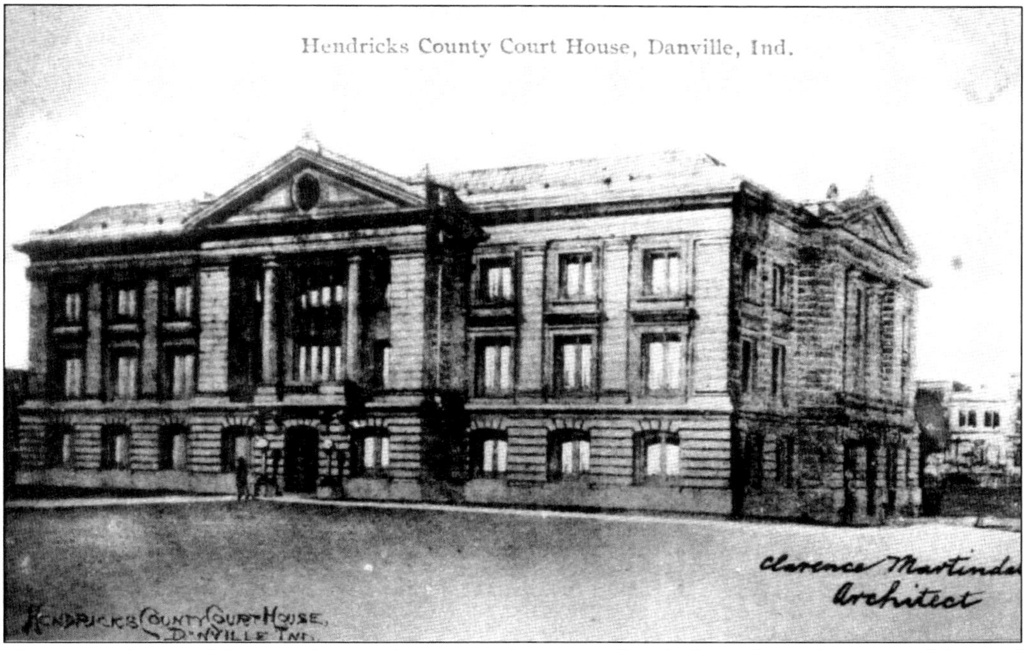

Upon completion of the courthouse, this postcard was issued with the architect's name emblazoned across the souvenir. All four sides of the building were equally emphasized with the only difference being the additional length of the north and south elevations. It was considered to be one of the finest-looking buildings in all of the state of Indiana. (Hendricks County Museum.)

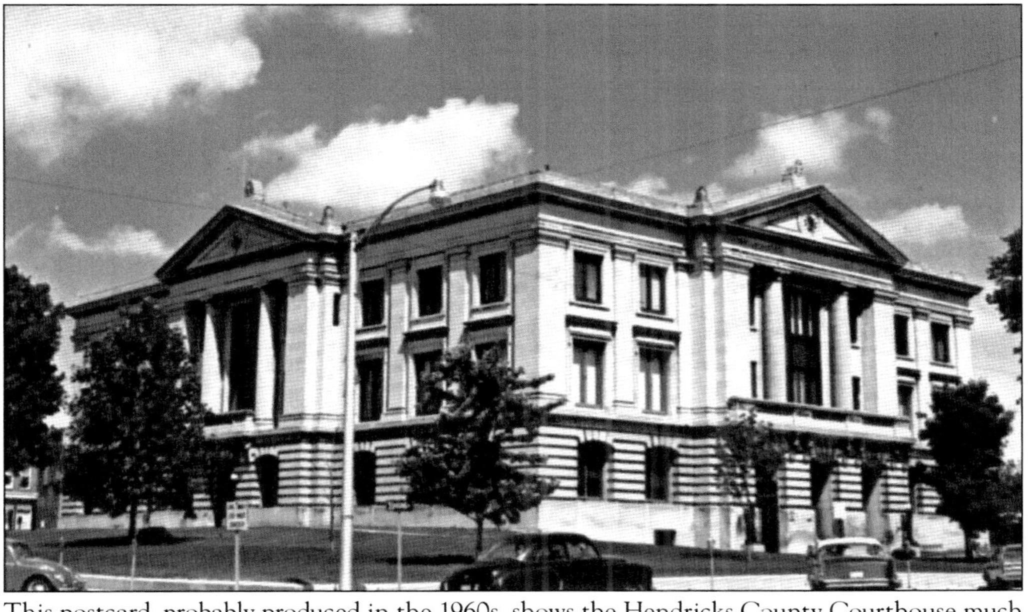

This postcard, probably produced in the 1960s, shows the Hendricks County Courthouse much as it appears today. The county commissioners maintain the building much as it appeared when it was built. Modern air-conditioning required the placement of a unit on the south lawn in a landscaped area. A prominence high above the south door blew down in a terrific storm. The interior of the building has been rearranged many times. (Hendricks County Museum.)

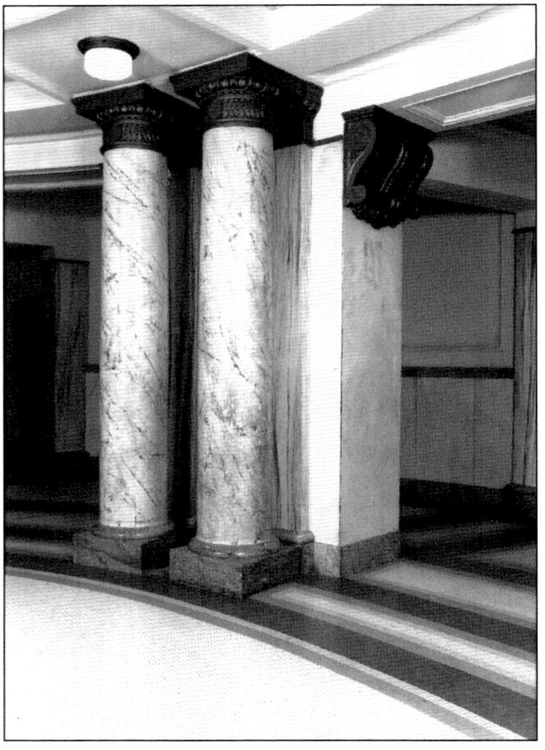

Marble columns adorn the first floor of the courthouse, extending through the rotunda up to the mosaic above the third floor. During many elections large blackboards were placed here to track election returns—votes were counted and the results displayed throughout the night. The rotunda is the crossroads of the courthouse; lawyers, citizens, litigants, and taxpayers all cross paths. (Judy Pingel.)

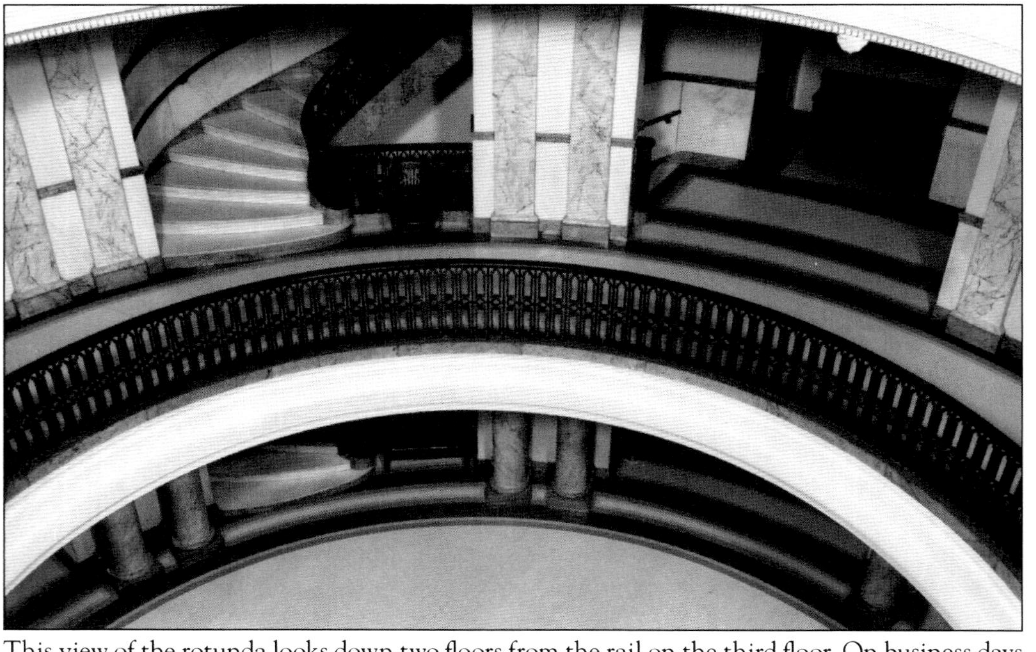

This view of the rotunda looks down two floors from the rail on the third floor. On business days there are often large numbers of people congregating in the public areas of the building. The private offices are populated by a small number of hardworking, public-spirited people doing the work of a constantly growing county. (Judy Pingel.)

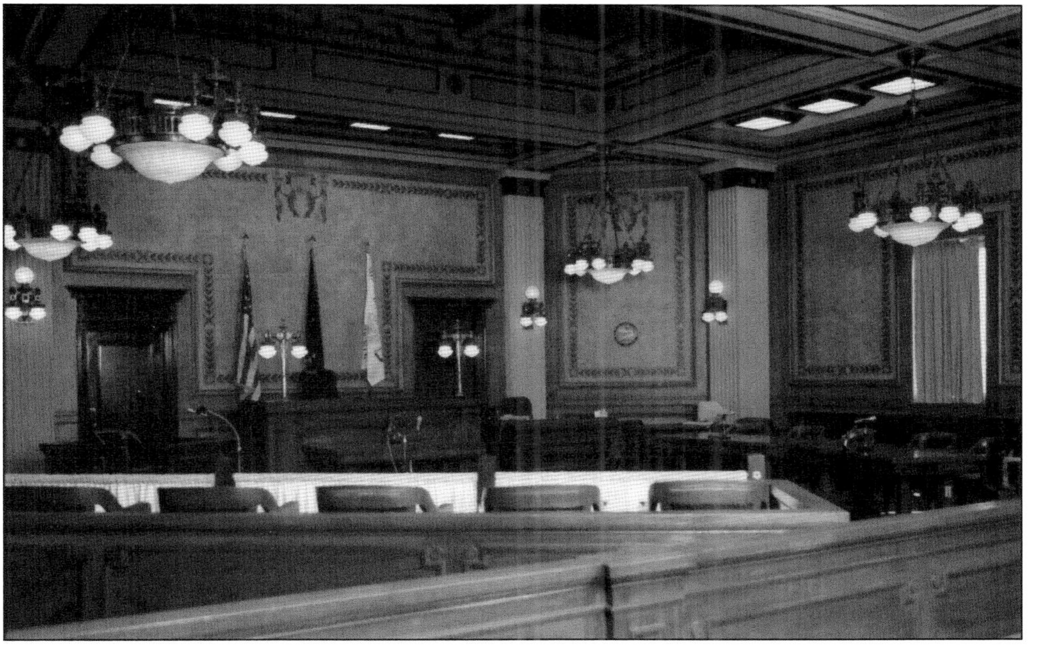

The circuit court room is on the third floor of the courthouse. It has the largest spectator space available in the county. This view looks out from behind the jury box, where jurors sit on civil or criminal cases. To the right are the counsel tables where attorneys for the plaintiff and defendants sit. The court reporter sits between the counsel tables and the bench. The witness sits in the witness box seen at left. Elected in 1978, the circuit court judge is Jeff Boles. (Judy Pingel.)

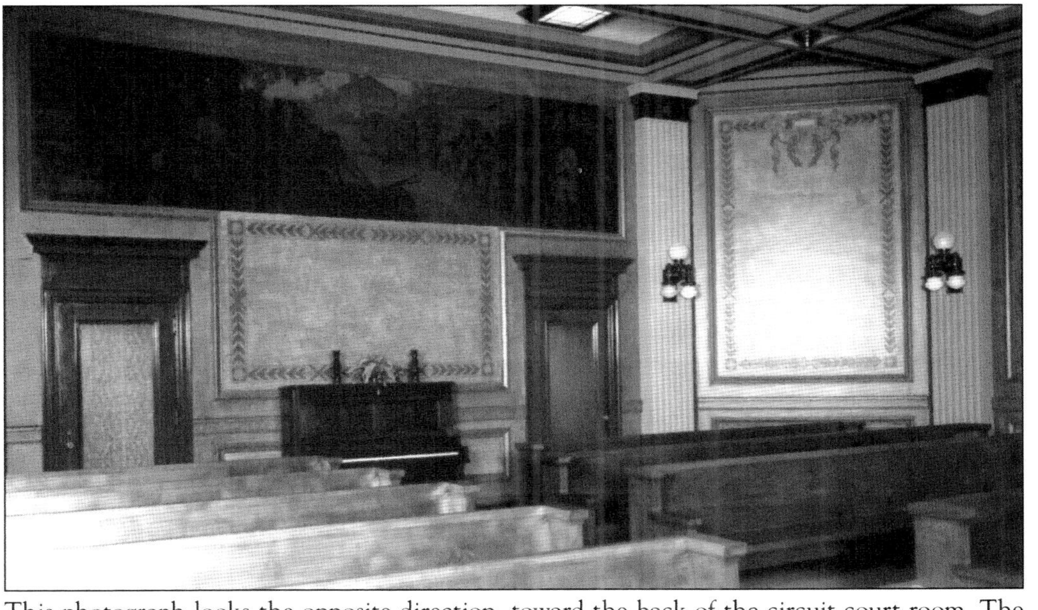

This photograph looks the opposite direction, toward the back of the circuit court room. The spectator seats open on the right to the door out of the court room. The piano is there as a historical curiosity, probably because this is the largest room in the building. And the mural on the wall says Judge Boles "is worth more than the whole building." (Judy Pingel.)

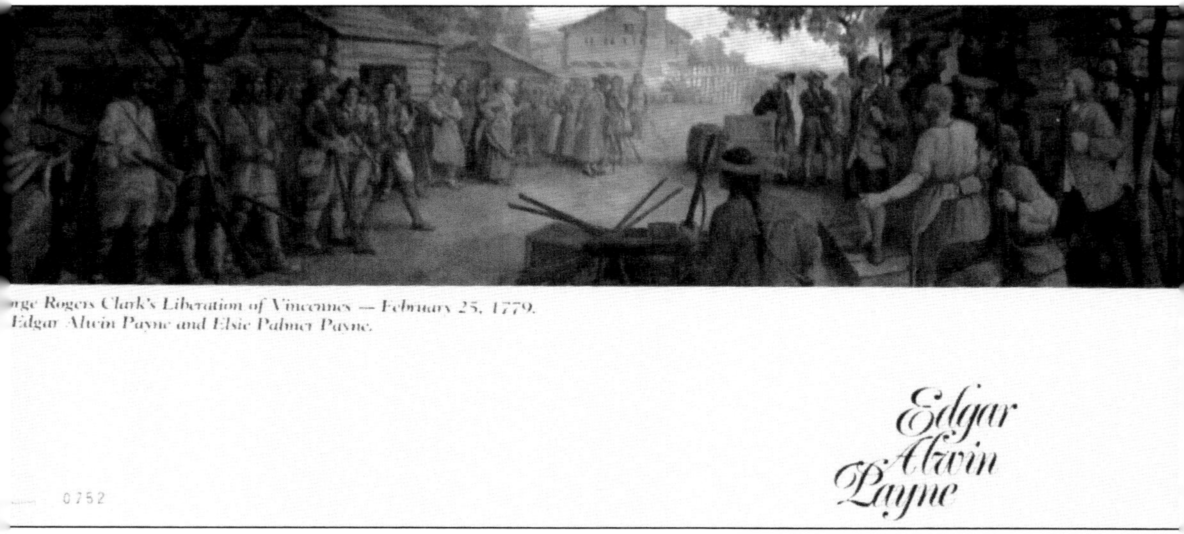

The circuit court mural is titled *George Rogers Clark's Liberation of Vincennes—February 25, 1779.* Painted by Edgar Alwin Payne and Elsie Palmer Payne in 1914, this mural was planned as an integral part of the Hendricks Circuit Court. Painted on canvas with oil, it measures 4 feet, 5 inches by 18 feet, 8 inches. It is priceless as it is the only remaining example of the collaborative work of the Paynes. (Judge J. V. Boles, Hendricks Circuit Court, and Hendricks County.)

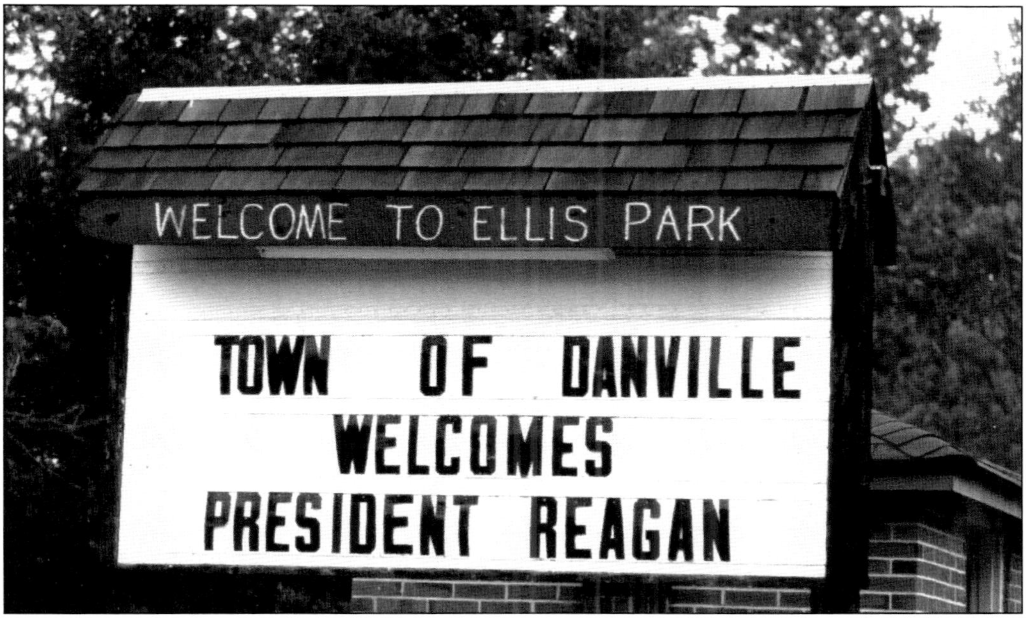

During the week leading up to July 13, 1987, word began to circulate that somebody important was going to visit Danville. Soon it became clear that the rumor was true—the "somebody important" was none other than Ronald Reagan, president of the United States. The sign at Ellis Park was used as a community message board and offered a greeting to the only president to visit Danville! (Hendricks County commissioners and Hendricks County.)

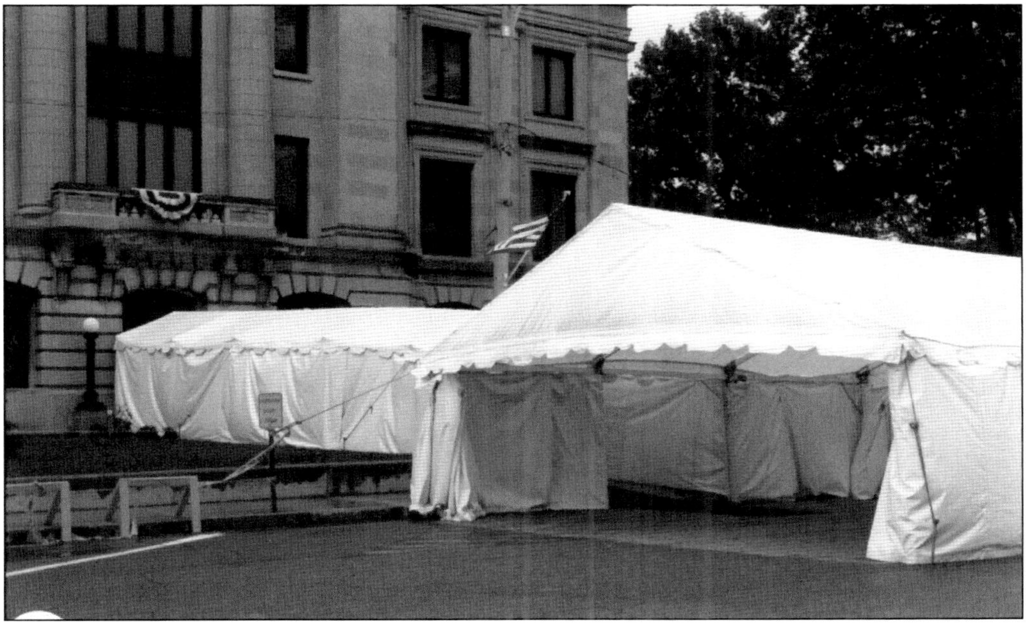

Early in his presidency Ronald Reagan was the object of an assassination attempt at the Washington Hilton Hotel. The Secret Service developed new methods to protect the president, including use of a tent to shield the president when he was not in his protective limousine. (Hendricks County commissioners and Hendricks County.)

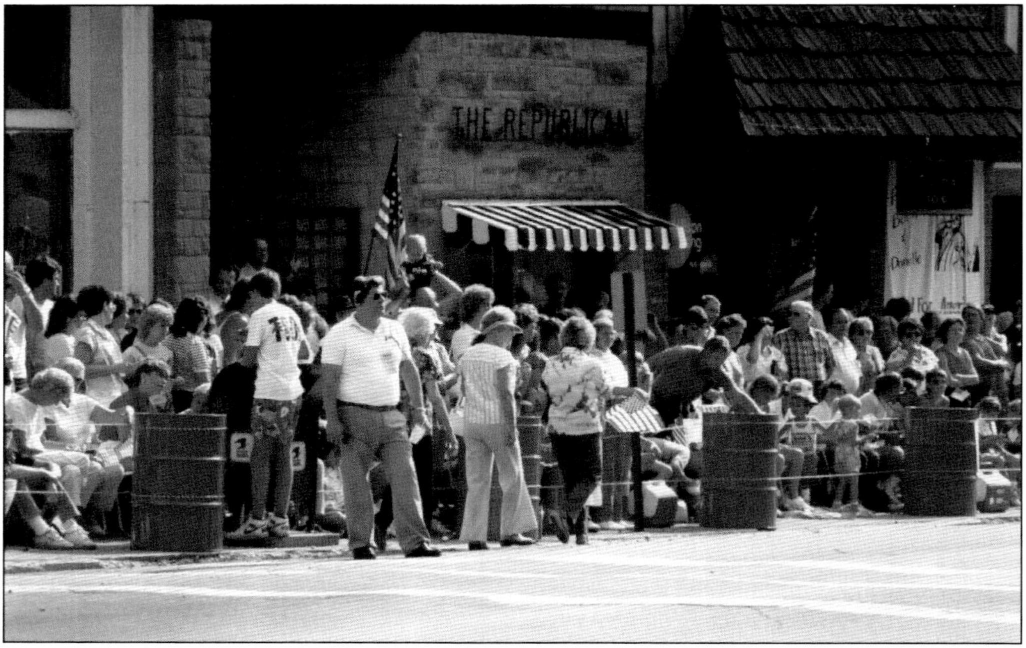

Danville and Hendricks County turned out in force to get a glimpse of the president. This picture, taken on East Main Street in front of the Basket Shop and the Danville Republican, shows people lining the sidewalks long before the presidential motorcade was due into town. This photograph also shows some of the security that was used to control the massive crowd. (Hendricks County commissioners and Hendricks County.)

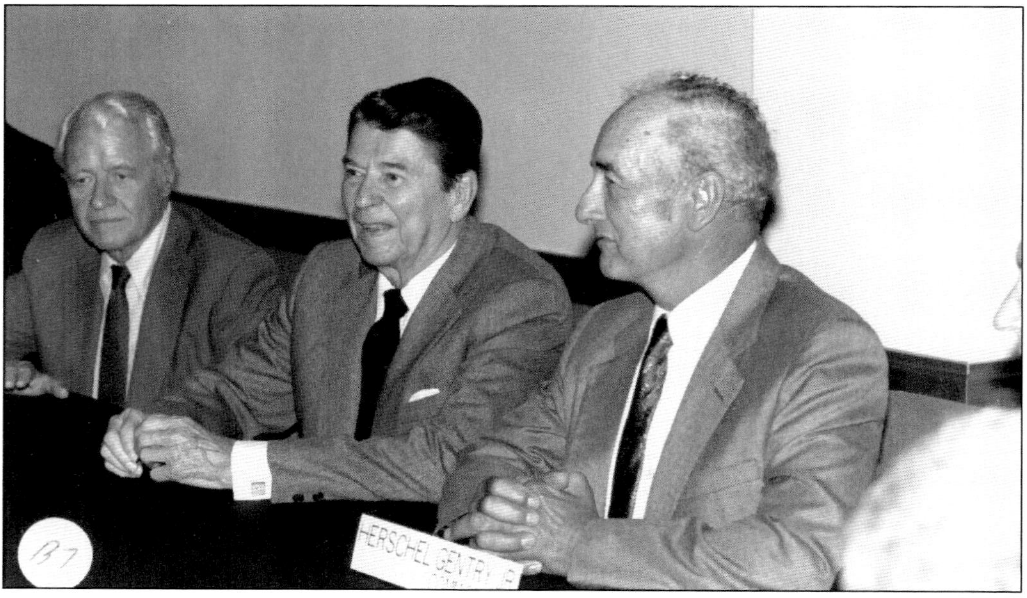

Before speaking to a limited crowd in the rotunda of the courthouse, the president met with Gov. Bob Orr and 16 other elected officials, including the county commissioners, in a room on the third floor of the courthouse. On the president's right is Governor Orr, and Commissioner Herschel Gentry Jr. is on his left. (Hendricks County commissioners and Hendricks County.)

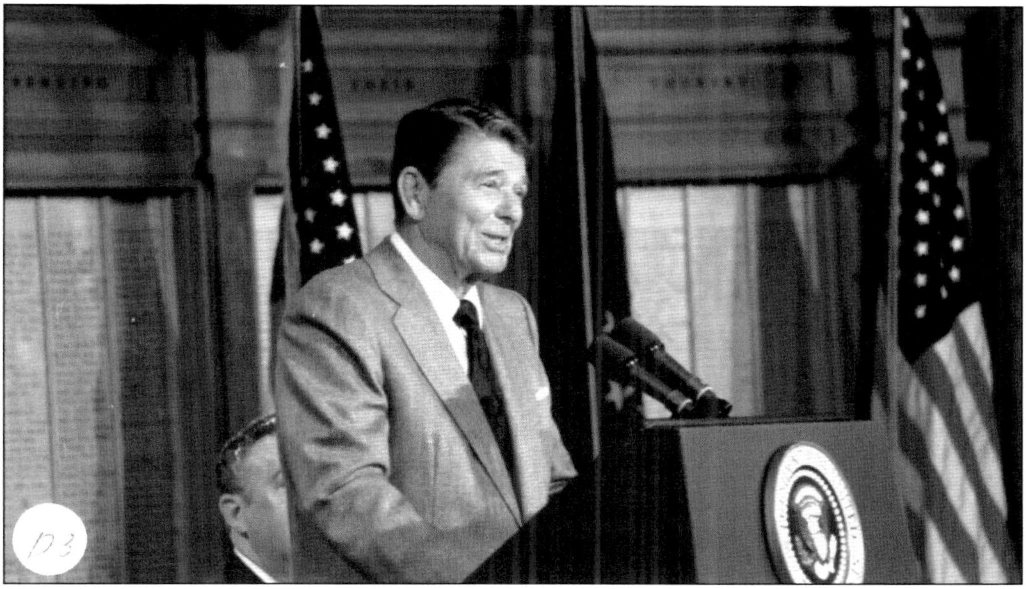

One hundred and forty-three people gathered in the rotunda of the courthouse to hear the president discuss his economic bill of rights—freedom to work, freedom to enjoy the fruits of one's own labor, freedom to own and control one's own property, and freedom of a free market. (Hendricks County commissioners and Hendricks County.)

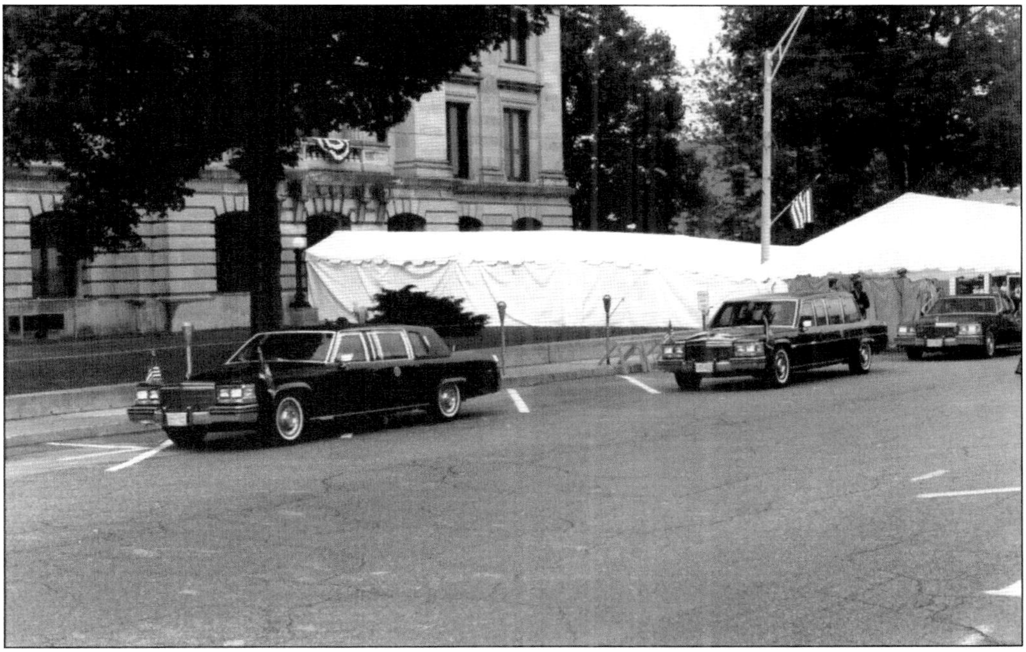

As the president's motorcade, led by 26 police motorcycles, assembled for departure via the west side of the courthouse square, people lined Main Street to get a final peak at the president. After addressing the national meeting of the National Association of Counties at the convention center in Indianapolis, the president returned to Air Force One and jetted back to Washington. (Hendricks County commissioners and Hendricks County.)

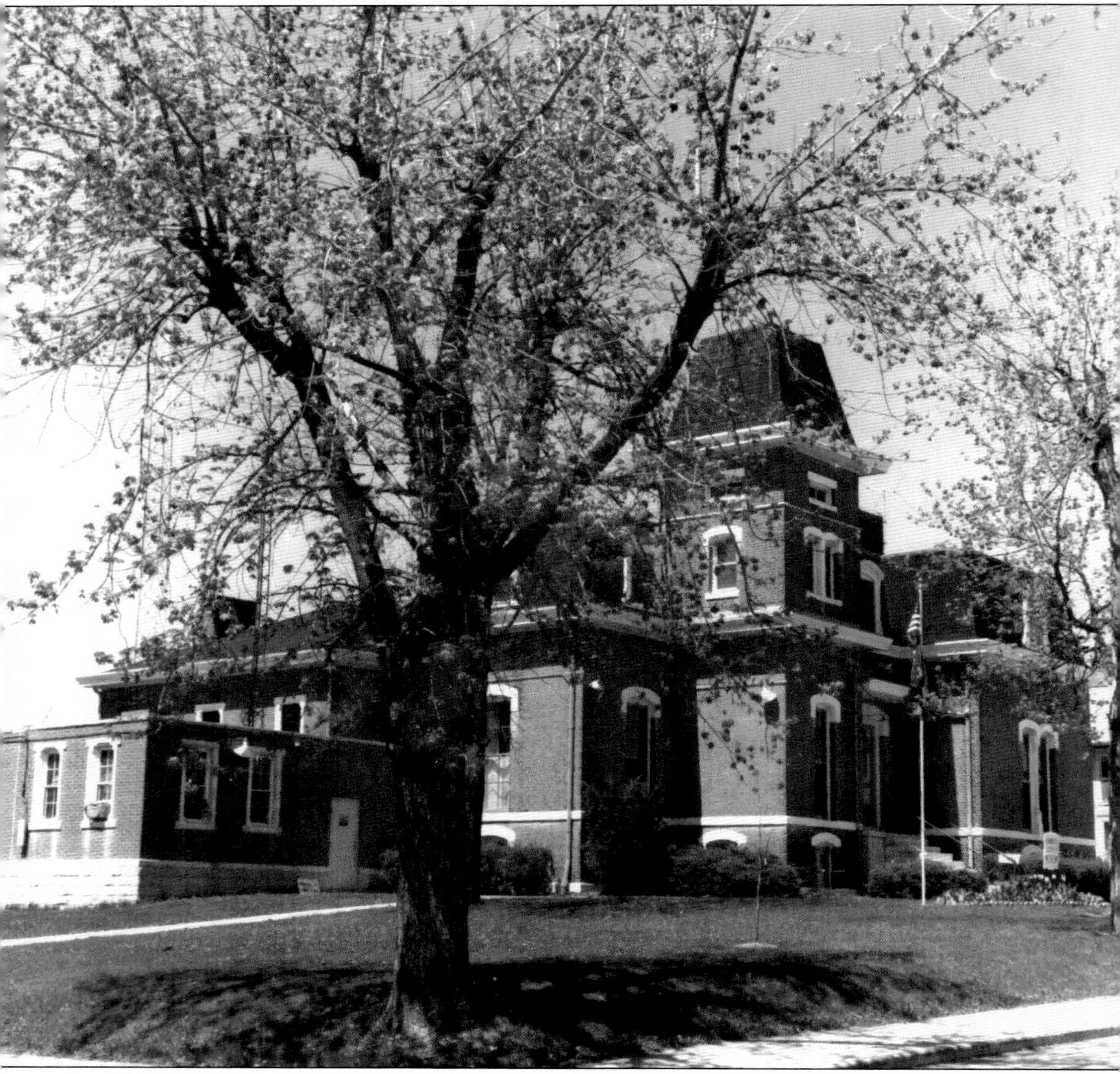

This is a contemporary view of the same building that is still owned and maintained by Hendricks County. It is now the home of the Hendricks County Museum, with the Friends of the Hendricks County Historical Museum Inc. responsible for the renovation and remodeling of the exhibit areas. The two-story brick structure is the only surviving example of the Second Empire style of architecture in Hendricks County. The Second Empire style was popular after the Civil War and has as defining elements a central tower and mansard roof. The museum was the first building in Hendricks County to be placed on the National Register of Historic Places. An exterior renovation of the building, which included restoration of the decorative band of rosettes on the mansard roof, was completed in 1996. The Hendricks County Museum is the largest repository in the world of a collection in regard to Central Normal College/Canterbury College, which was located in Danville from 1878 to 1951. The museum collection includes a large number of items relating to domestic life, agriculture, and education in the growth and history of Hendricks County. (Hendricks County Museum.)

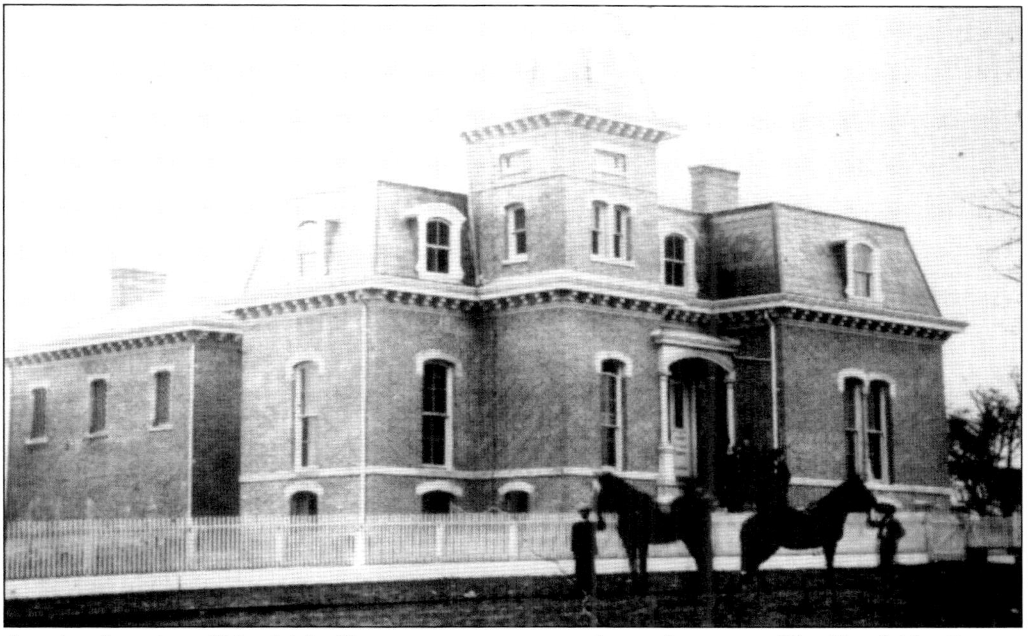

Another function of Hendricks County government was law enforcement. The Hendricks County sheriff's residence and jail, built in 1866 at an approximate cost of $30,000, served as the county jail until 1975. The trees around it are not very big, and there are no hitching posts, requiring the men to hold the horses until they are to be ridden away. (Hendricks County Museum.)

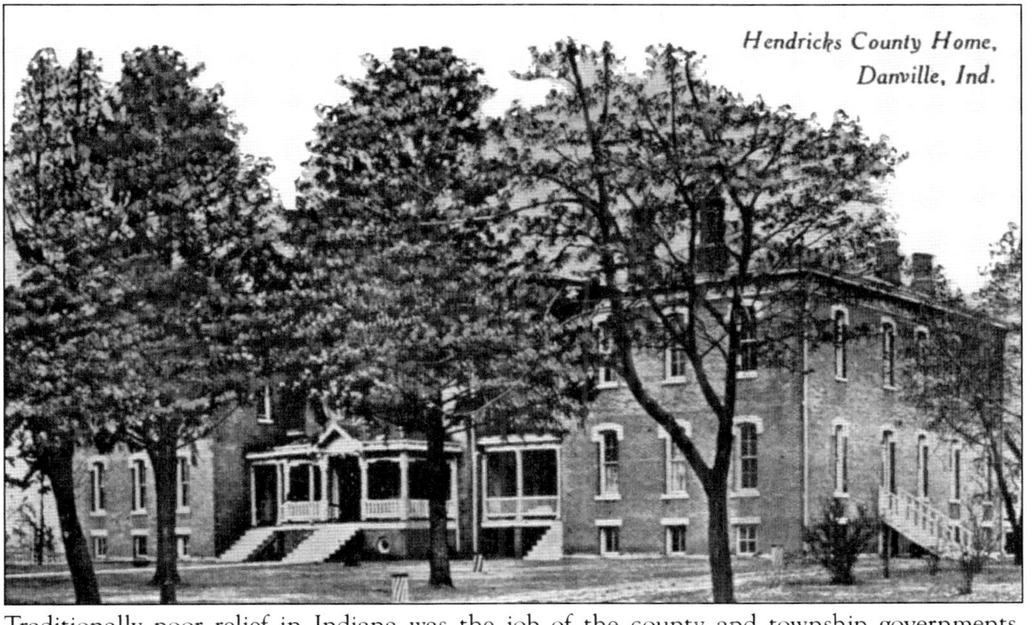

Traditionally poor relief in Indiana was the job of the county and township governments. Accordingly, the Hendricks County Home was built as the prototypical poor farm, where people could live and work when they had no other place to go. With the changes brought about in the social structure, it is one of several options now available for persons in need. (Indiana Room, Danville-Center Township Public Library.)

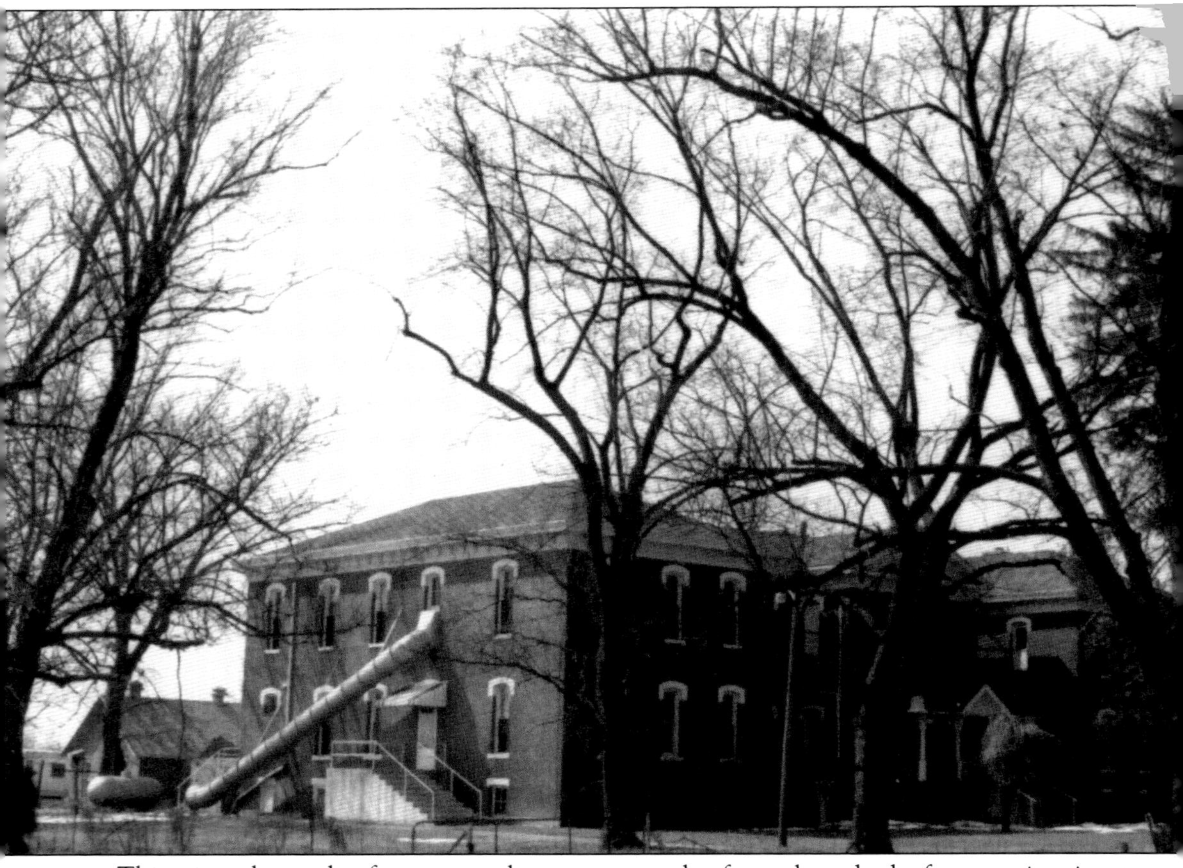

This view shows the fire escape that was once the favored method of evacuation in an emergency. The Hendricks County Home is now a unique housing facility in a historic homelike setting. The home is surrounded by a large yard with many mature trees and many flowers in the summer. In cooperation with outside providers, the home provides for the needs of residents facing mental and behavioral challenges. (Guilford Township Historical Collection, Plainfield-Guilford Township Public Library.)

Three

TRANSPORTATION

Transportation is a crucial key to what the residents of Danville have been in the past and to what they are today. When Danville was founded in 1824, it was done so by people who could walk or move a bit faster on horseback or in horse-powered equipment. The led to an insulation from the outside to the extent that each town and its surrounding residents had to be almost completely self-sufficient. It took a long time to get anywhere, and most things just were not worth it.

With the advent of the roads, crude though they were, people could travel to other places as long as they buried their reservations about the crudity and length of the trip. Railroads, however, really opened up the world. People from all over the country could come to Danville with relative ease and comfort. And crops, livestock, and the few things manufactured could go all over the country as well.

The governor of Indiana could, and did, live in Danville and commute to work each day at the statehouse in Indianapolis. Students could come from all over the country to Danville to attend Central Normal College. And they did.

Then, at the beginning of a new and wondrous century (20th) the electrically powered interurban provided clean, fast, and efficient transportation from town to town and even across state lines. A person could ship products, and they could make the trip themselves.

The automobile, however, gave a driver personal freedom that he or she did not have while waiting on mass transit with a schedule. The interurban system died, and then passenger train service all but died.

Danville now has a new airport. Will it significantly change the style of residents lives in Danville? And what of new regulations and restrictions on internal combustion engines coming from Washington? Will they restrict travel as it was in the days of pioneers in Danville and Hendricks County? The history of that has yet to be written.

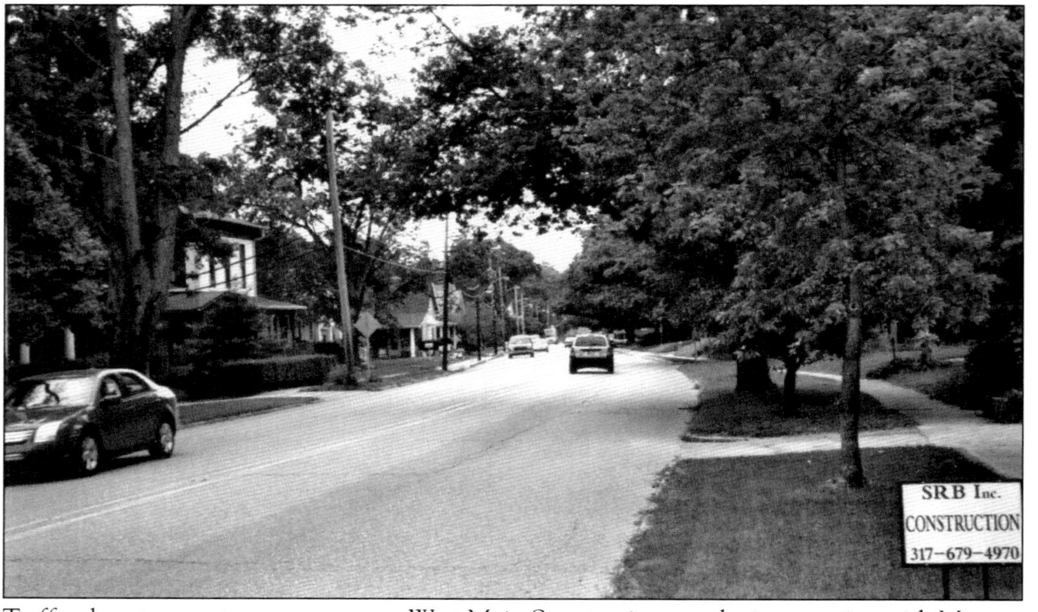

Traffic almost seems to never cease on West Main Street as it nears the intersection with Morgan Street. This is the gateway from the west into downtown, and whether by horse or by car, it has always been a main entryway into town. Traffic flow in the 21st century only seems to slow down a few times in the middle of the night. It is difficult to believe that at one time it was a dirt road that saw little traffic. (Author's collection.)

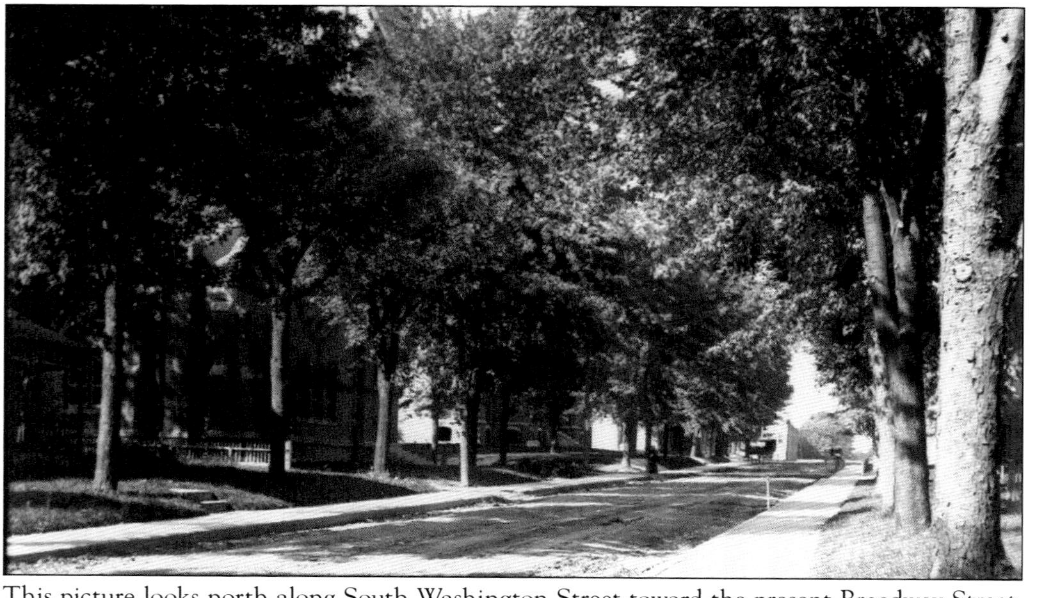

This picture looks north along South Washington Street toward the present Broadway Street, with what was then the Danville Methodist Church at the left with the strange-looking tower that will be examined more later. This street has all the appearance of a packed-dirt road that is not paved at all. It is difficult to determine, but there may be some gravel on the road. This is just one and a half blocks from the courthouse square. (Indiana Room, Danville-Center Township Public Library.)

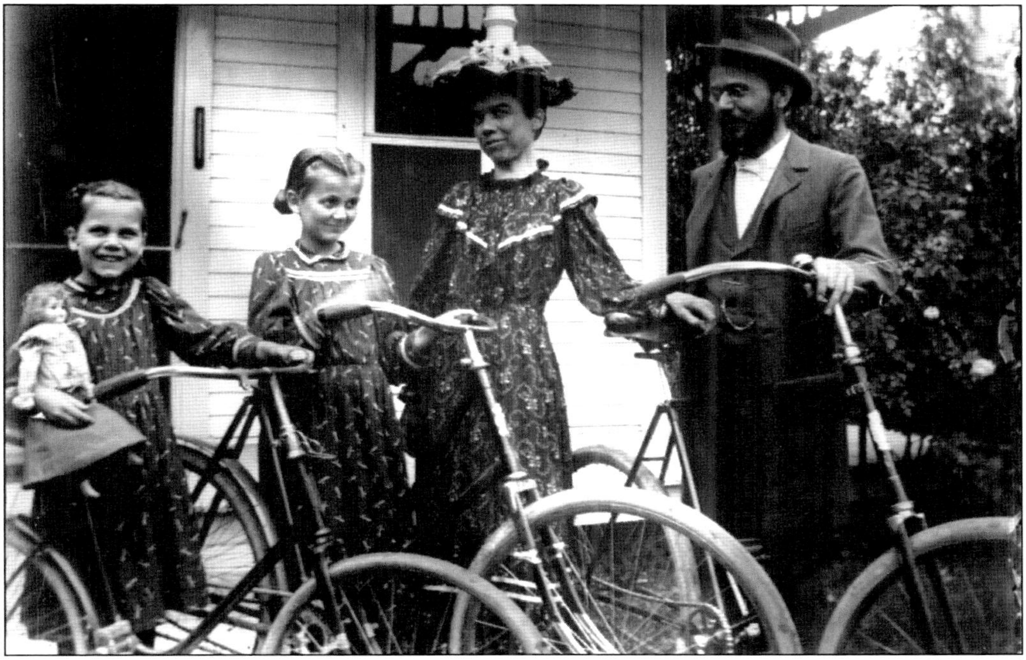

Nothing was better for a bicycle ride than the nonpaved roads around town. Here the well-dressed Charles Hargrave family prepares to depart with the girls in their long dresses, the mother in her hat, and the father with his vest, coat, and hat all in place. Also getting to make the trip was the well-dressed doll. (Indiana Room, Danville-Center Township Public Library.)

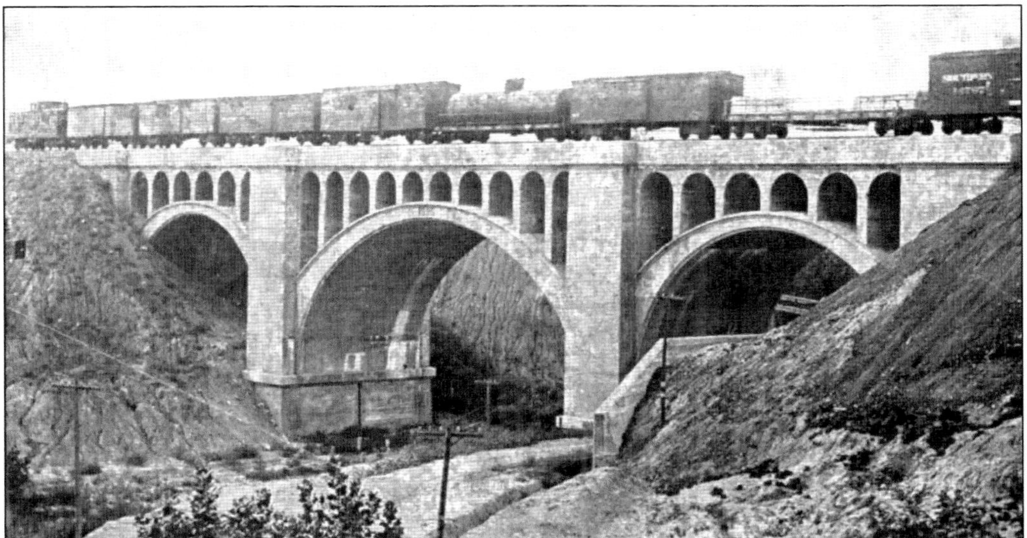

As of 2009, this railroad bridge over White Lick Creek in the southeast part of Danville is still reported to be haunted. One story says that an Irish workman fell into the concrete of the bridge as it was hardening, leaving him encased in the support structure of the bridge. Another story says that a young woman threw her baby to its death as the train passed over the bridge. Cries, moans, and screams are allegedly heard in the vicinity of the bridge. (Hendricks County Museum.)

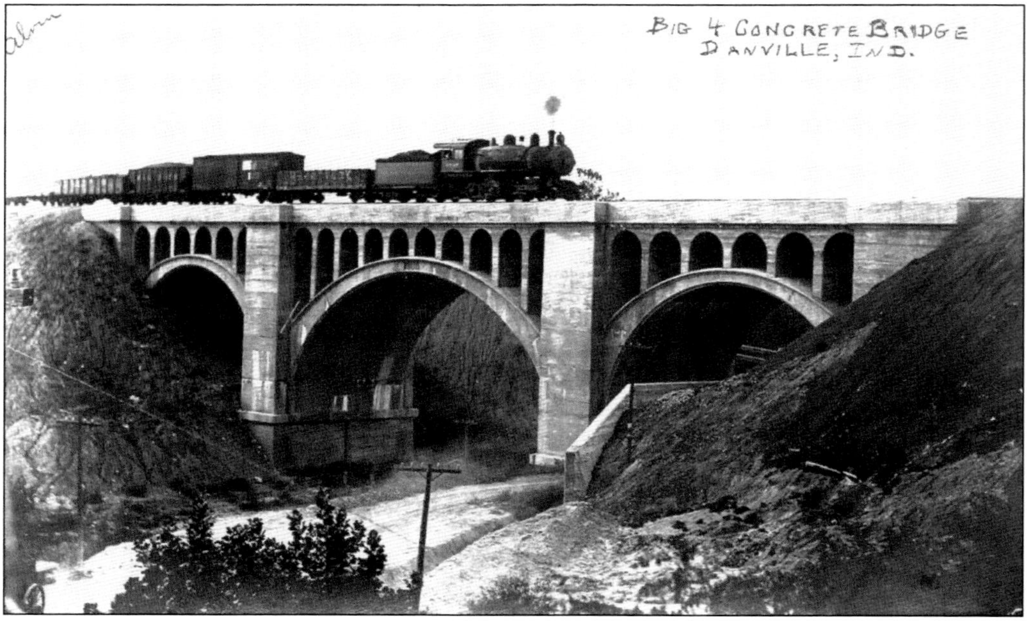

A steam engine pulls a freight train westward across the Big Four bridge just to Danville's southeast. The Big Four linked Cleveland, Cincinnati, Chicago, and St. Louis. Danville farmers and manufacturers could determine where they might get the best price for their products and ship them to that location. (Indiana Room, Danville-Center Township Public Library.)

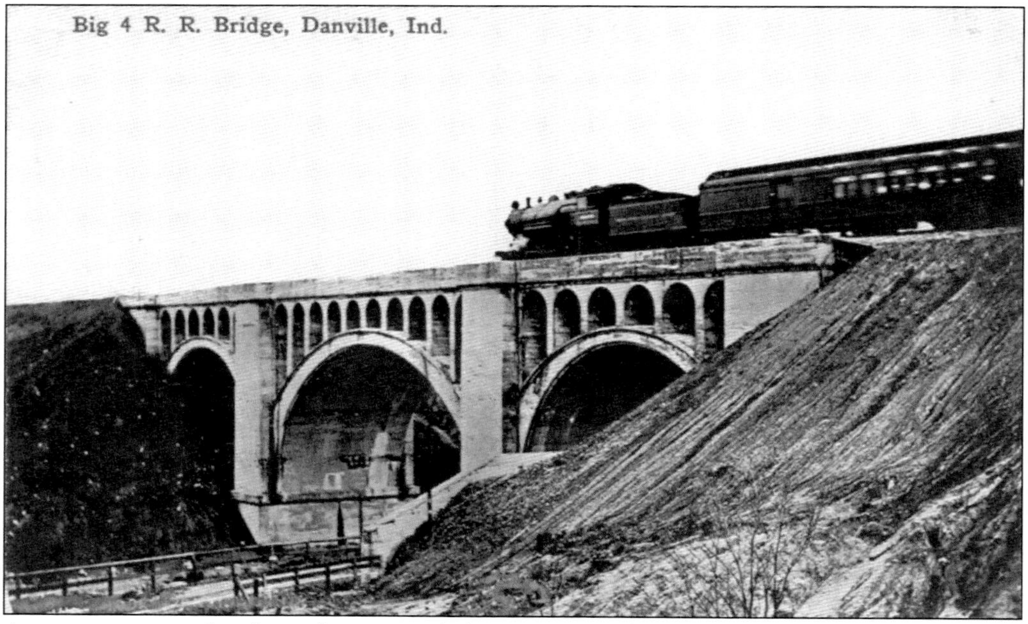

A passenger train heads to the east and the great cities beyond. It is possible, however, that the Danville passengers are heading no farther east than Indianapolis. Passenger trains were the first mass transit form of commuting. Later in this book a story is told of a famous Danville commuter. Passenger trains, however, gave Central Normal College a huge market from which to find educational prospects. (Indiana Room, Danville-Center Township Public Library.)

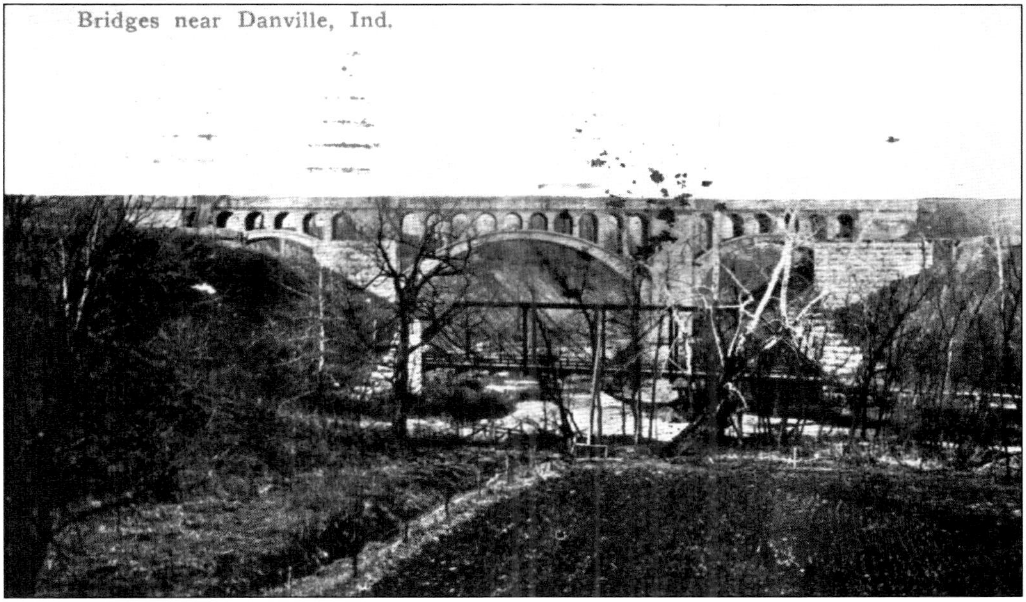

At some point after the construction of the Big Four bridge the town of Danville extended Broadway Street to connect to the road that ran under the Big Four bridge that the locals call the "Twin Bridges Road." Of course, the bridges are not twins at all, but there are two bridges there. Actually, the twin for the Big Four bridge is a few miles to the east as the train line approaches Avon and the Big Four yard. (Hendricks County Museum.)

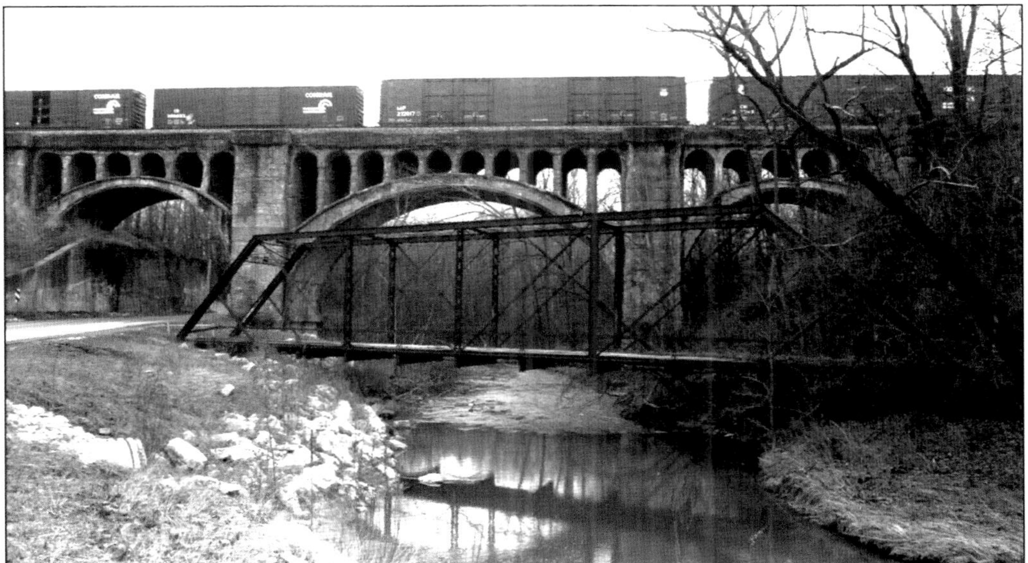

This is a modern photograph of a Conrail freight train going over the twin bridges. The access from Broadway Street has now been cut off, and much traffic flows through this intersection, even though the car lane through the railroad bridge is only one car length wide. This location is no longer southeast of Danville. The Kroger store, only a few hundred yards away, makes this area very much a part of today's Danville. (Indiana Room, Danville-Center Township Public Library.)

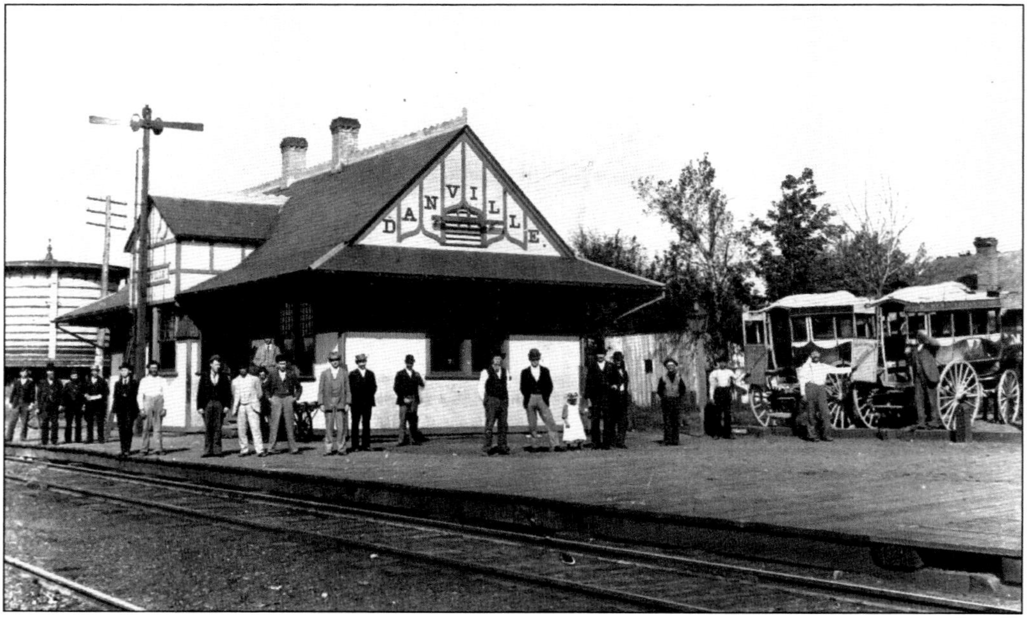

This is a photograph of the Danville railroad station in 1890. Of course steam engines have to fill up their water tanks; notice a large water tank to the left. The passenger train appears to be coming from the east as everyone's attention is directed that way. Members of the large group of travelers are all well dressed, and there are several horse-drawn coaches to carry the passengers into town. (Hendricks County Museum.)

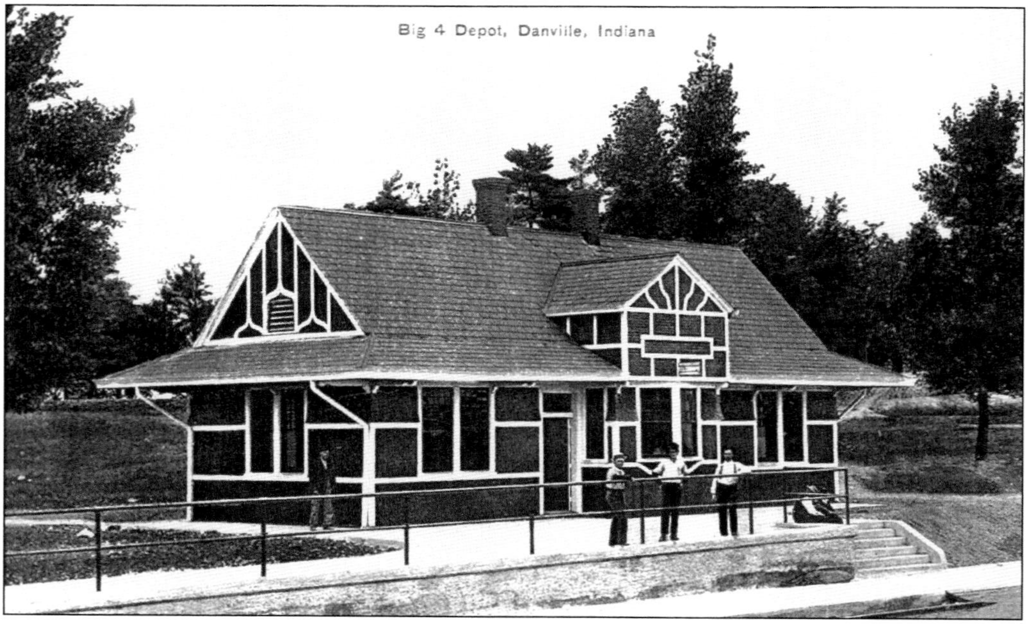

A much smaller crowd awaits the train in this picture. The color scheme of the depot has changed substantially from the previous picture, and the terrain looks a bit different as well. During the long history of train service to Danville the depot remained at the same place so far is as known. (Indiana Room, Danville-Center Township Public Library.)

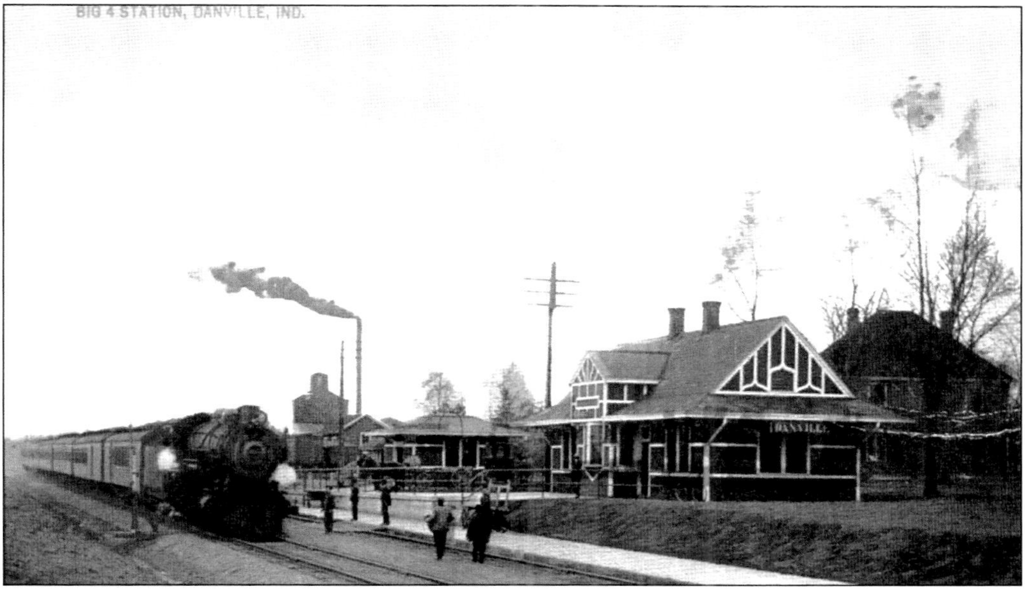

The railroad line and depot on the south side of Danville were completed in the 1850s. The railroad connected Danville to the rest of the world. A postcard from the author's family tells how his great uncle, then attending Central Normal College in the early part of the 20th century, was going to catch a passenger train headed west for home in southern Illinois. He would walk the three miles to their farm for the final leg of the trip. Due to the railroad, Central Normal College had a wider base of potential students to draw from than did many colleges. (Indiana Room, Danville-Center Township Public Library.)

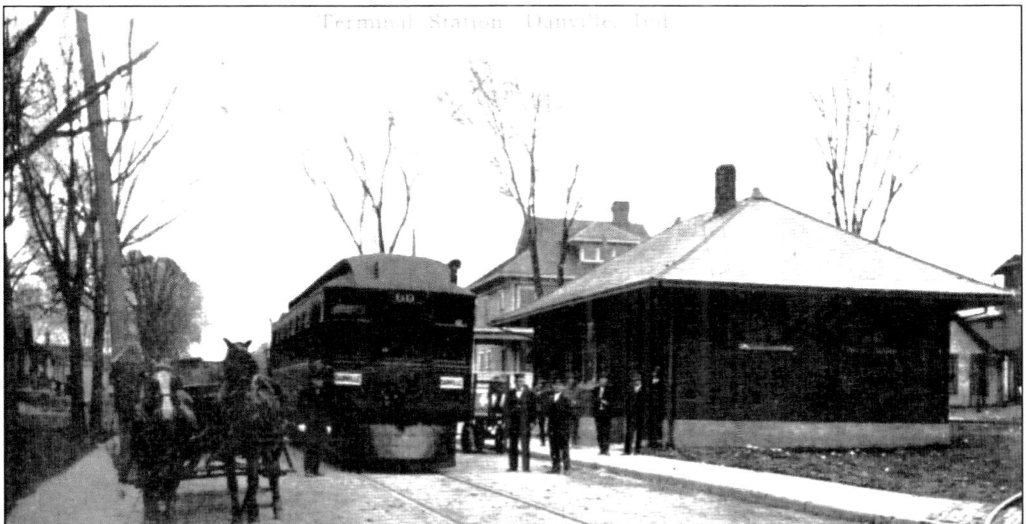

Between 1906 and 1930, Danville was connected to a vast network of interurbans—electric trolleys that extended over much of Indiana. Interurban service was provided from Danville to Indianapolis hourly. The track ran through what is now Danville's Ellis Park; a bridge over White Lick Creek was torn down in 1961. The interurban terminal in Indianapolis was one of the largest in the country, and from there a rider could make connections to travel around the state of Indiana. (Hendricks County Museum.)

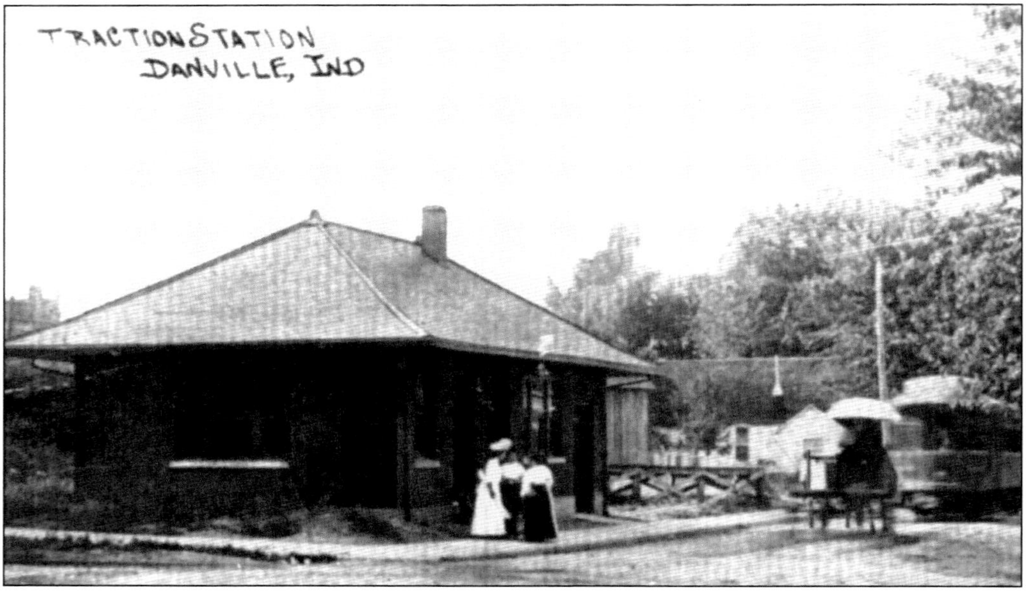

The Hackleman Auto building at the corner of Marion and Indiana Streets is all that is left of this wonderful mass transit system. This building was constructed as the interurban station where the electric trip from Danville began. The rise of the automobile, as well as legislation unfavorable to the interurban industry, made the interurban a money-losing proposition, and the service died in October 1930. (Hendricks County Museum.)

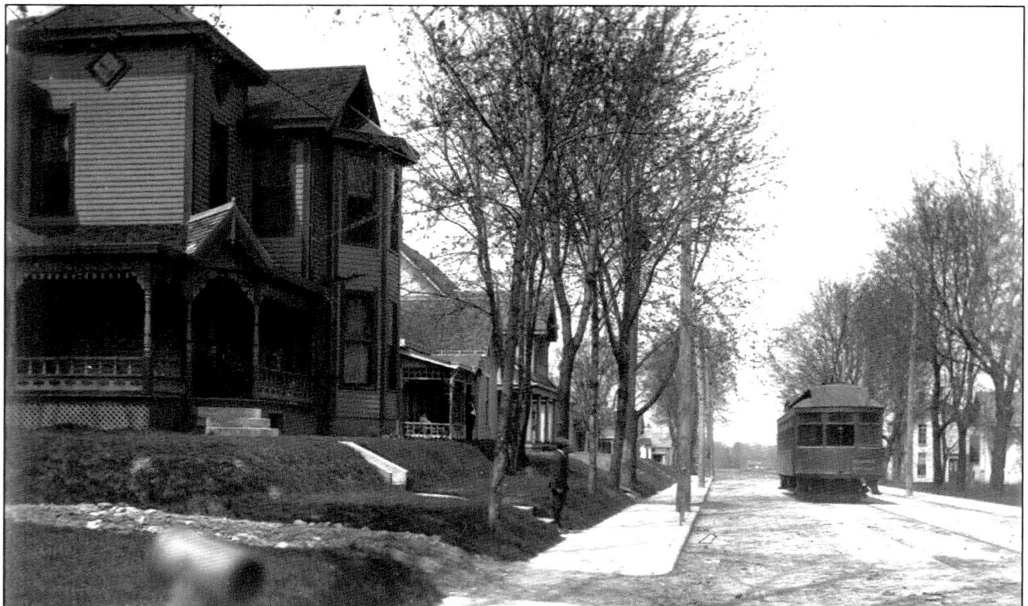

This photograph on Indiana Street shows the interurban coming up past the house of Prof. Charles Hargrave, prominent on the left. The interurban left its station at Marion and Indiana and went down Indiana to make a turn to the east to go through what would eventually be Danville's Ellis Park. That, however, would come later. (Indiana Room, Danville-Center Township Public Library.)

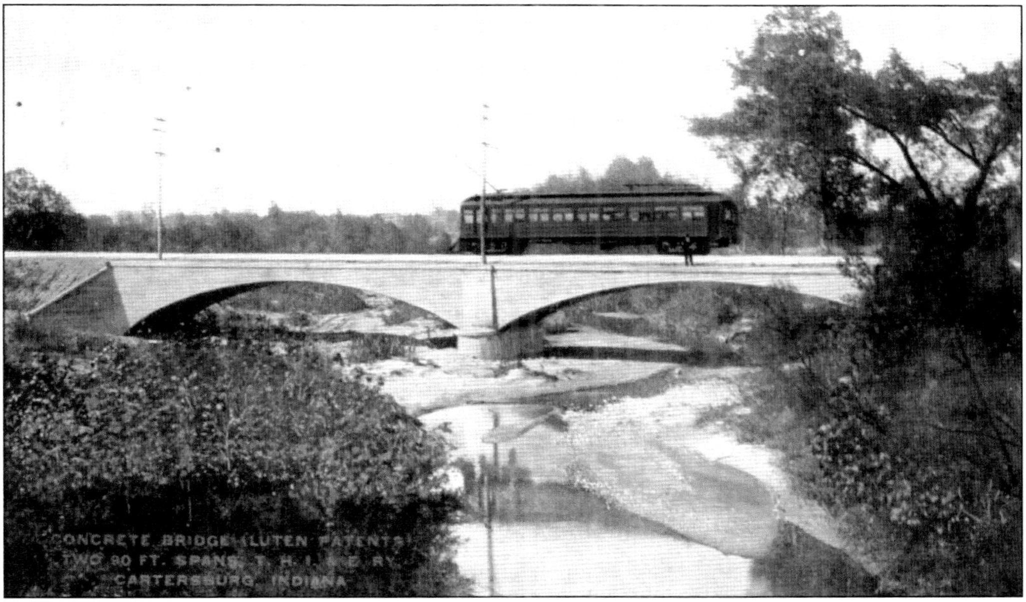

This picture is illustrative of the look of the interurbans as they went down the track and across bridges. They were electrically powered and had an angled pole at one end to go up and get the current. This is the same company that ran the line through Danville, although this picture purports to be in the Cartersburg area a few miles south of Danville. (Hendricks County Museum.)

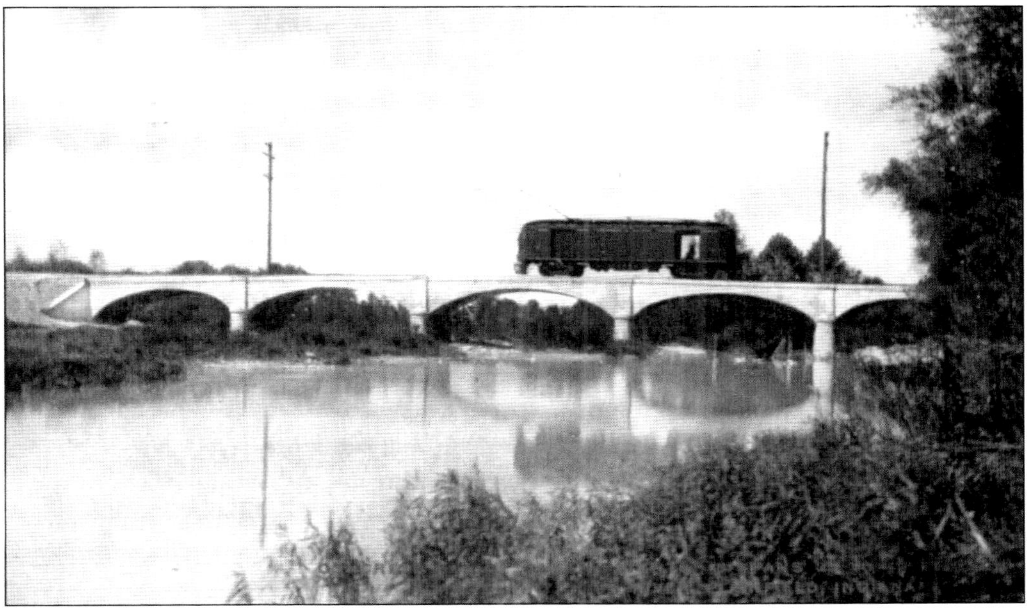

This photograph, purportedly near Plainfield a few miles southeast of Danville, represents a totally different type of interurban. This appears to be a vehicle patterned after a locomotive's baggage car, and it carries cargo but no people other than the operator. Even the names of the interurban companies suggested that they attempted to be railway companies in all means possible. (Hendricks County Museum.)

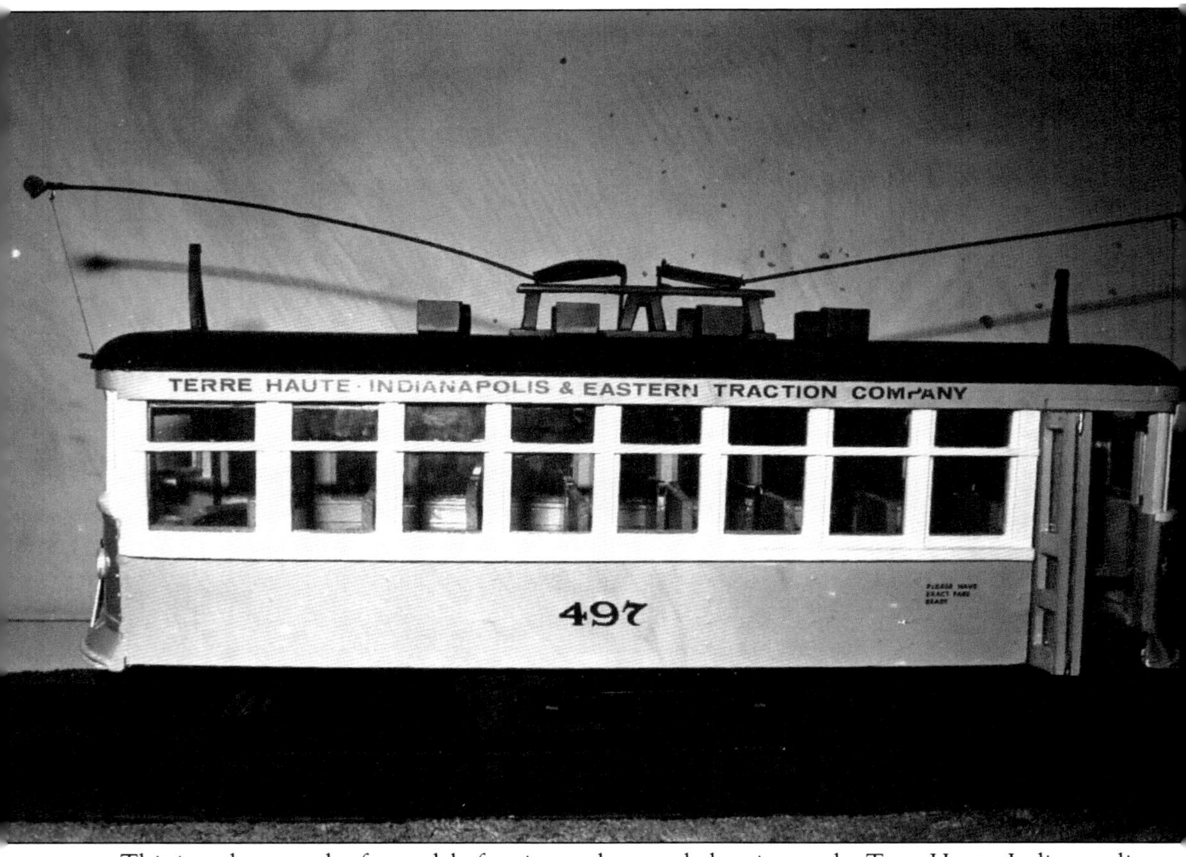

This is a photograph of a model of an interurban car belonging to the Terre Haute, Indianapolis and Eastern Traction Company, the company that provided service to Danville. The model was made by Eugene Davidson. This company provided service to and from Terre Haute, Sullivan, Clinton, Paris (Illinois), Brazil, Greencastle, Indianapolis, Martinsville, Danville, Lebanon, Frankfort, Lafayette, Crawfordsville, Greenfield, Knightstown, New Castle, Cambridge City, Richmond, and Dayton (Ohio). They advertised hourly local and fast limited service as well as "fast freight service to all points reached." (Robert Davidson.)

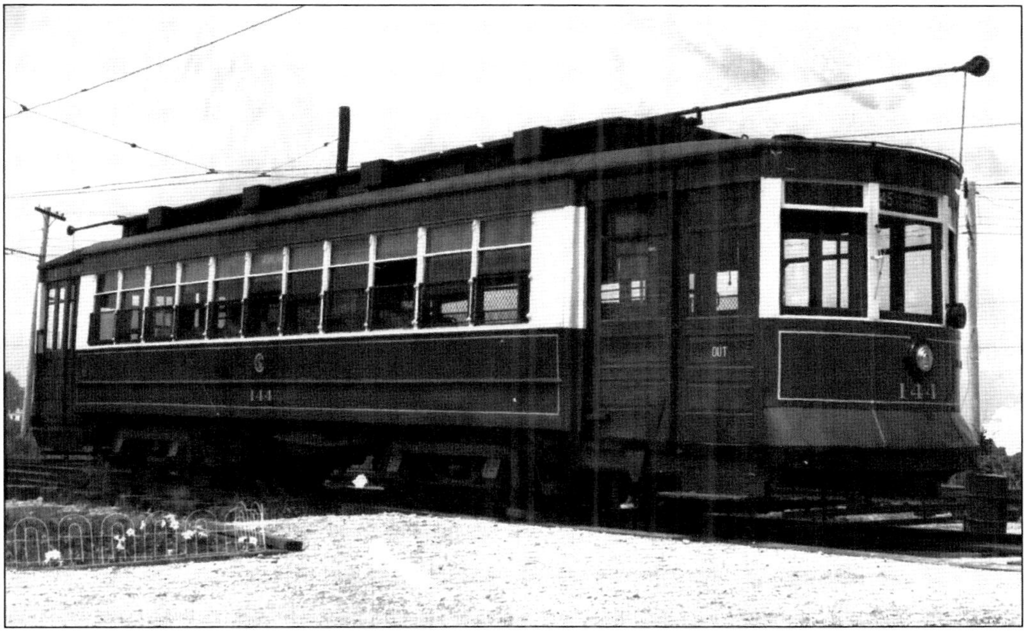

This is a close view of an interurban parked on a siding. The wheels rode on track similar to railroad track although the gauge may have been different. Notice that the pole is folded down but can be reached up to contact the electric lines and power the vehicle. The seats would reverse in case it was necessary for the back end of the interurban to go forward. This interurban belongs to an unknown company. (Robert Davidson.)

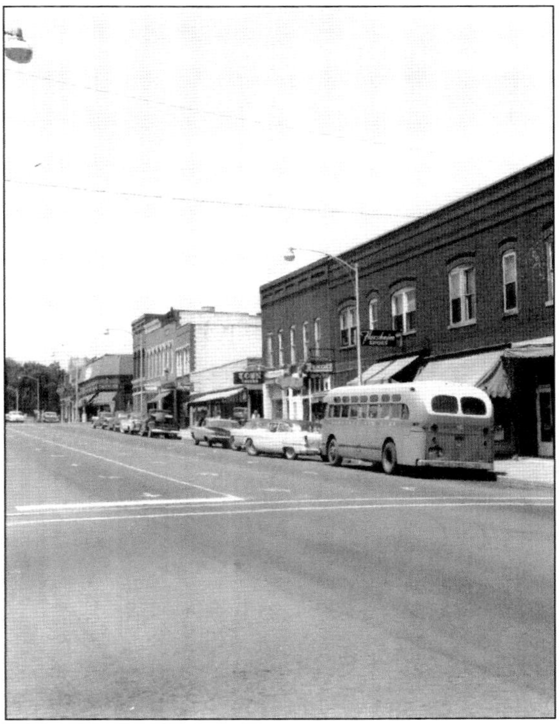

The interurban ceased running to Danville in 1930. Leighton B. Platter operated the Danville Bus Line possibly as early as 1936. The bus left from the corner of Main and Washington Streets, shown. It departed Danville early in the morning and several times during the day, bound for the bus station in Indianapolis. (Hendricks County Museum.)

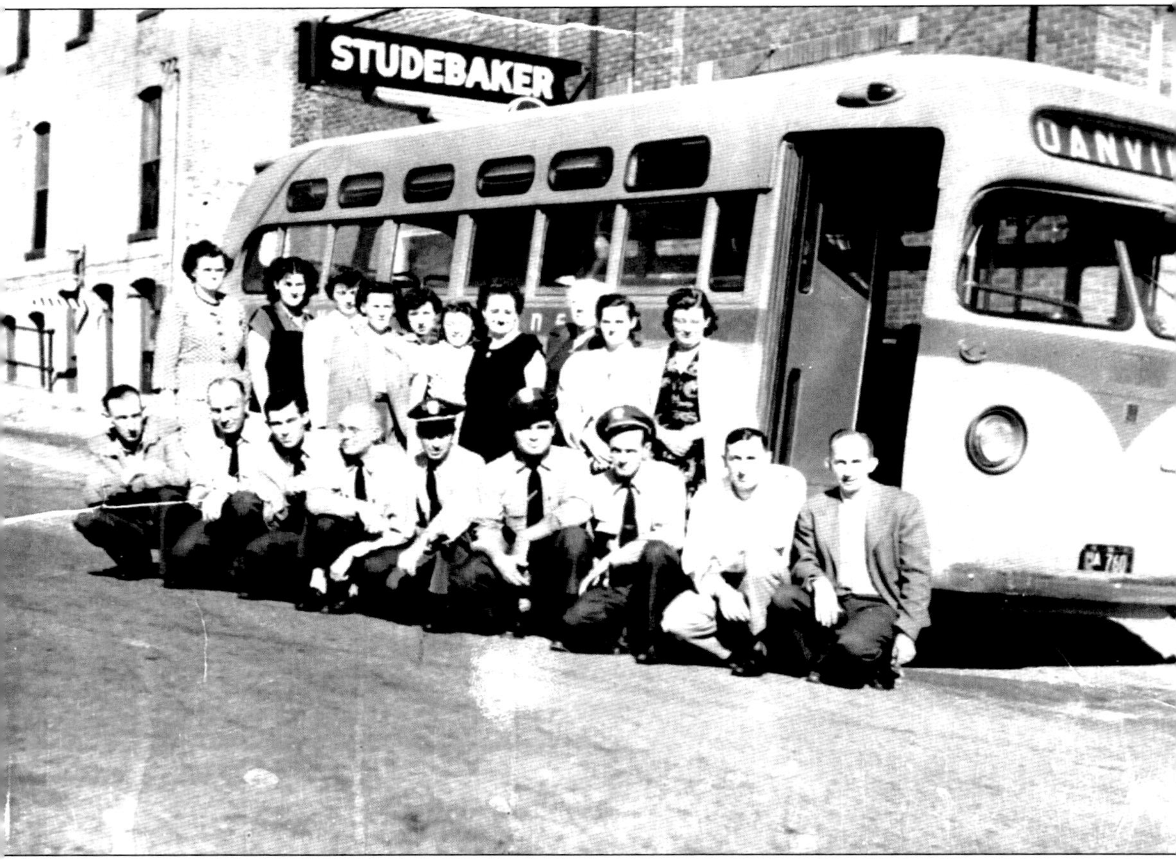

This is a picture of one of the buses of the Danville Bus Line, as well as its employees. This is believed to have been taken about 1950. As cars became more prevalent in the 1960s, the ridership and income of the Danville Bus Line declined. However, tragedy struck when a fire struck the storage shed and burned up most of the buses. Accordingly, in 1968, the Indianapolis Transit Inc. acquired the bus line and its routes. In 1975, the Indianapolis Public Transportation Corporation (IndyGo) acquired the routes but discontinued service. Now that gasoline has hit $4 per gallon IndyGo is expressing interest in Danville commuters again. (Hendricks County Museum.)

Four

Danville Schools and Central Normal College

Early in its history the residents of Danville placed a great emphasis on education. Two institutions of higher learning, the Hendricks County Seminary and the Danville Academy, failed. However, early on the morning of May 10, 1878, at the instigation of Prof. W. F. Harper of the Central Normal School of Ladoga, 50 farm wagons from Danville arrived at Ladoga and "stole" the whole school, including equipment, students, faculty, and baggage. Central Normal College was installed in the prior facility belonging to the Hendricks County Seminary and the Danville Academy. One day of study was lost. From 1878 to 1951, the college was a Danville institution, turning out more than 75,000 graduates who went into leadership roles in fields such as education, business, law, and politics. So far as is known it is the only college that was ever "stolen."

The college impacted the life of Danville. Unlike colleges of today, there were no dormitories or fraternity houses. Students lived in extra rooms in the homes of Danville residents at prices established by the college to make Central Normal College affordable. The students had their meals at the family table in the home. In addition to the meager rent that was paid, a barter system was established wherein the students did household chores for their new extended family including washing dishes and clothes, cleaning the home, caring for the children, and cooking meals. Residents essentially got a college-age stepchild, and many warm family-type relationships were established. This lifestyle of Danville residents was greatly enriched.

Danville residents have always supported education for their own children too. In 1829, when Danville was only five years old, the first brick schoolhouse was built. Despite troubles, such as schoolhouses burning in 1872 and 1878, Danville kept building schools and educating children.

In 1880, a class of one senior was graduated from the Danville Public Schools. In 1881, the number was up to three. From 1885 to 1892, school was held in the Presbyterian church, which still exists on Main Street as the Masonic temple. Danville continues to emphasize the education of its youth as the key to the future.

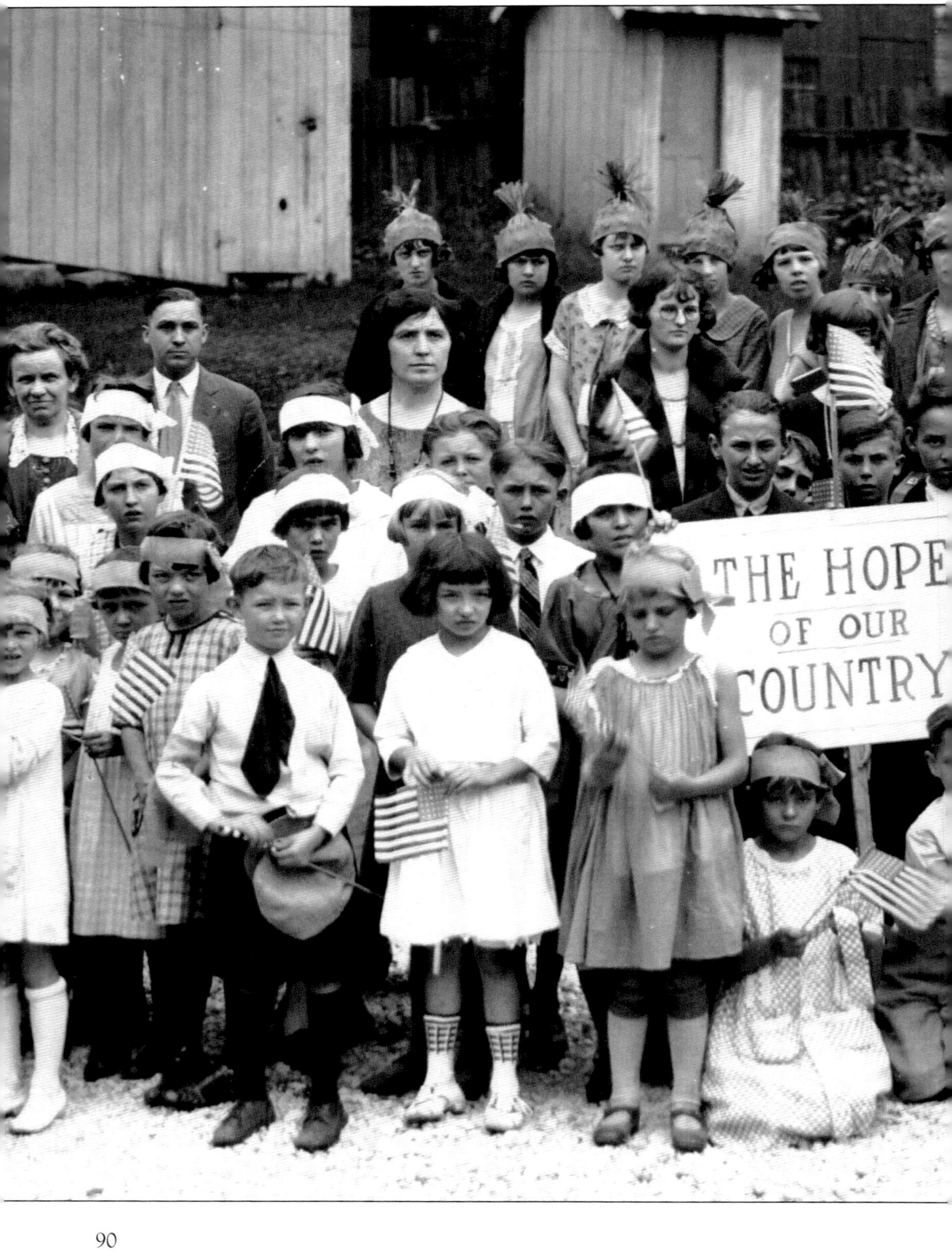
THE HOPE
OF OUR
COUNTRY

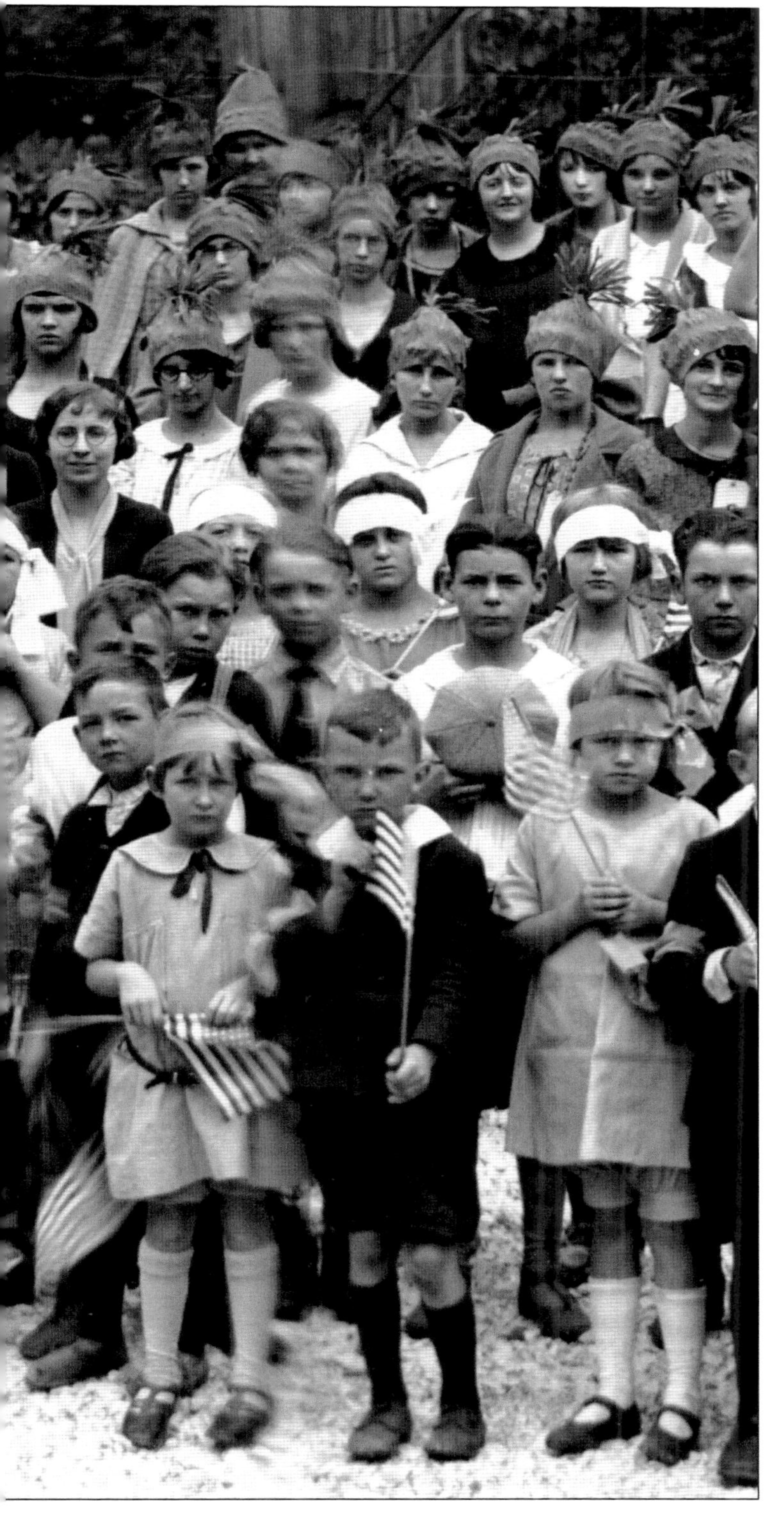

The entire school population, grades 1 through 12, of Danville gathers together to have their picture taken in 1924. Danville has always considered its youth and their education to be the hope of the future, and so Danville built a school when the town was only five years old and Danville continues to support education today. (Hendricks County Museum.)

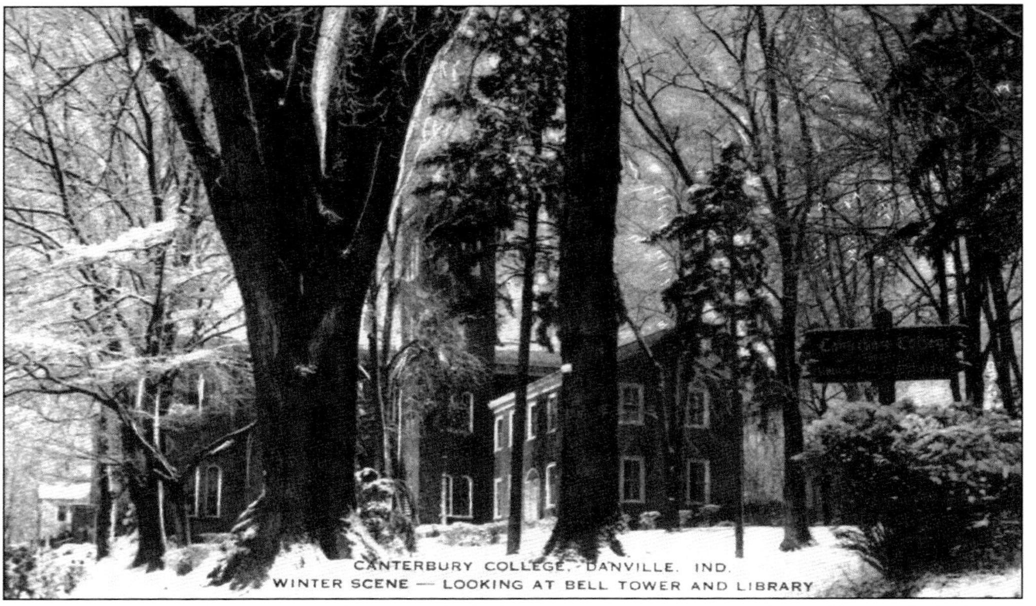

Buildings acquired by Central Normal College upon moving to Danville included one constructed in 1829 for the Danville Seminary and one or more that had been built for the Danville Academy in 1860. The Danville Academy closed in 1868, and in 1878, Central Normal College moved in. The Central Normal College (and later Canterbury College) library was also known as Recitation Hall. The administration building was originally called Chapel Hall. (Indiana Room, Danville-Center Township Public Library.)

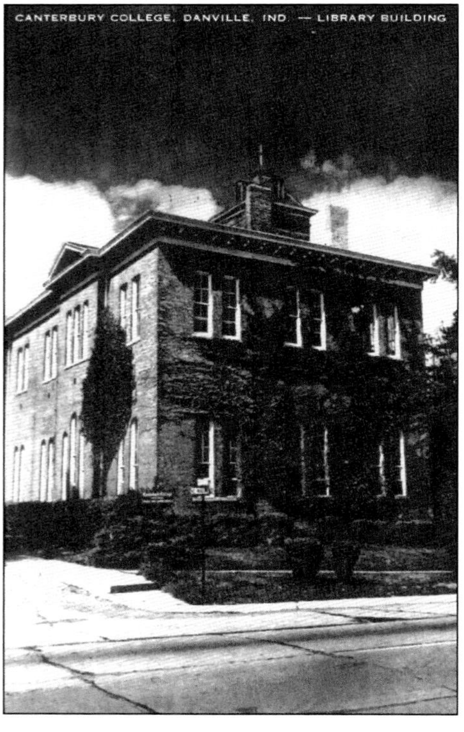

This view shows the library building from the west. The tower is barely visible above the roof. Ivy covers much of the south side of the building, shown. For a long time the college library was housed in the administration building. After the Episcopalians took over the college the library moved into Recitation Hall. The building sat at the corner of Main and Wayne Streets. (Indiana Room, Danville-Center Township Public Library.)

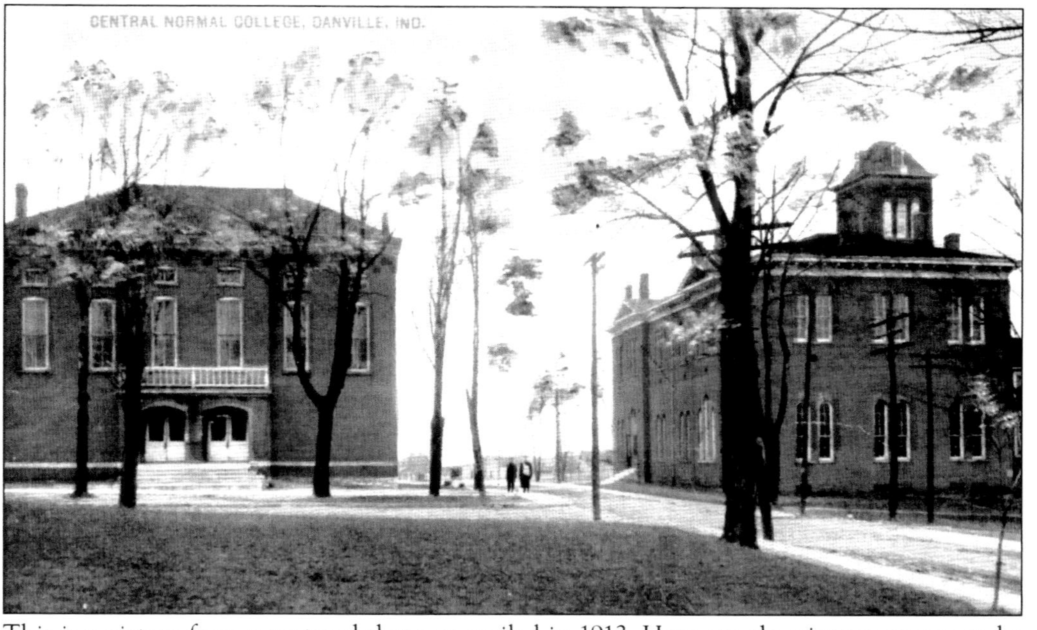

This is a picture from a postcard that was mailed in 1913. However, the picture appears to be of a campus much younger. Wayne Street runs between the college buildings and goes on past the people on the sidewalk toward the north. Main Street is between the campus and the trees through which the scene is viewed. (Hendricks County Museum.)

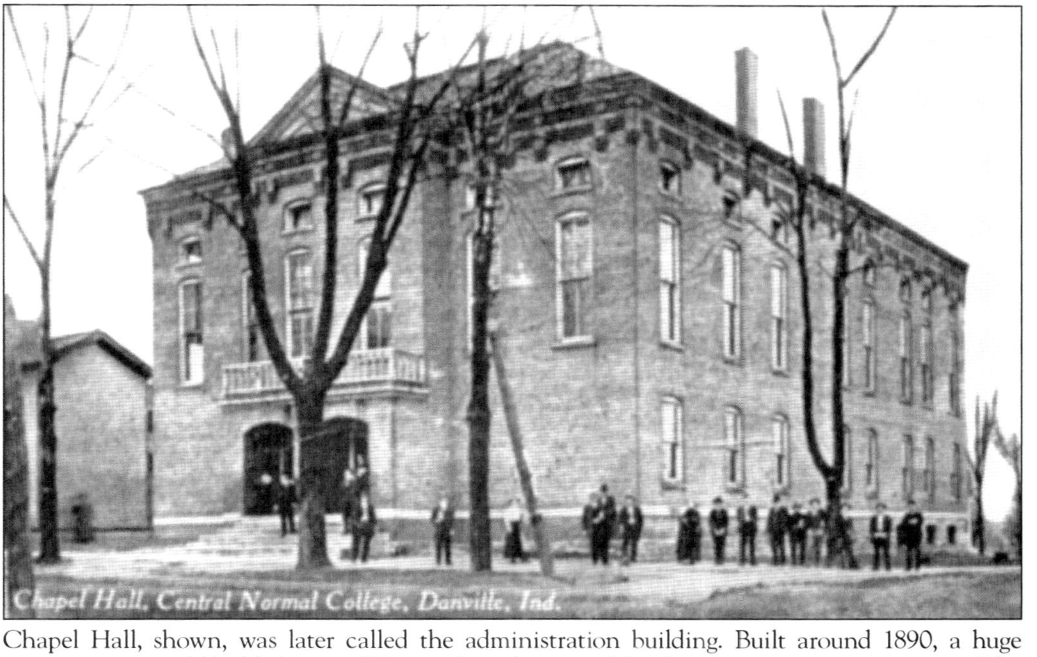

Chapel Hall, shown, was later called the administration building. Built around 1890, a huge upstairs room could hold almost 1,000 people and was used for chapel services every morning. The building also held the college offices and the bookstore. At the dawn of the 20th century, Central Normal College had trained more teachers than Indiana University, Purdue University, and the forerunners to Ball State and Indiana State Universities combined. (Hendricks County Museum.)

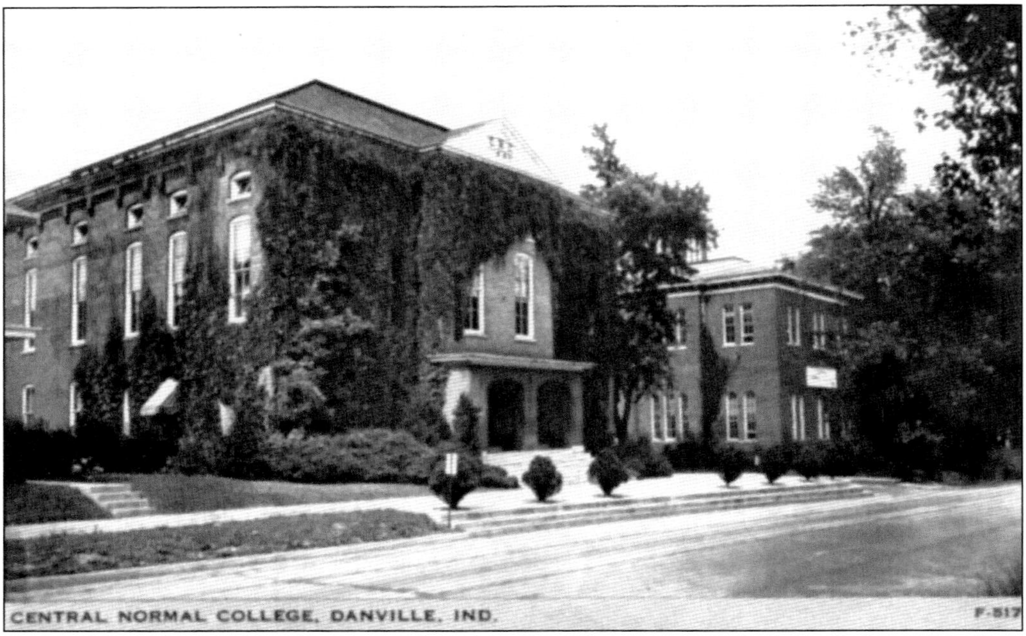

Pictured from the south and west are Chapel Hall and Recitation Hall. Central Normal College thrived modestly with a stable student body of around 1,000 students per year between 1878 and the end of World War II. Although it struggled financially toward the end, Central Normal College was affordable and never received tax support. Many teachers got their credentials during summers at Central Normal College. (Hendricks County Museum.)

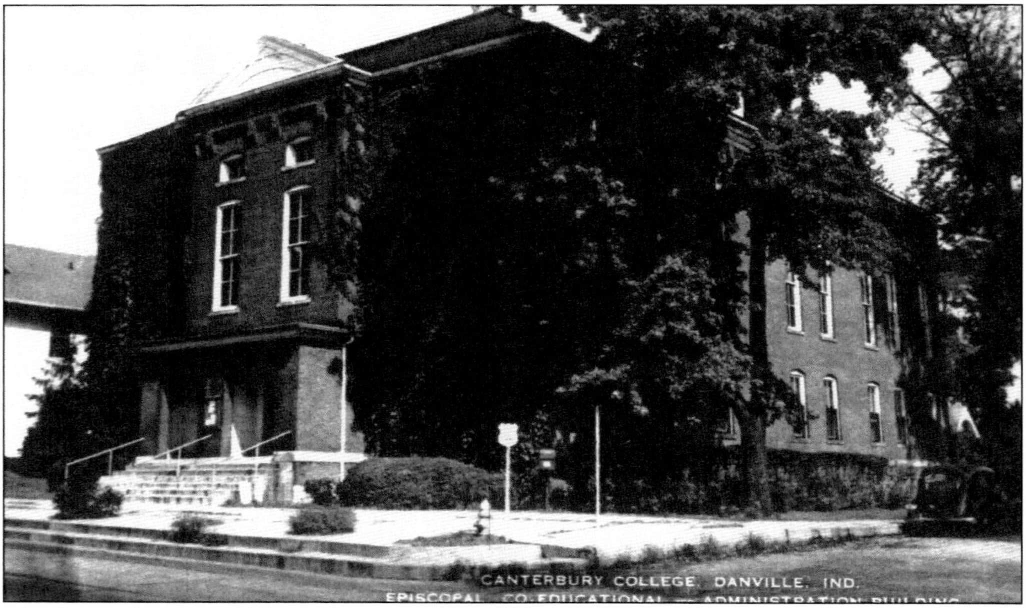

The former location of the administration building, shown from the south and east from Main Street, has sat empty as a parking lot for many years, since demolition of this building. The white building behind it was last used as a child care center. It had been used for housing students in the college days. (Indiana Room, Danville-Center Township Public Library.)

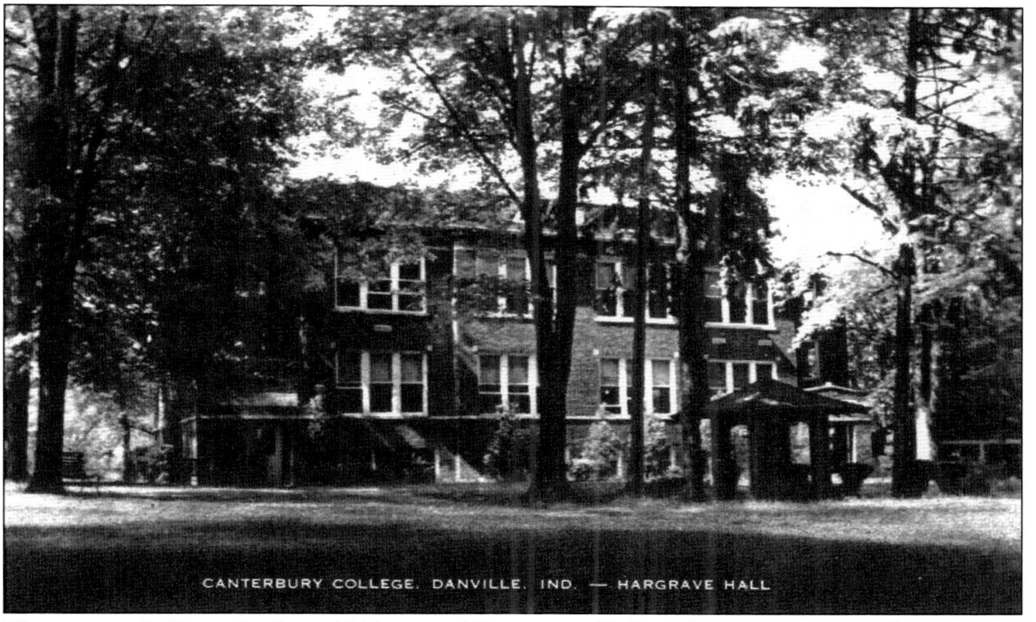

The science hall was built in 1915, east of Recitation Hall, to house classrooms, laboratories, and a small gymnasium. Upon the death of Charles Hargrave, a member of the science faculty, the science building was renamed Hargrave Hall. The well house seen in the picture stood until a few years ago when a tree came crashing down in a storm and destroyed it. (Indiana Room, Danville-Center Township Public Library.)

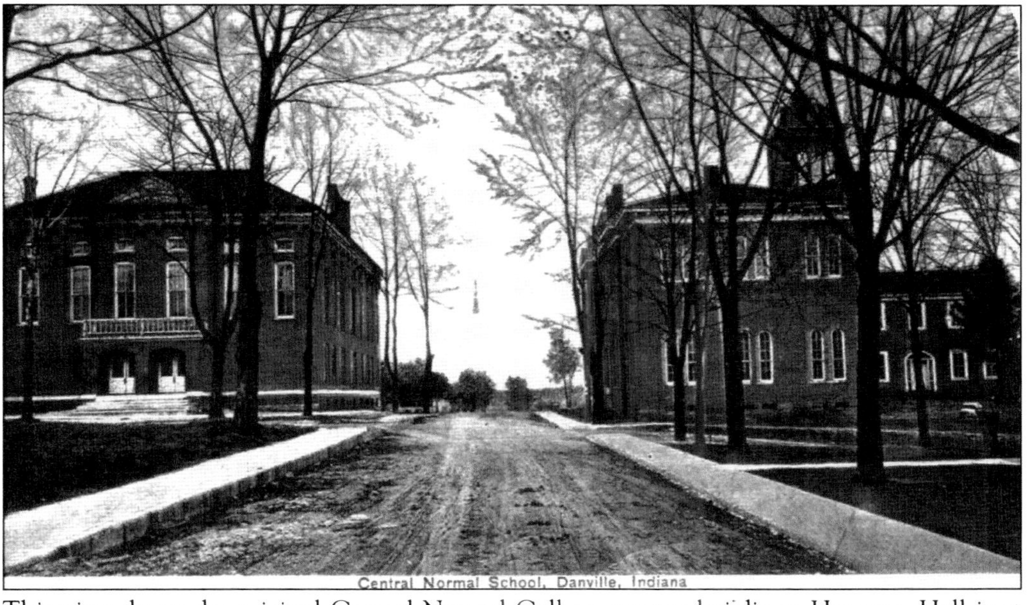

This view shows the original Central Normal College campus buildings: Hargrave Hall is at right (east), and the next buildings are gymnasiums—one still sits just beyond Recitation Hall where the leafy tree stands, north up Wayne Street. (Indiana Room, Danville-Center Township Public Library.)

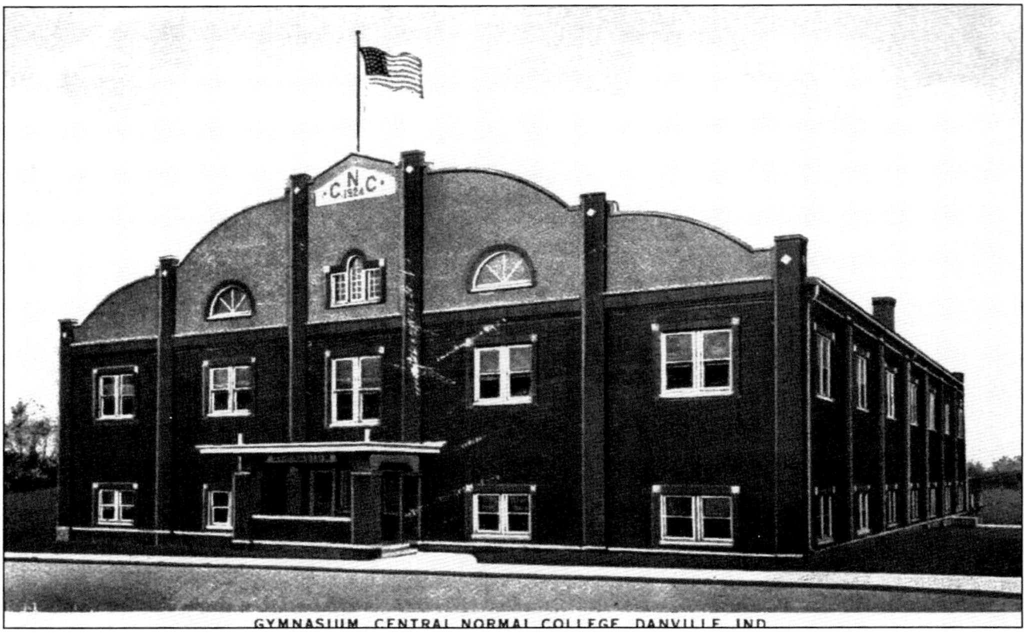

In 1924, Central Normal College built this gymnasium on North Wayne Street. Central Normal College was competitive in football and basketball—the Purple Warriors spread their fame far and wide. Long before the days of the NCAA, the local team had Danville residents cheering their team on in Chicago for days. The Danville Browns semiprofessional baseball team also garnered town support. On a morning in 1936, the gymnasium caught fire. The students were saved, but the building was a total loss. (Indiana Room, Danville-Center Township Public Library.)

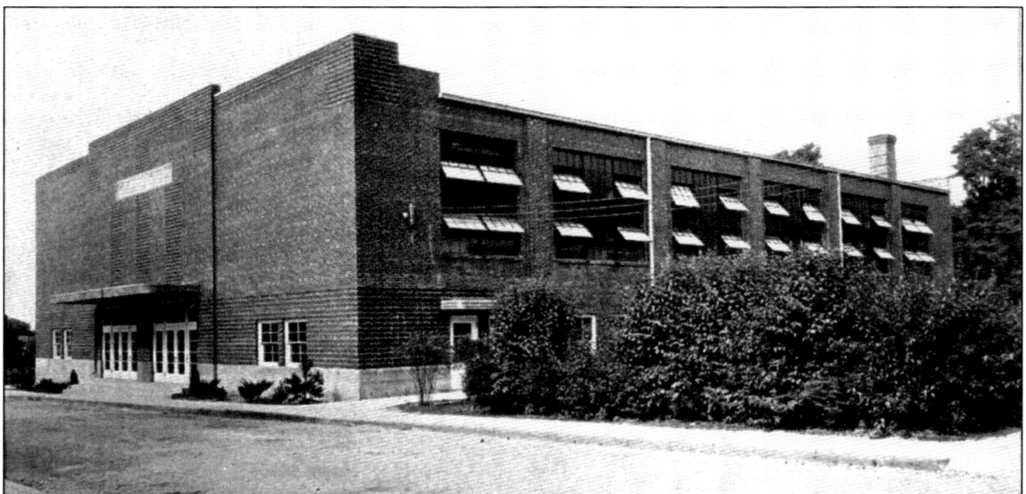

In 1936, the gymnasium pictured here replaced the one that burned. Student labor got the job done, and the college found $15,000 to fund it. This gymnasium still exists, attached to the building that later became Danville High School and then Danville Middle School. A new Danville Middle School has been built, and this property has been deeded to the Town of Danville. (Indiana Room, Danville-Center Township Public Library.)

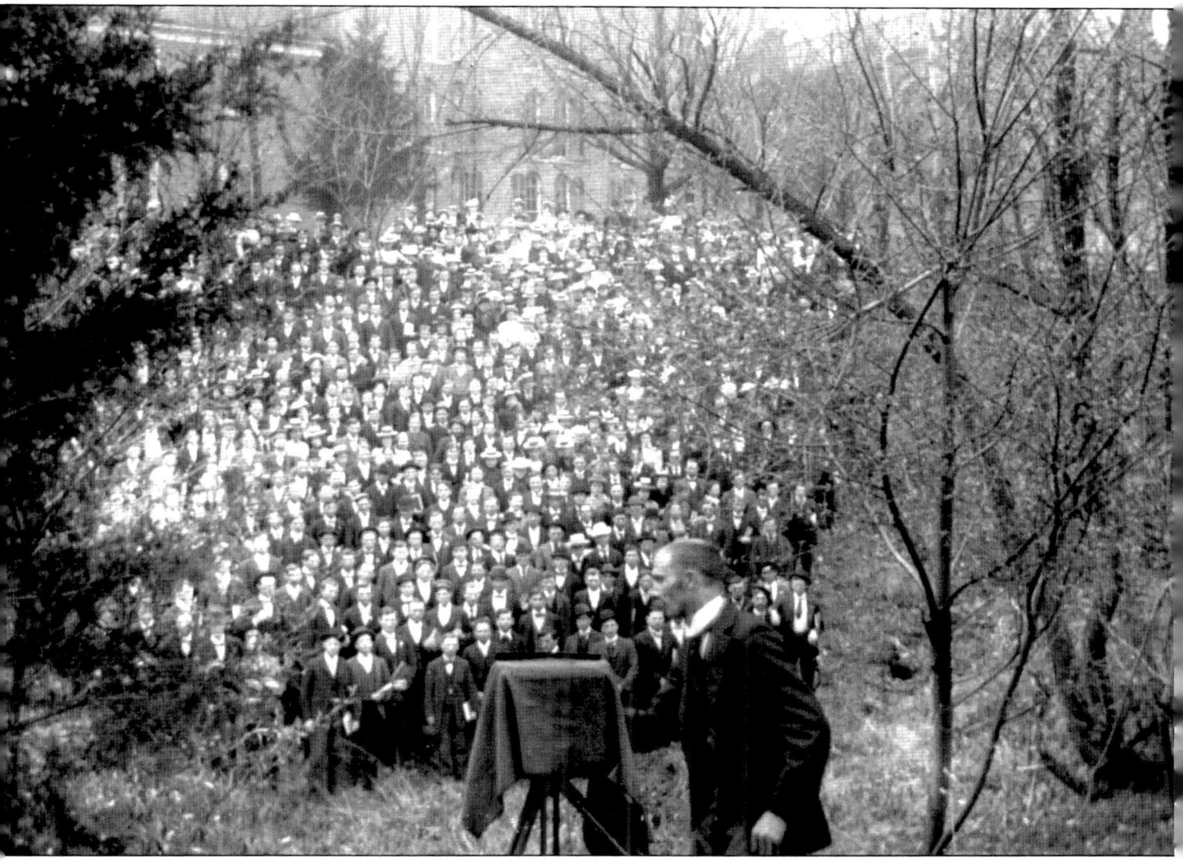

This photograph, believed to have been taken by Prof. Charles Hargrave, shows a photographer taking a picture of the Central Normal College graduation class of 1899 in front of the university buildings, gathered against the east side of Recitation Hall. (Indiana Room, Danville-Center Township Public Library.)

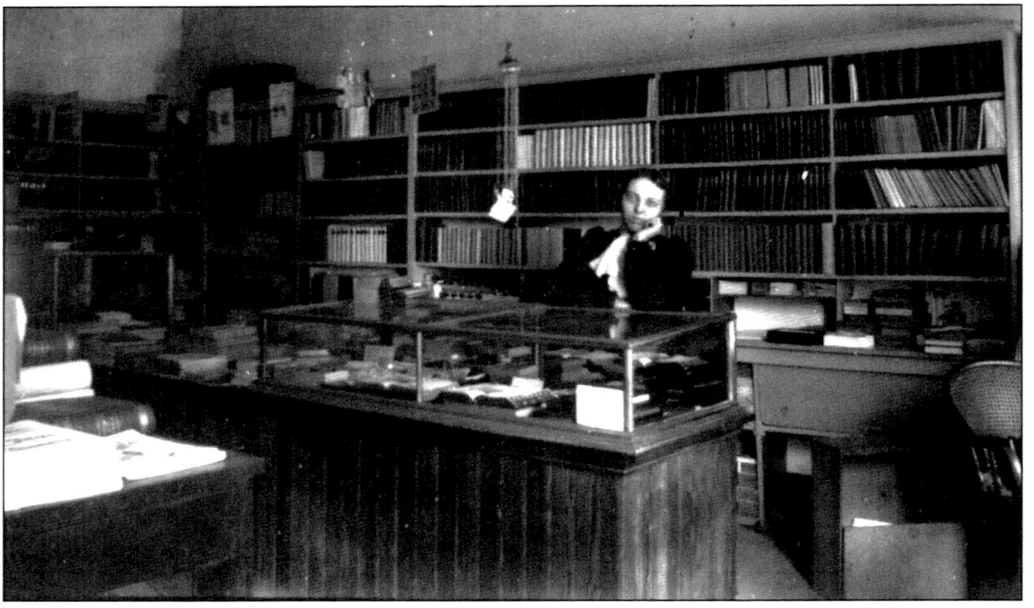

The Central Normal College bookstore was in Chapel Hall, and here Pearl Relander keeps track of her store. Many materials had to be stocked in a fairly crowded space. However, the students were provided what they needed and many students of Central Normal College went on to become famous in education, law, government, and business. (Indiana Room, Danville-Center Township Public Library.)

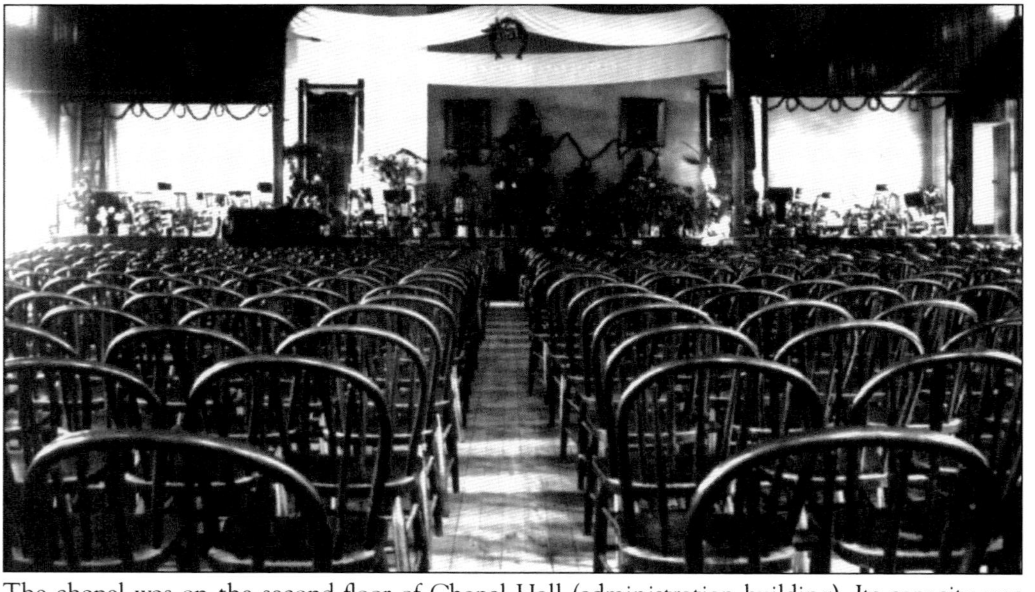

The chapel was on the second floor of Chapel Hall (administration building). Its capacity was about 1,000 people, and it was undoubtedly the largest room in Danville. In this photograph it is decorated for commencement in 1897. Central Normal College had its first commencement in 1876, and commencement was not an hour-long ceremony. Many times the commencement took the entire day with readings and presentations on many aspects of scholarly and society interests such as science, poetry, and the arts. (Indiana Room, Danville-Center Township Public Library.)

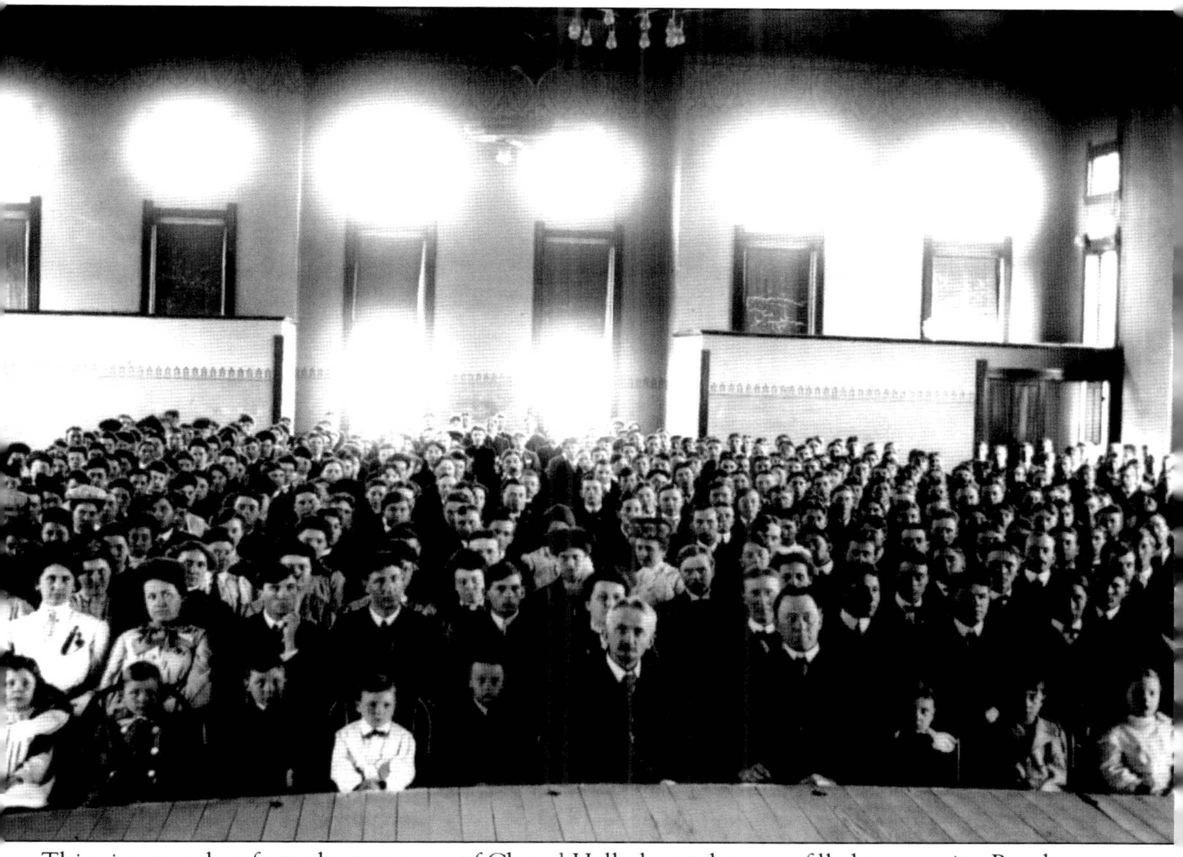

This picture, taken from the stage area of Chapel Hall, shows the room filled to capacity. People are standing in the wings on both sides in the back, and young children have claimed several seats in the front row. (Indiana Room, Danville-Center Township Public Library.)

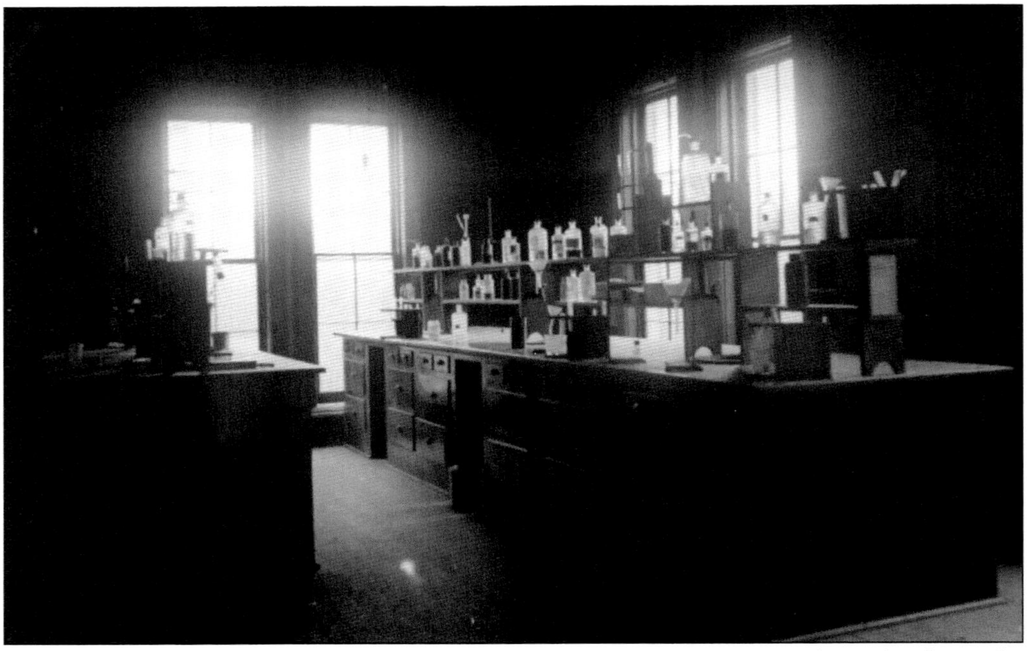

Science was a great emphasis of Central Normal College and many other schools as the 20th century began. This pictures the chemistry laboratory in 1908 at some location in Recitation Hall. The windows make it appear to be a bright day outside, but the lighting inside still appears to be inadequate. Many of the things on the laboratory table appear familiar to chemistry students of today. (Indiana Room, Danville-Center Township Public Library.)

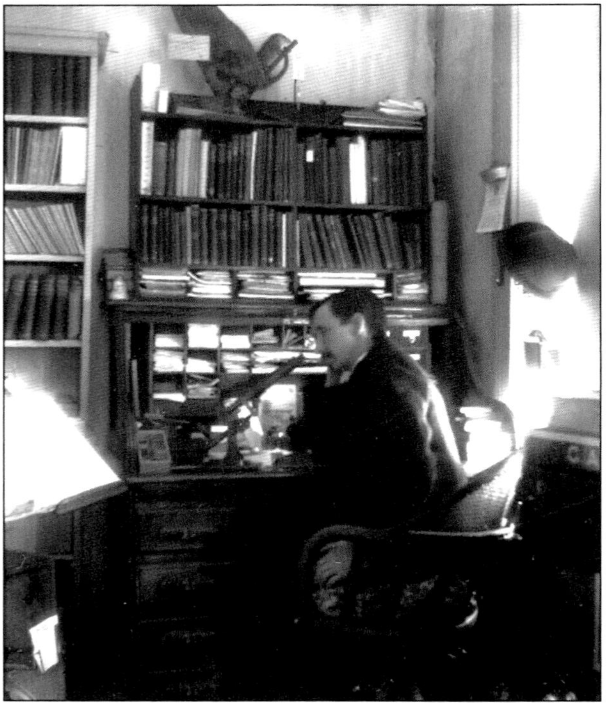

Prof. Charles Hargrave came to Central Normal College as a student, married a student, and stayed on as a professor of science. He held many other offices on campus, including president. He spent many years as the registrar and is reputed to be able to call about 75,000 Central Normal College students over the course of many years by name. Here Hargrave appears to be looking through a microscope on his desk—surrounded by his books. (Indiana Room, Danville-Center Township Public Library.)

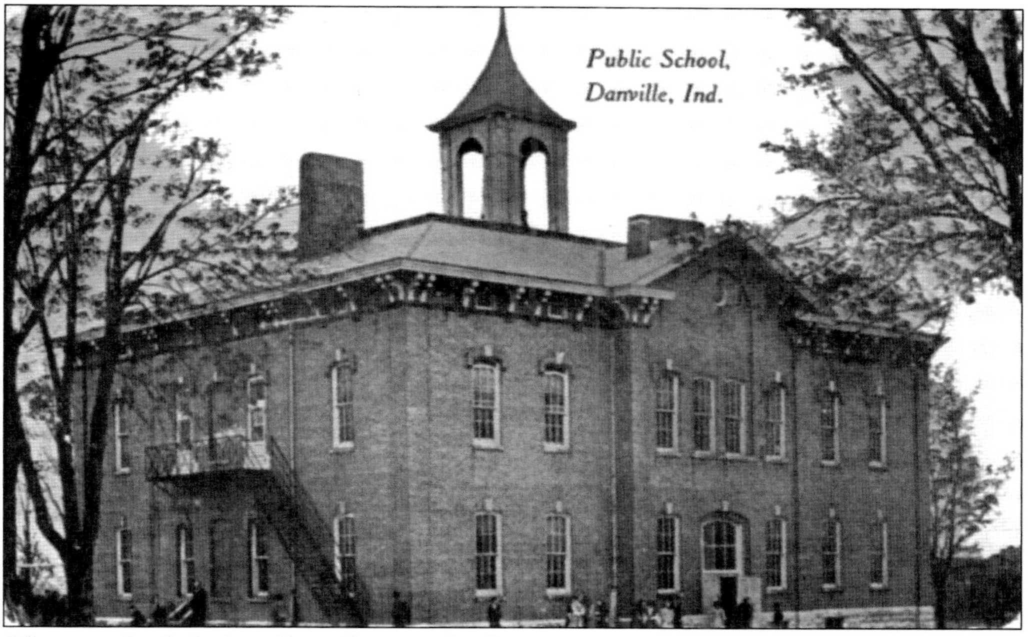

Of many schools built in Danville since the first went up in 1829, many burned or disappeared without photographic record. The Mattie Keeney School, an elementary school built in 1900 just north of today's Hendricks County Government Center, operated as the Danville Elementary School for many years. When the building to its south was completed, all 12 grades moved into the new building. The Mattie Keeney School and the high school at Clinton and Cross Streets were disbanded and then demolished. (Indiana Room, Danville-Center Township Public Library.)

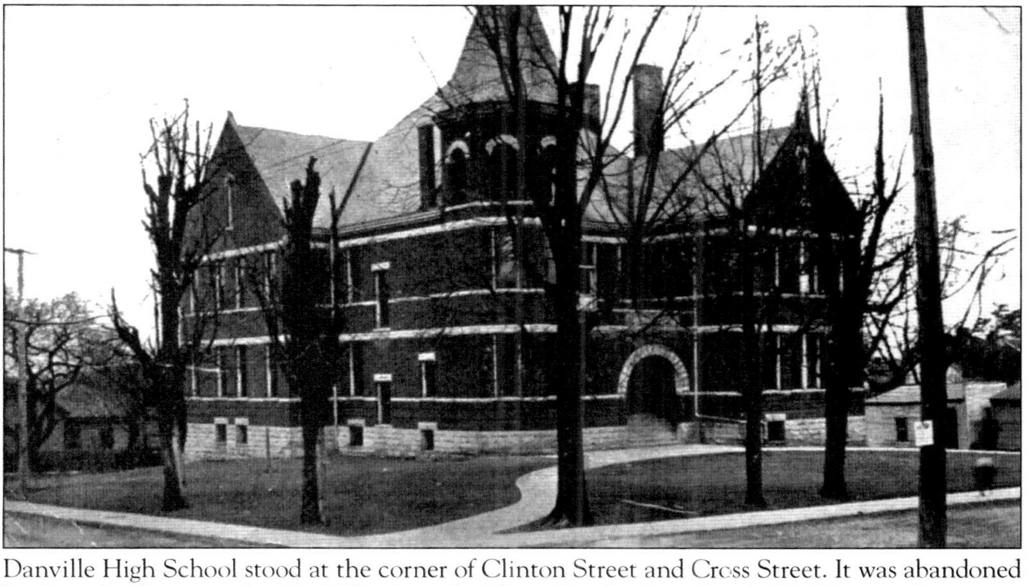

Danville High School stood at the corner of Clinton Street and Cross Street. It was abandoned by the school corporation in 1929 when the 12-grade school on South Washington Street was completed. This building had no gymnasium; the students used the Danville Christian Church gymnasium one block north. This building was sold and used as an auction house. (Indiana Room, Danville-Center Township Public Library.)

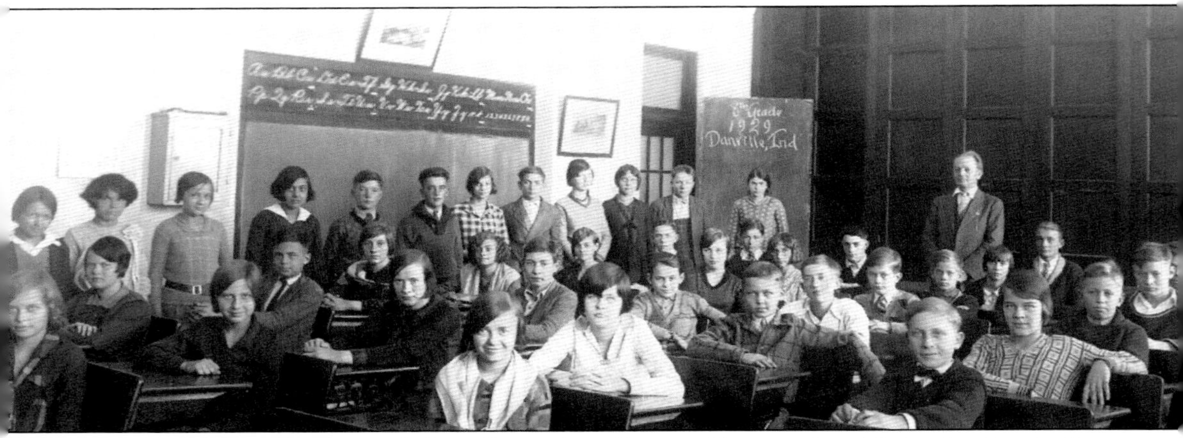

Pictured here is renowned Danville teacher Chester Clement Bosstick in the Mattie Keeney School with the 1929–1930 eighth-grade class. He came to Danville in 1917 to serve as principal of the Danville grade schools. Bosstick established the first Boy Scout troop in Danville and was the scoutmaster for many years. He inaugurated the Danville Halloween Festival to discourage Halloween destruction. It survived for more than 50 years and became the largest project of the Danville PTA, raising thousands of dollars for Danville playground equipment and involving hundreds of parents, students, teachers, and townspeople over the years. From left to right are (standing) Helen Kersey, Frances Wiggam, Virginia McManigell, Flora Everling, Robert Parker, James Christie, Virginia Smith, Paul Jones, Christine Pritchett, Laura Morgan, Ralph Heagy, and Louise Bain; (first row) Mary June Pierson, Morgan Swain, Juanita Edwards, Frances Hoke, Margaret Cummings, Maurice Newman, and Louis Armstrong; (second row) Catherine Dean Harvey, Maybelle Miles, Mabel Meeks, Basil Kersey, John Airhart, Virginia Cox, Mildred Johnson, and Amos Young; (third row) Ethel Vannice, Martha Dale Watson, Richard Kimberlin, Earle Hites, Leon Ludlow, Bueford Majors, Dorothy Pritchett, and Henry Landon; (fourth row) George Harper, Wilma Walls, Harold Rose, James Neff, ? Collier, and Mary Ellen Borders. (Indiana Room, Danville-Center Township Public Library.)

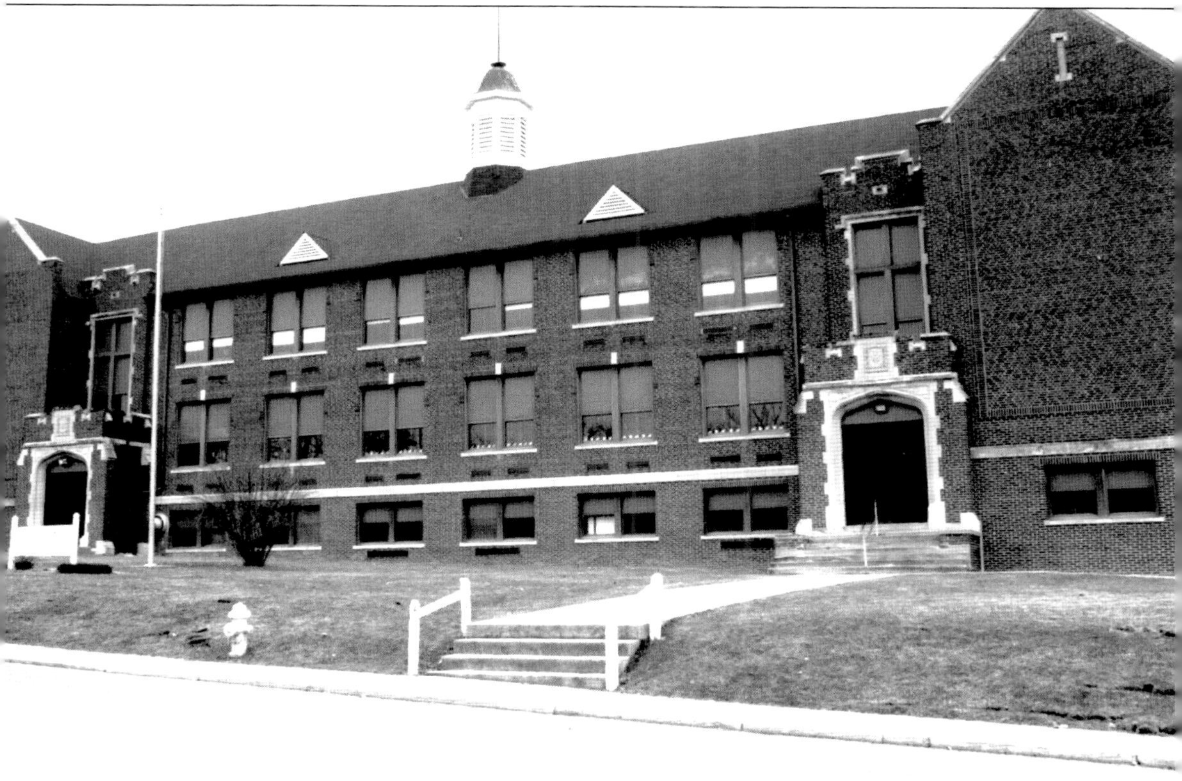

This building housed all 12 grades of Danville schoolchildren from 1929 through 1959. It had two floors plus a basement that contained classrooms, laboratories, and a gymnasium that had a stage and so it could double as an auditorium, a cafeteria, and areas to teach industrial arts and home economics. When the former Central Normal College buildings were demolished/renovated/attached, the high school (and for a while eighth grade) moved to that location and grades one to seven (and then eight) stayed in this building. (Guilford Township Historical Collection, Plainfield-Guilford Township Public Library.)

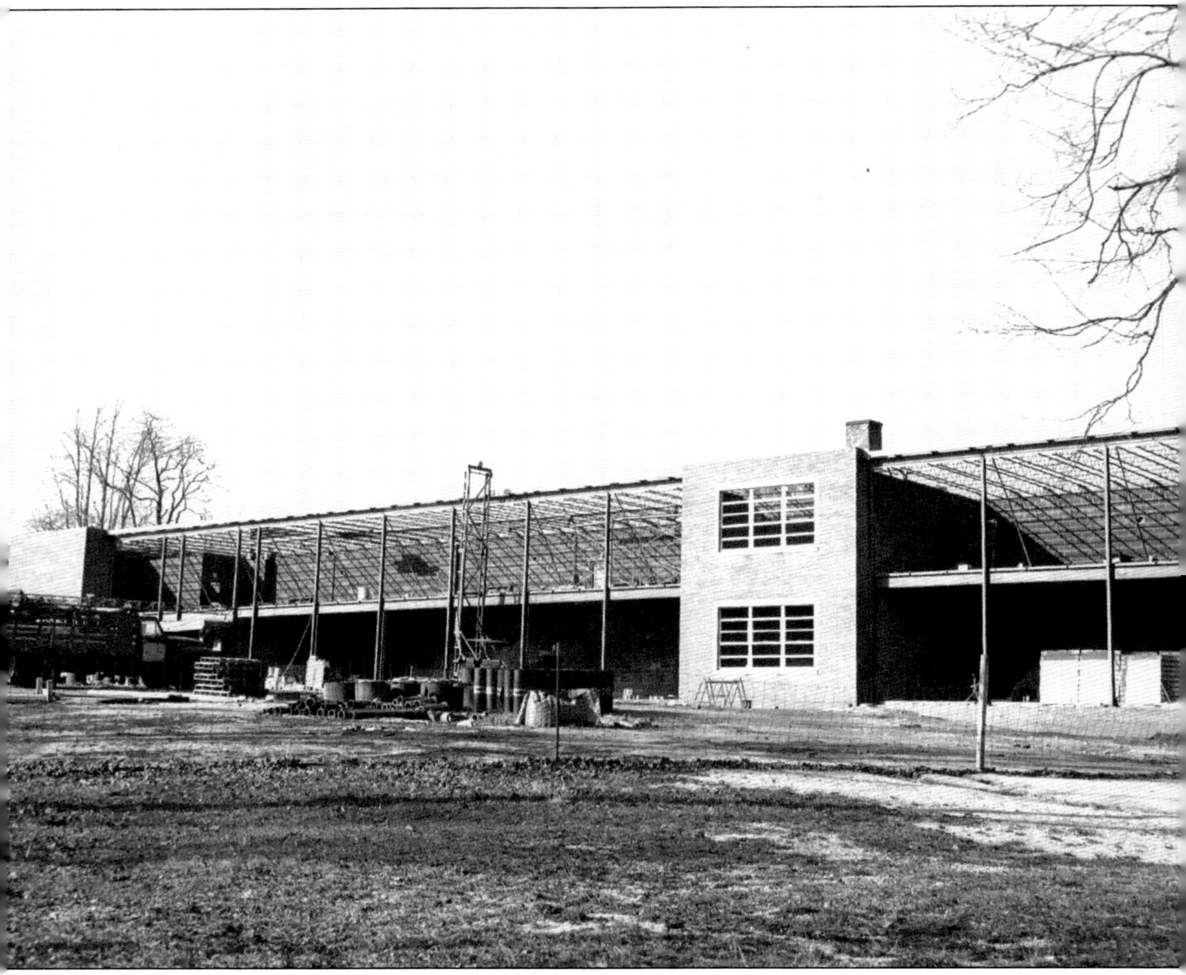

The time is about 1958. The site is the home of the former Central Normal College–Canterbury College. Recitation Hall (library hall) has been torn down. Chapel Hall (administration building) has been torn down. The gymnasium and Hargrave Hall have been left standing, and the two are being connected in this picture with the mating of the gymnasium with the back of the far left part of the new building, and the new building is then extended eastward to join with Hargrave Hall. (Indiana Room, Danville-Center Township Public Library.)

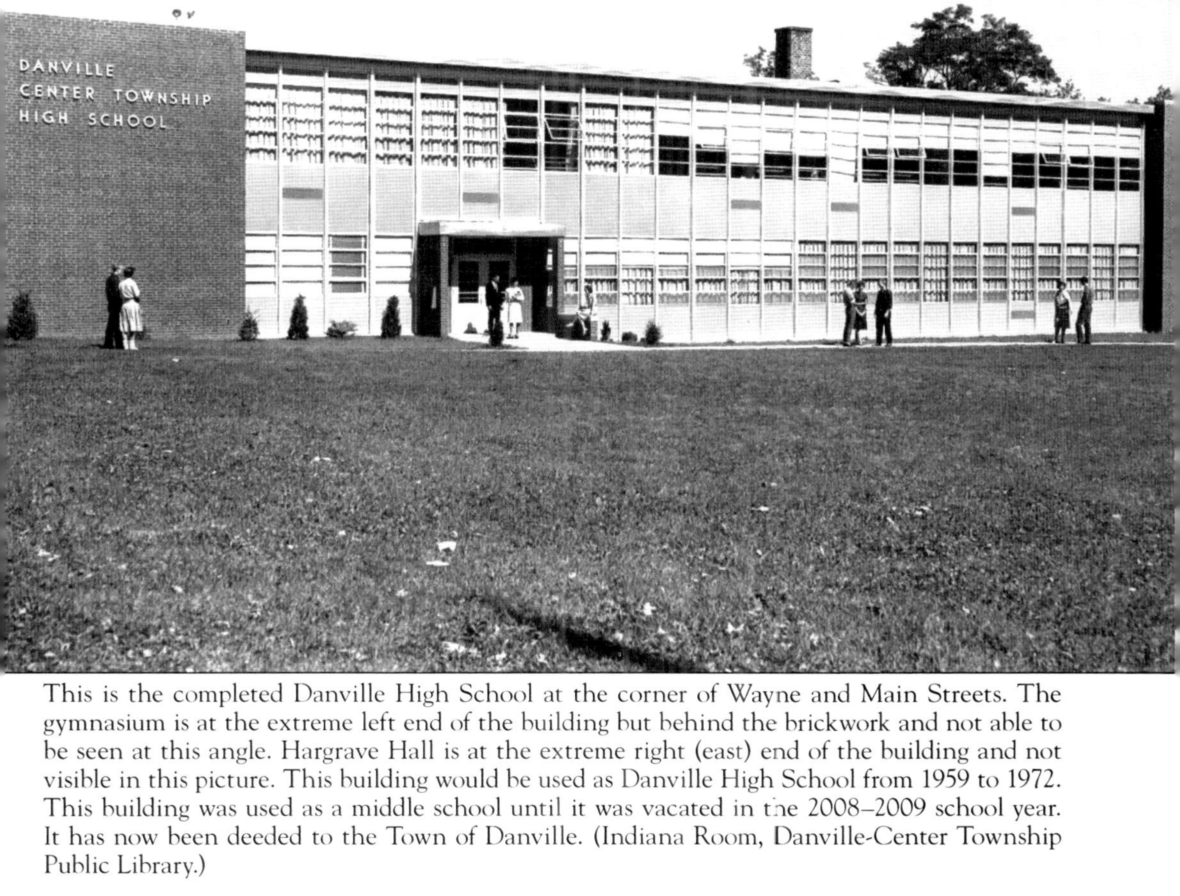

This is the completed Danville High School at the corner of Wayne and Main Streets. The gymnasium is at the extreme left end of the building but behind the brickwork and not able to be seen at this angle. Hargrave Hall is at the extreme right (east) end of the building and not visible in this picture. This building would be used as Danville High School from 1959 to 1972. This building was used as a middle school until it was vacated in the 2008–2009 school year. It has now been deeded to the Town of Danville. (Indiana Room, Danville-Center Township Public Library.)

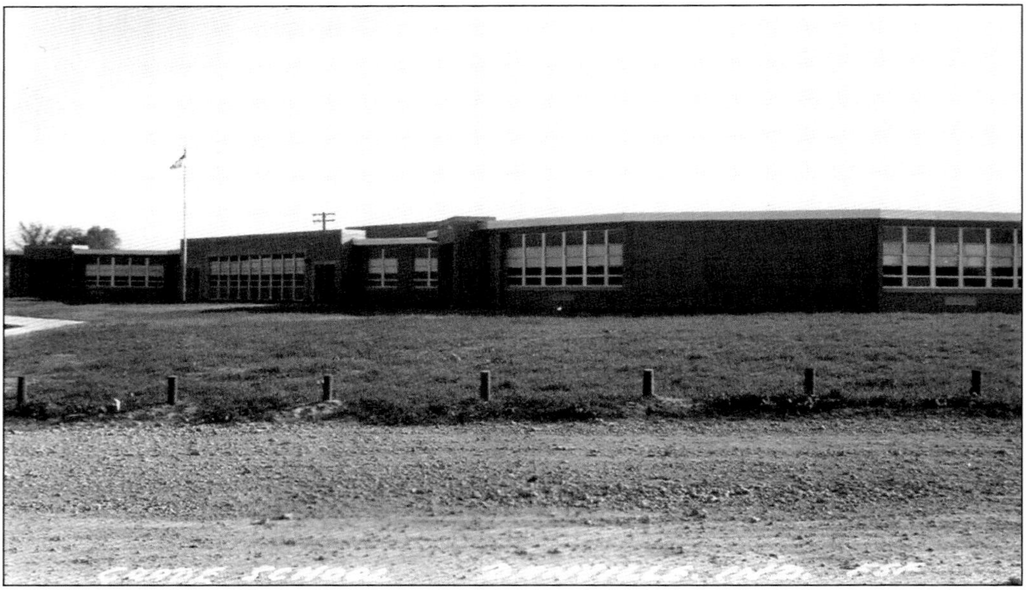

Danville North Elementary School was built in 1963 at Urban Street and Old North Salem Road. The image on page 22 shows this location in the days when it was a hay field. The Danville–Center Township schools were consolidated, pursuant to state law, with the New Winchester–Marion Township schools. New Winchester students through grade eight were brought to North Elementary along with kids from the north side of Danville. (Indiana Room, Danville-Center Township Public Library.)

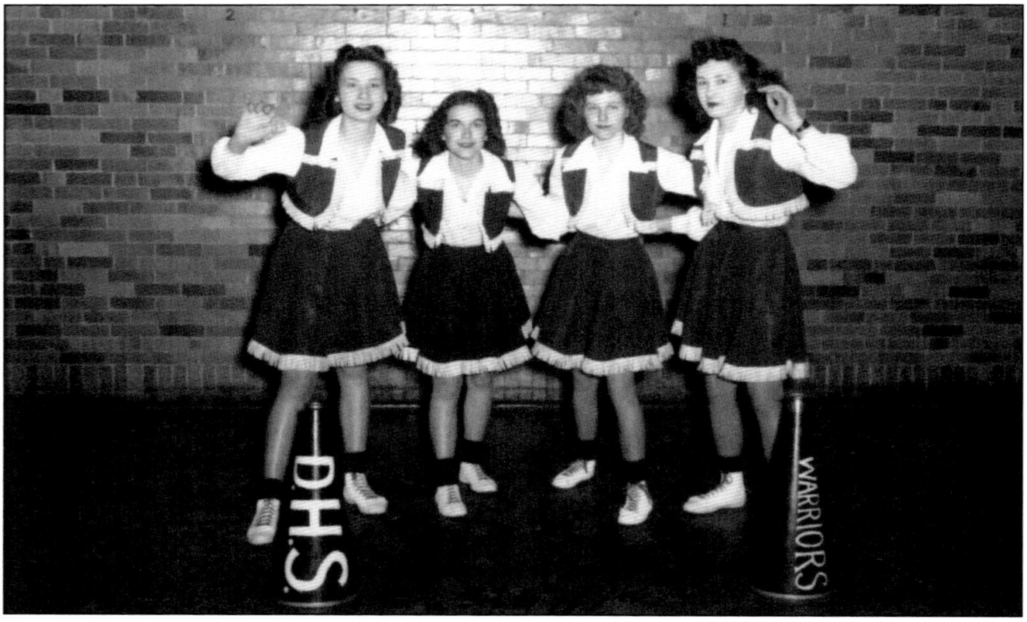

Danville school students have always had spirit. This is a picture inside the school gymnasium that served all 12 grades from 1929 to 1959. Perhaps the reader can see the contour of the brick wall behind the cheerleaders who are identified from left to right as Dean Harris, Barbara Goodwin, Virginia Tincher, and Bessie Harris. (Danville Community School Corporation.)

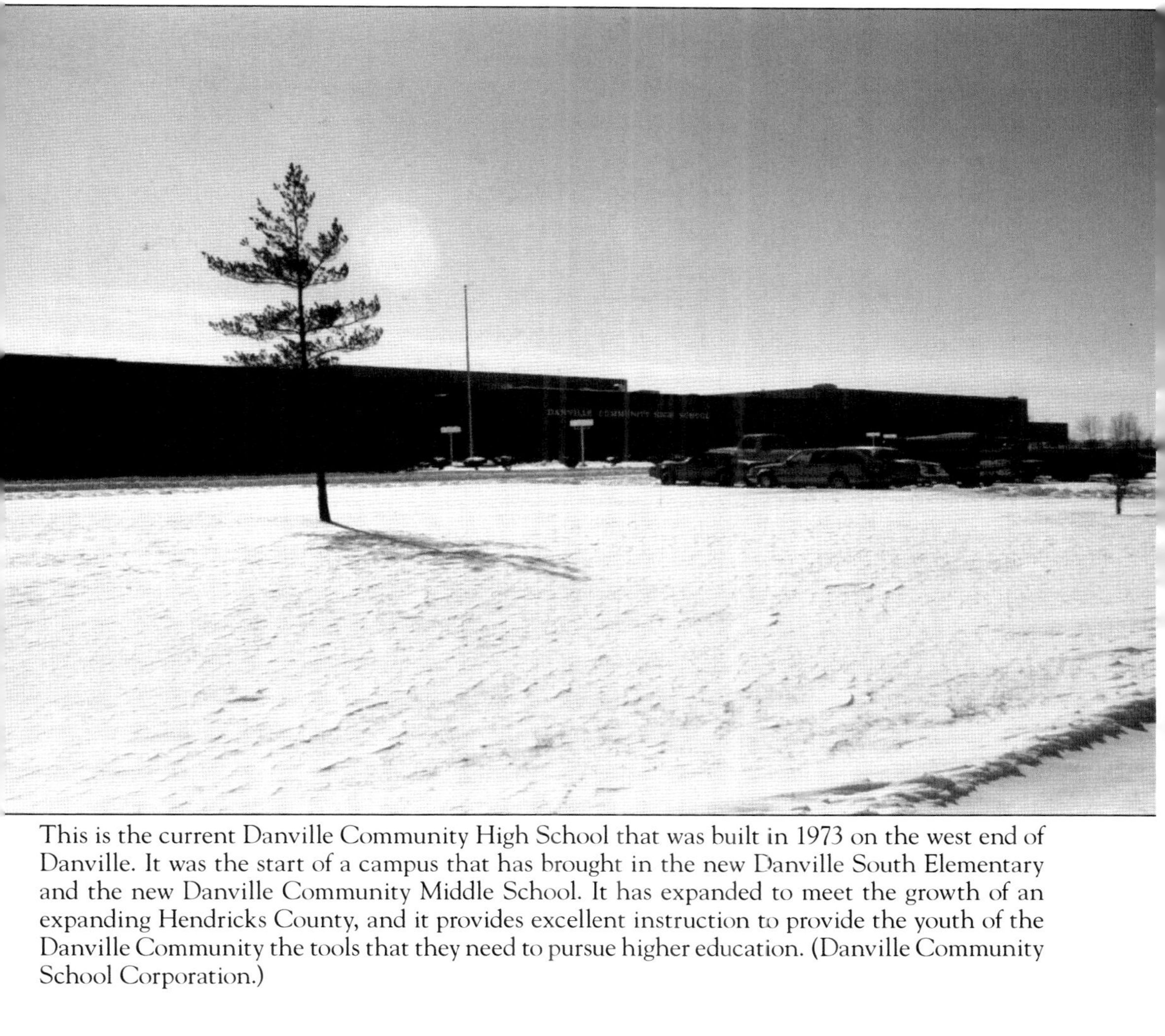

This is the current Danville Community High School that was built in 1973 on the west end of Danville. It was the start of a campus that has brought in the new Danville South Elementary and the new Danville Community Middle School. It has expanded to meet the growth of an expanding Hendricks County, and it provides excellent instruction to provide the youth of the Danville Community the tools that they need to pursue higher education. (Danville Community School Corporation.)

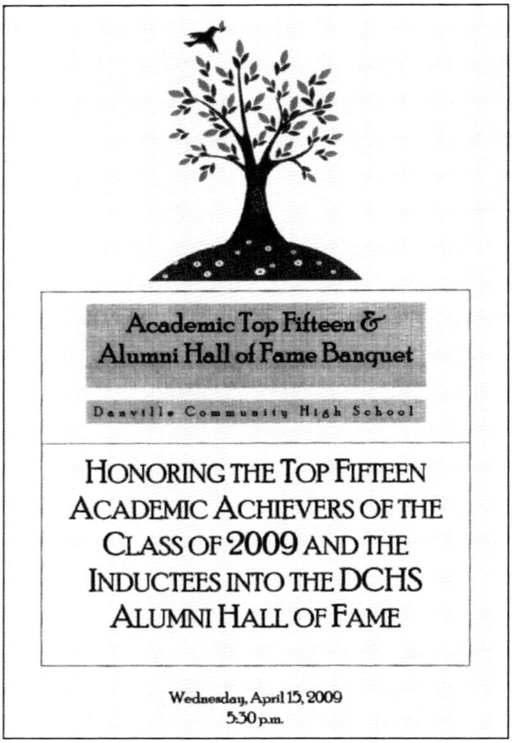

Danville High School has instituted a wonderful program to recognize its top academic talent by recognizing the top 15 graduating members of its senior class. In addition, they have joined this with a program that recognizes former Danville graduates who have left their mark on the world. This is the cover from that program in the year in which this book was written and published. (Danville Community School Corporation.)

TOP FIFTEEN AND HONORED GUESTS

Whitney Baenziger Steve Cassady	Undecided Danville Community High School	Biomedical Engineering Science Teacher
Philip Baldwin Jeremy Livingston	Rose-Hulman Danville Community High School	Mechanical Engineering Percussion Director
Nikki Cullison Robin Bess	Purdue University Danville Community High School	Veterinary Technologist Student Council Advisor
Elissa Dillon Maggie Rockwell	Indiana University Danville Community High School	Pre-Optometry P.E./Health Teacher
Brandon Doub Steve Johnson	Hanover University Danville Community Middle School	Elementary Education Teacher/Coach
Jordan Dougherty Becky Richard	Indiana University Danville Community High School	Undecided Math Teacher
Matthew Hollars Gage Brogan	Purdue University Floyd Central High School	Mechanical Engineering Social Studies Teacher
Mackenzie Knotts Jamie Young	Purdue University Danville Community High School	Undecided Math Teacher
Emma McEvilly Karen Mayo	Indiana University Danville Community High School	Nursing Choir/Music Teacher
Nicholas Phipps Jennifer Miller	Purdue University Danville Community High School	Pre-Dentistry English Teacher
Britni Plummer Robb Dure	Ball State University Danville Community High School	Music Education Band Director
Kelsa Reynolds Linda Guyer	Butler University Danville Community High School	Pre-Pharmacy Retired Business Teacher
Luke Robinson Dick Burrows	Purdue University Danville Community High School	Engineering Social Studies Teacher/Coach
Paul Schmidt John Finlay	Indiana University Danville Community School Corp.	Computer Science Technology Dept./District Technician
Heather Watts Bob Smith	Purdue University Danville Community High School	Nursing Spanish Teacher

This is the list of Danville's "top fifteen" as recognized in the year 2009, the year that this book was written and published. The student, the student's probable major, and probable college are listed. Then the student lists an honored guest, a faculty member or some other person whom the student recognizes has been instrumental in that student's success. Where that honored guest works and what they do is also listed. It is a wonderful way to recognize the valuable role that teachers and mentors play in the Danville community. (Danville Community School Corporation.)

Five

Homes, Churches, Suburban Life, and Other Interruptions

A quick view of Danville shows many churches to which people have devoted substantial time and money. They have built substantial homes and a library and a hospital. Many of them are not known outside Danville, but some of them have wide renown.

"Big Sam" Thompson grew up in Danville and is enshrined in the National Baseball Hall of Fame in Cooperstown, New York. Thompson remains first in runs batted in per game, edging out Lou Gehrig. John Hanson Craig had the title of the "heaviest man alive" at 907 pounds. He made his home in Danville when not on tour with the circus. Poet James Whitcomb Riley frequently visited Danville via the interurban to visit friends.

John V. Hadley, a lawyer and judge in Hendricks County after the Civil War, wrote a book about his imprisonment and escape from a Confederate prison called *Seven Months a Prisoner* that was recently relied on, in part, to write the book and the movie called *Cold Mountain*.

On Good Friday of 1948, a tornado swept toward Danville from the southwest, flattening everything in its path. Large portions of Danville were devastated, including many residential areas and the Christian church. Most residents rebuilt, but their homes now included basements as tornado refuges. Even today when digging in many yards pieces of tin roof and pieces of glass from that day are turned up with a shovel.

You never know what kind of a surprise might interrupt your day!

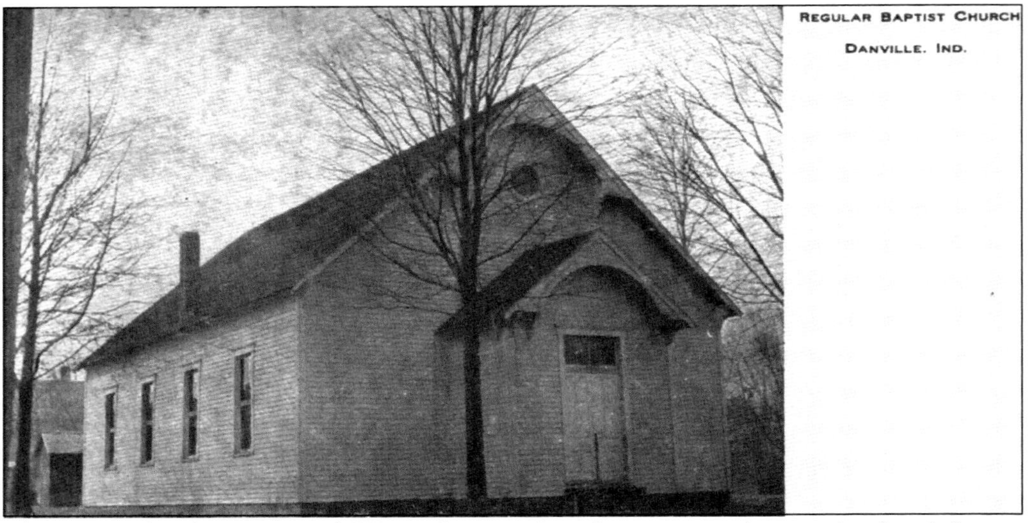

The Baptist church sat on North Wayne Street and was known to residents as the church "across the street from the high school gym." However, when Central Normal College decided to build a gymnasium on North Wayne Street north of Recitation Hall in 1924, it bought the land from the Baptist Church. The Danville School system eventually bought the land on which the church stood, and it has been converted to a parking lot. The congregation survives as Hillcrest Baptist Church. (Indiana Room, Danville-Center Township Public Library.)

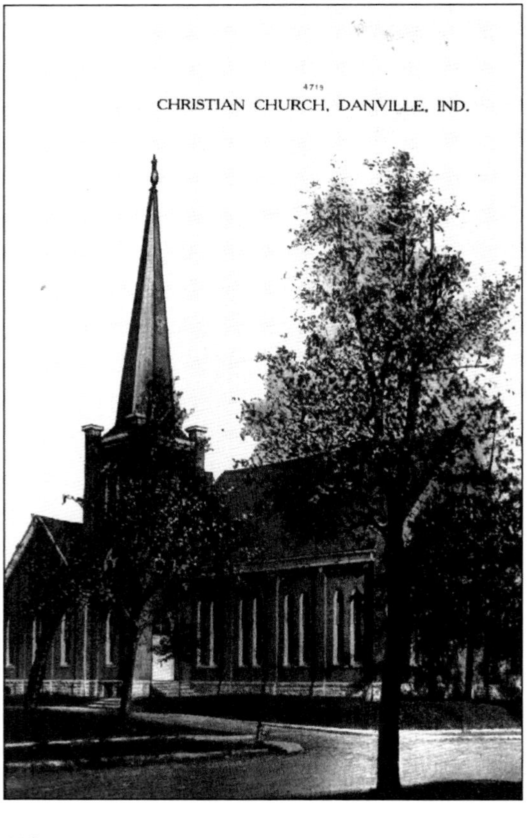

The Danville Christian Church sits on a prominent hillside as one approaches Main Street from the south. However, the church today is at least the third in the congregation's history. The church was organized around 1845. Its first building was farther east and south. The church building pictured was built at Main and Cross Streets in 1870–1874 at a cost of $15,000. The church bade farewell to the building following services on the last Sunday of March 1914; the building was razed. (Hendricks County Museum.)

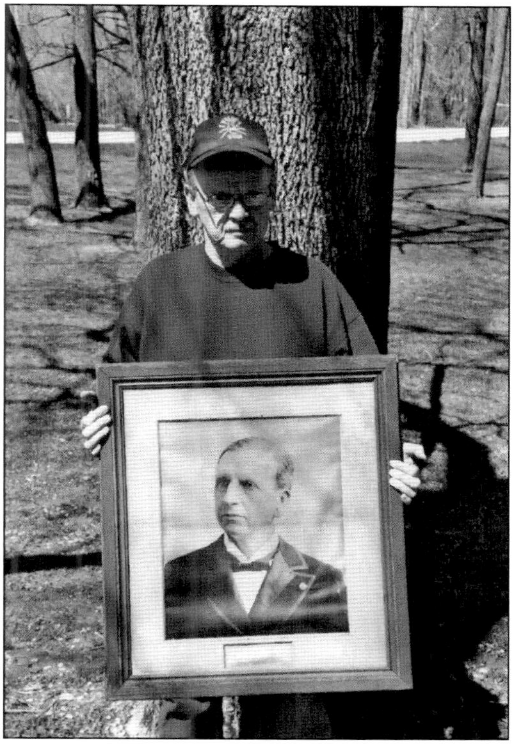

Ira J. Chase, pastor of Danville Christian Church, was born in New York, served in the Civil War, and then served churches in several states. He became the chaplain of the Indiana Grand Army of the Republic in 1886 and was elected lieutenant governor of Indiana in 1888. He served in this capacity until Gov. Alvin Hovey passed away on November 23, 1891. Chase assumed the duties of governor and ran for election in his own right. While governor he improved the state's road system and the Indianapolis Soldiers' and Sailors' Monument was constructed. After losing an election, Chase retired from office on January 9, 1893. Chase continued his service in the ministry while serving in government. Here Walter Anderson, who grew up in the Chase House, holds the picture of Governor Chase that hung over the front door of the house. (Author's collection.)

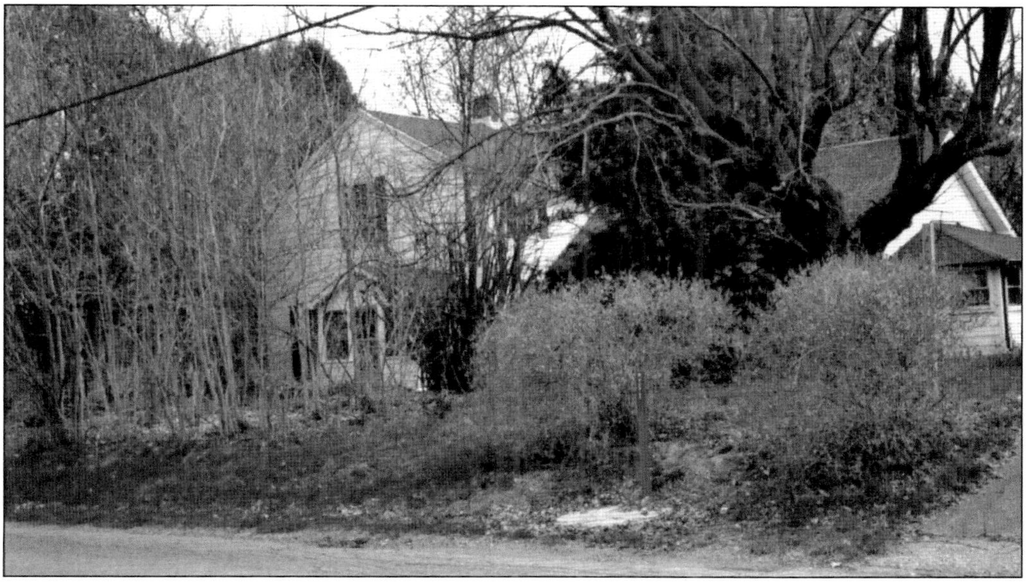

The home of Gov. Ira J. Chase stands on South Kentucky Street. Although Indiana law requires the governor to live in Indianapolis, Chase continued to reside in Danville, taking the passenger train back and forth between Danville and Indianapolis every day. Governor Chase was committed to maintaining his family home in familiar surroundings in consideration for his wife, blinded as a result of smallpox, which she contracted while serving as an army nurse during the Civil War in 1862. (Author's collection.)

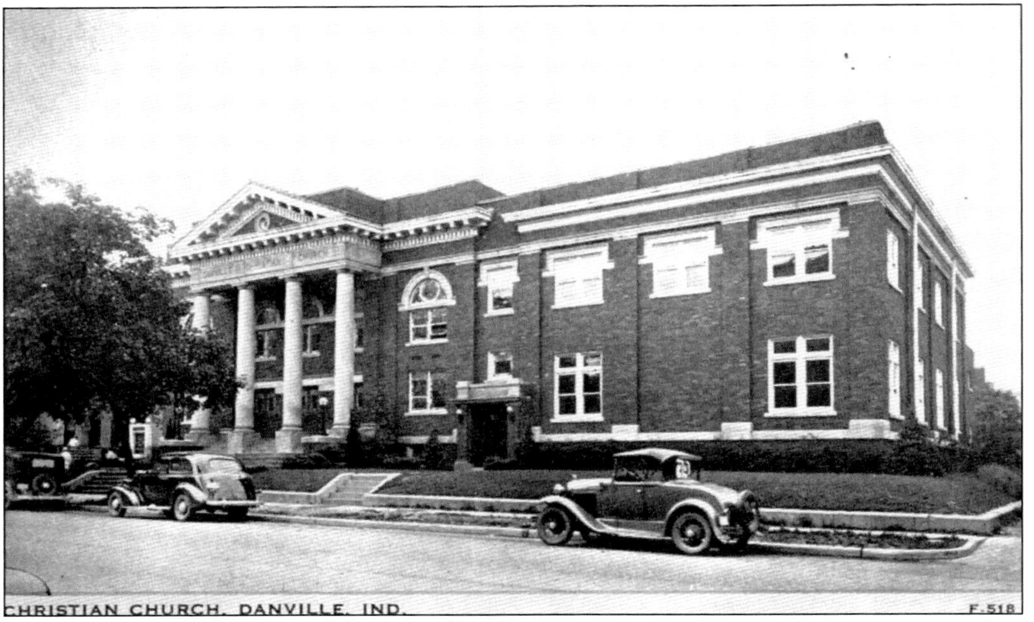

This is the present building of the Danville Christian Church, although the picture was taken when the cars on the street were not classic cars but cars in everyday use. The church is the only church that is downtown, and so it has hosted many community church services and dinners as well as many scouting groups over the years. The current pastor is Don Campbell. (Indiana Room, Danville-Center Township Public Library.)

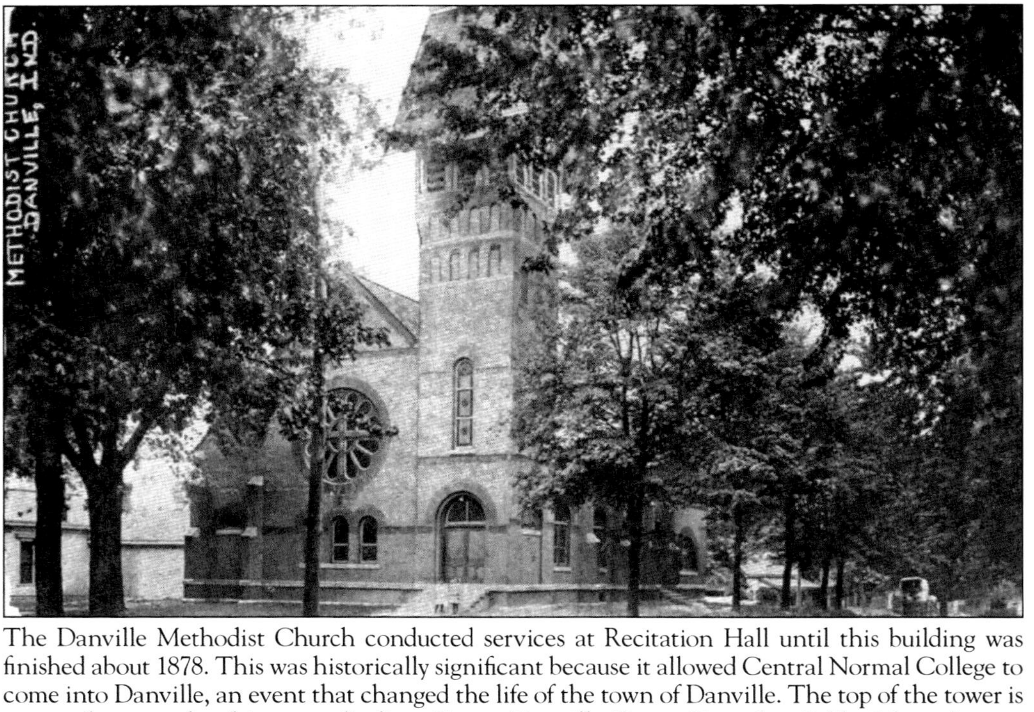

The Danville Methodist Church conducted services at Recitation Hall until this building was finished about 1878. This was historically significant because it allowed Central Normal College to come into Danville, an event that changed the life of the town of Danville. The top of the tower is extremely unusual architecture. (Indiana Room, Danville-Center Township Public Library.)

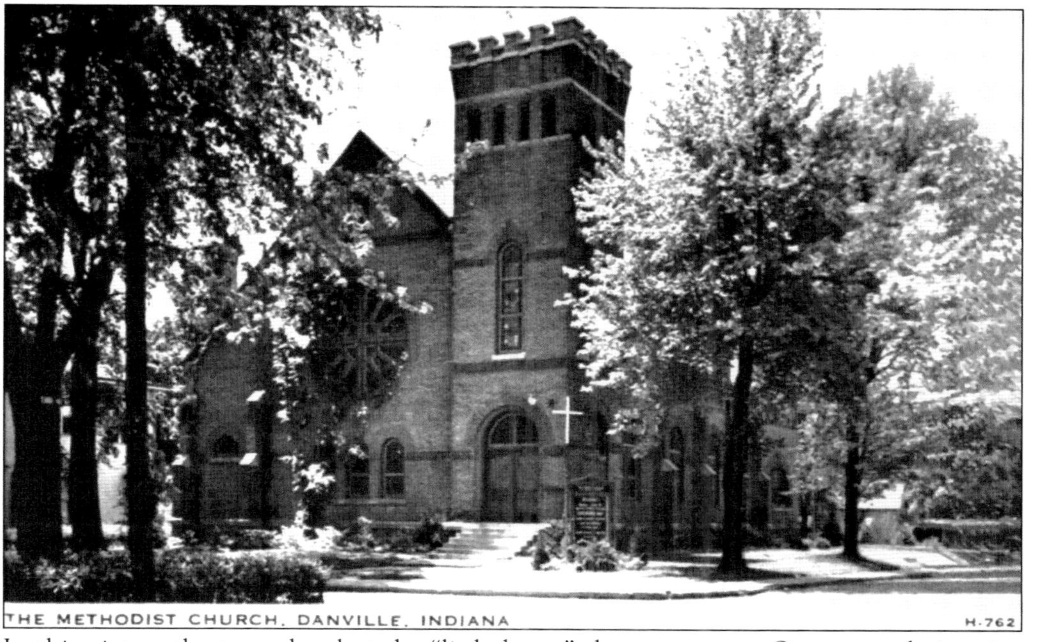

In this picture the tower has lost the "little house" that sat on top. One can only imagine the event that took this joyous decoration from view forever. (Indiana Room, Danville-Center Township Public Library.)

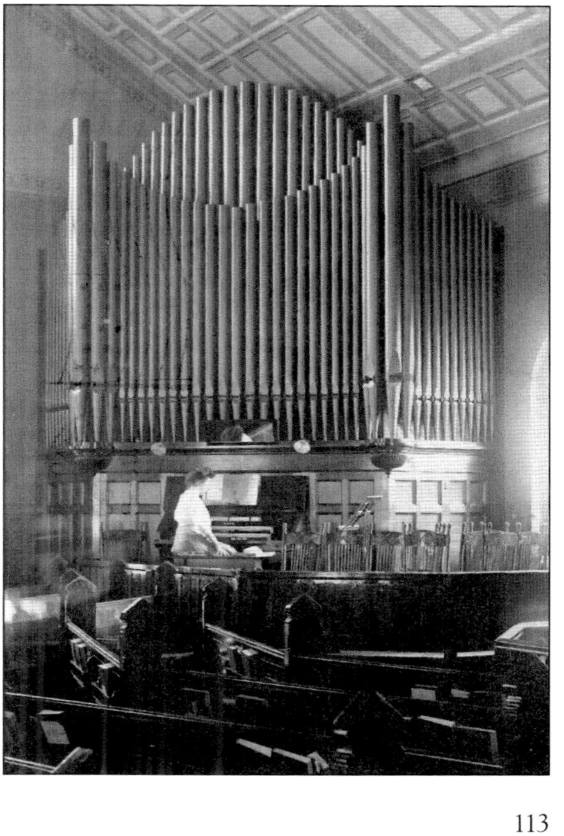

This massive pipe organ sat inside the Danville Methodist Church for many years. It is big enough that it must have shaken the rafters of the church, and perhaps the rest of the south side of Danville as well. (Indiana Room at Danville-Center Township Public Library.)

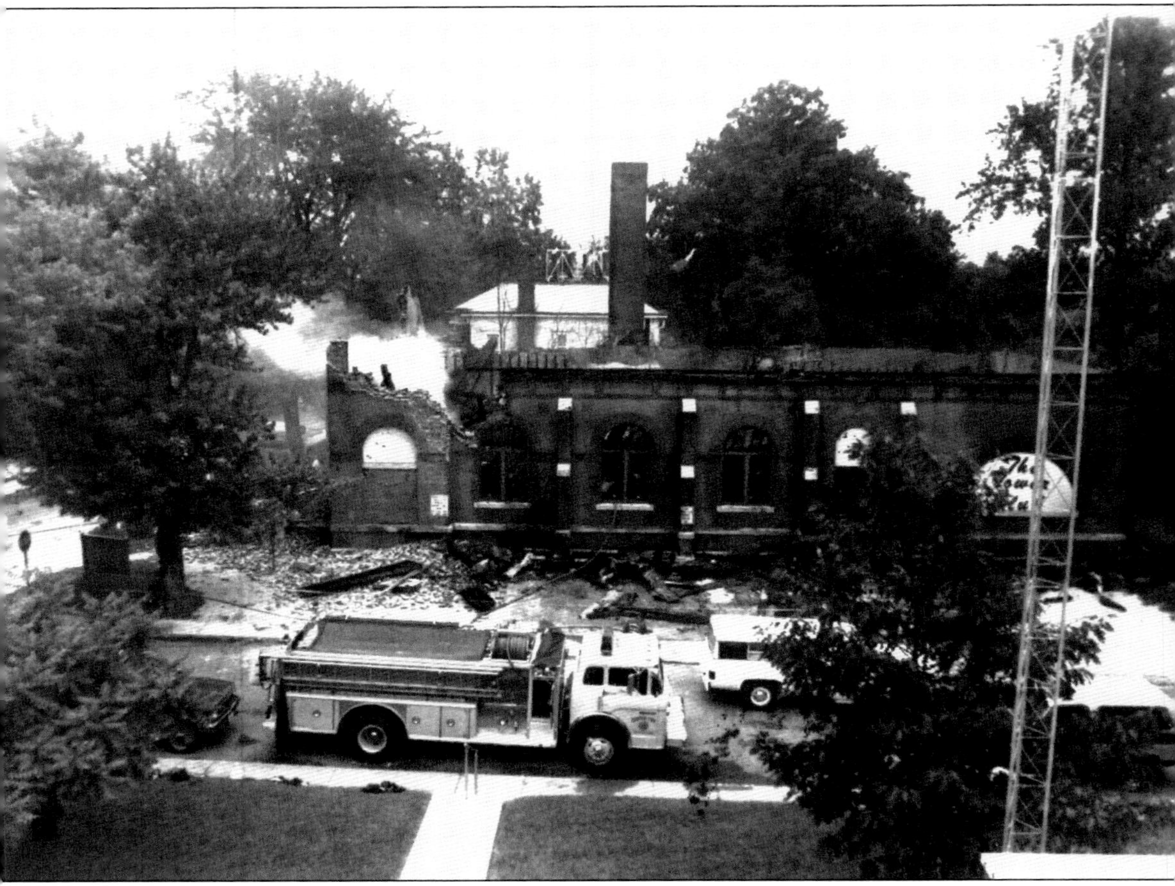

When the Methodist Church moved on to a new building, the 1878 building eventually was sold to a group running an exercise business. Because of the church tower they called it the Tower Club. Sadly, however, the building caught fire, and the Danville Fire Department is shown here battling the blaze. (Guilford Township Historical Collection, Plainfield-Guilford Township Public Library.)

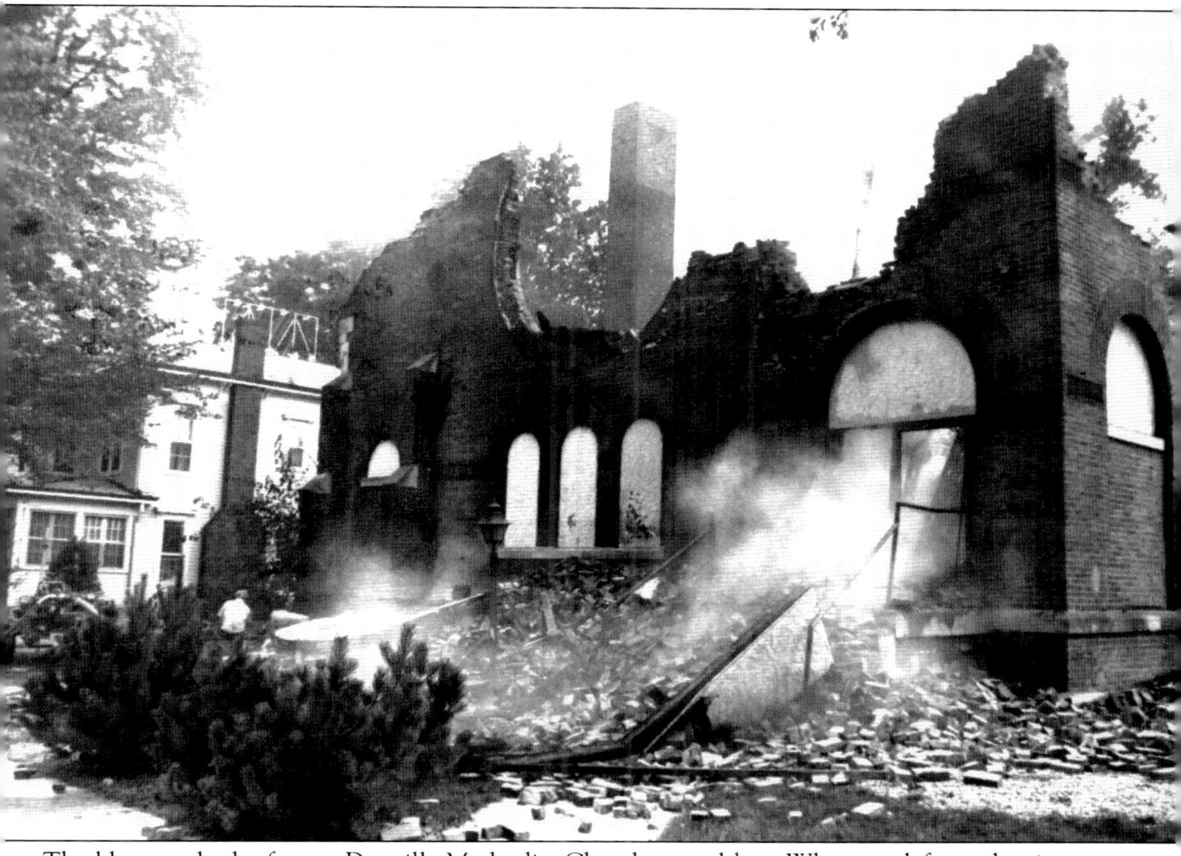

The blaze made the former Danville Methodist Church a total loss. What was left on the site was leveled and hauled away, and the site that had once stood so proudly became a parking lot. It is now a convenient place to park to visit the Hendricks County Museum, also located at the corner of Washington Street and Broadway Street in Danville. (Guilford Township Historical Collection, Plainfield-Guilford Township Public Library.)

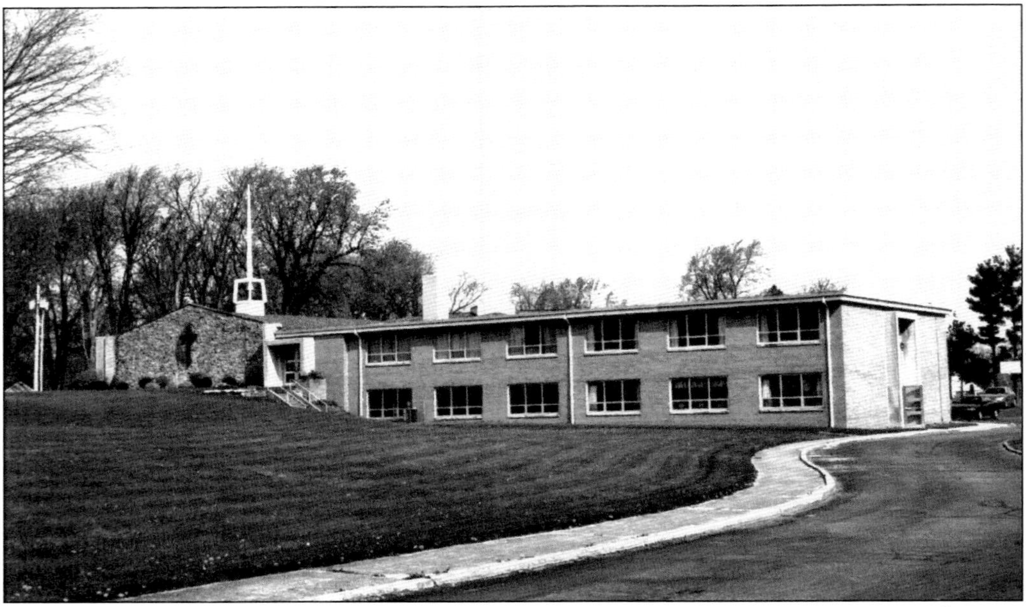

This is a current photograph of the Danville United Methodist Church. It is on West Mill Street in Danville and offers a variety of services to the community, including a food pantry. The pastor is Rev. David Powell. (Author's collection.)

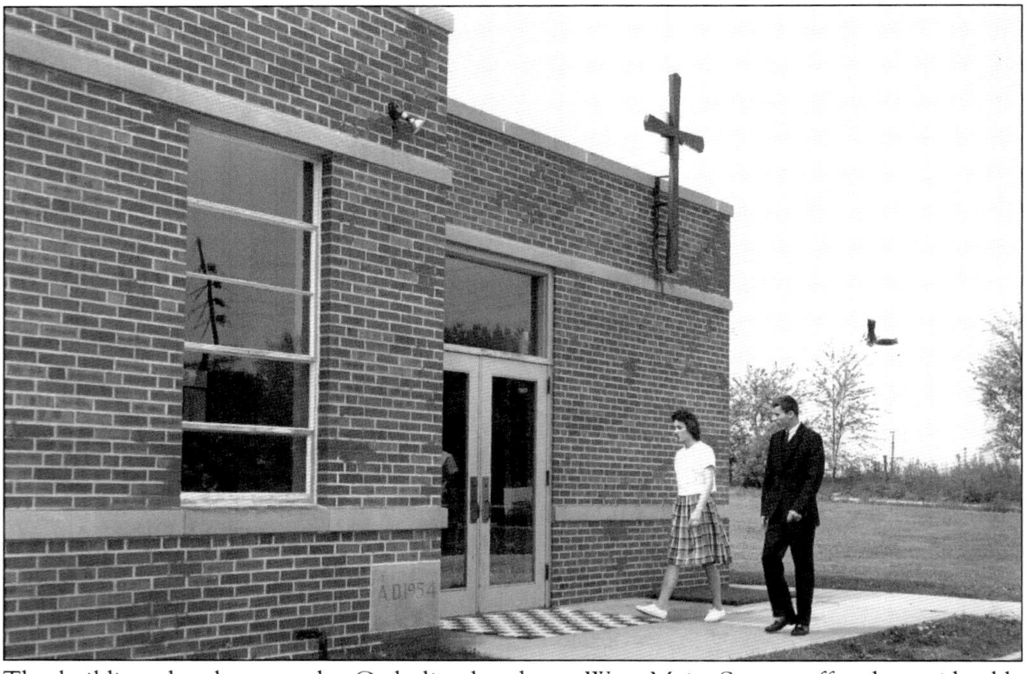

The building that became the Catholic church on West Main Street suffered considerable damage in the 1948 tornado. Accordingly, this building was built in 1954 as a church with thought of eventually turning this building into an educational complex. An unidentified man and woman approach the doors to go in and worship. (Indiana Room, Danville-Center Township Public Library.)

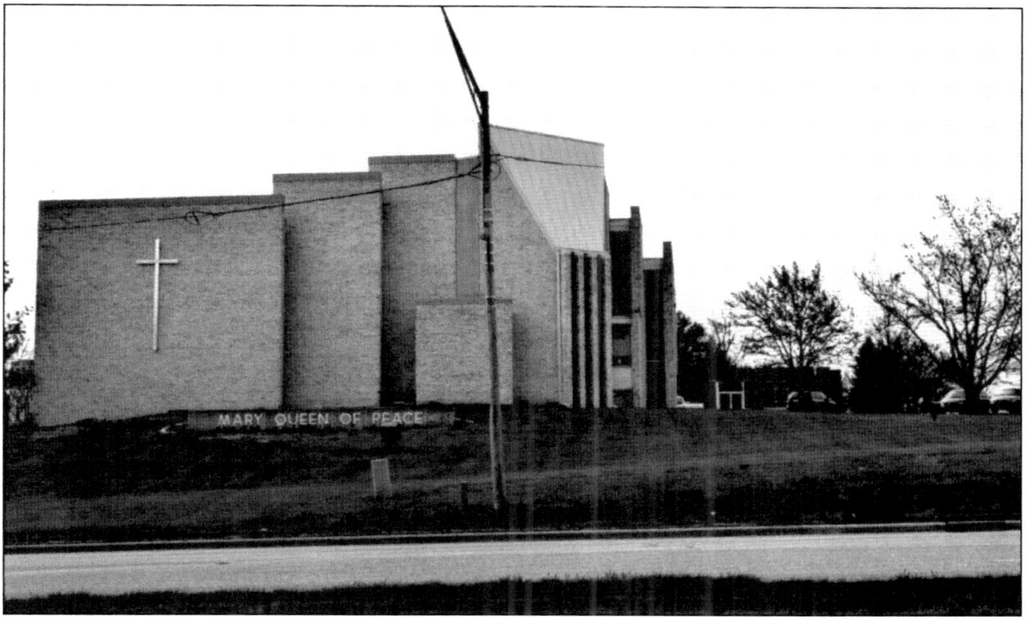

In 1990, the current Catholic church was built. It seats 400 people and sits on a total campus of eight acres. Mary Queen of Peace Parish currently serves 426 households, which includes 220 children. It sits at the corner of Mackey Road and West Main Street. (Author's collection.)

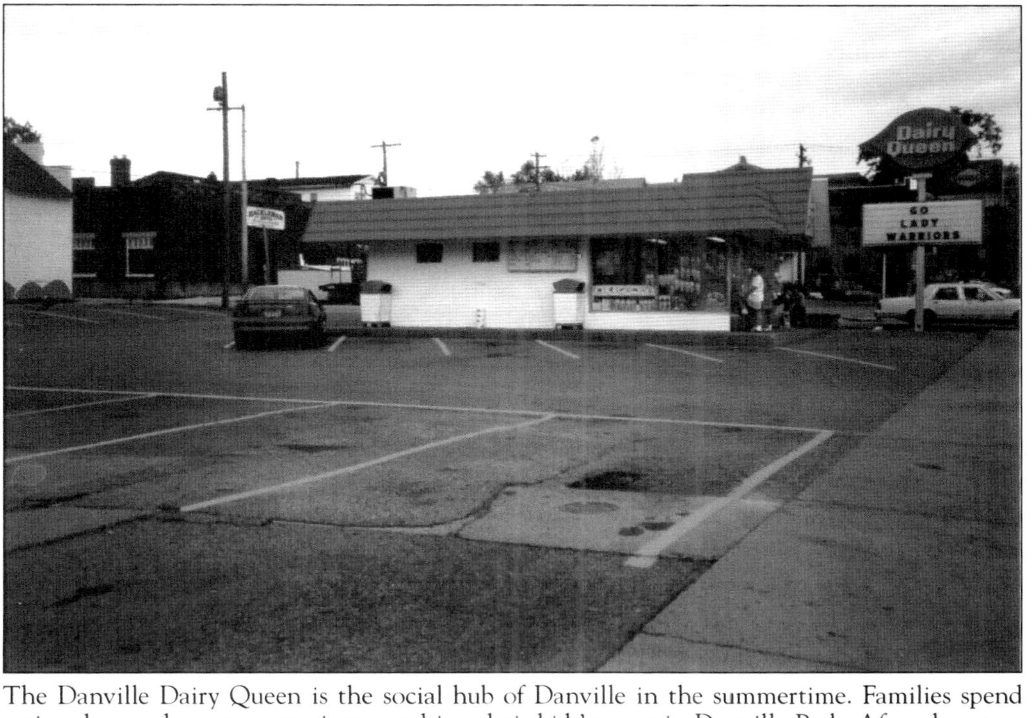

The Danville Dairy Queen is the social hub of Danville in the summertime. Families spend spring days and summer evenings watching their kids' sports in Danville Park. After the game the team and their families head to the Dairy Queen to celebrate victory or to cheer up. (Kathy and Larry Witte.)

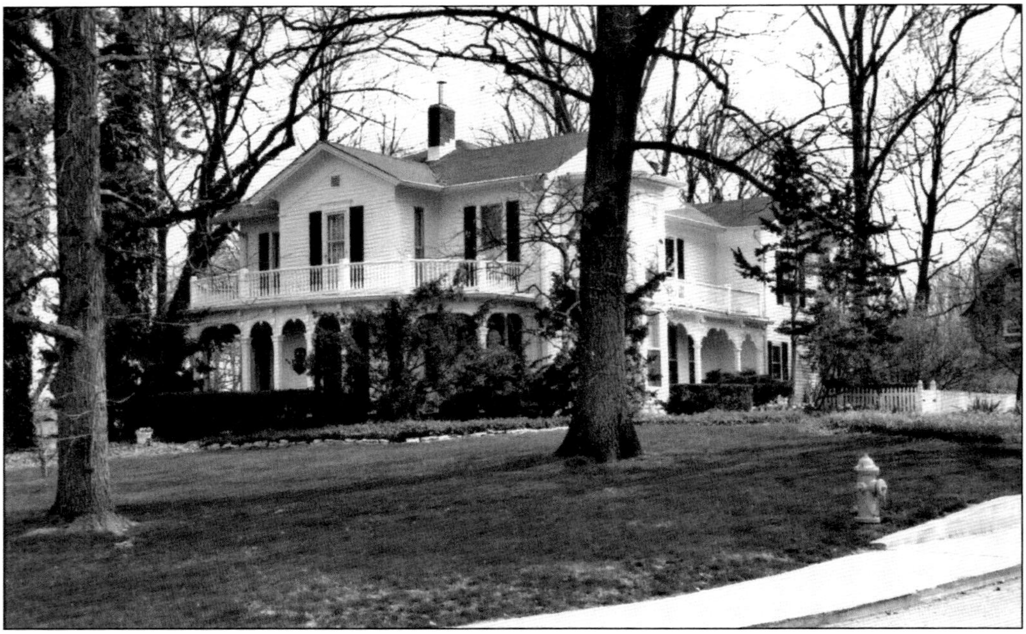

One of the most beautiful homes in Danville is the Judge John V. Hadley House on East Broadway Street. Judge Hadley fought in the Civil War, was a Confederate prisoner, escaped, wrote a book about it (*Seven Months a Prisoner*) upon which a fairly recent movie was predicated (*Cold Mountain*). He was a respected jurist, politician, and historian. (Author's collection.)

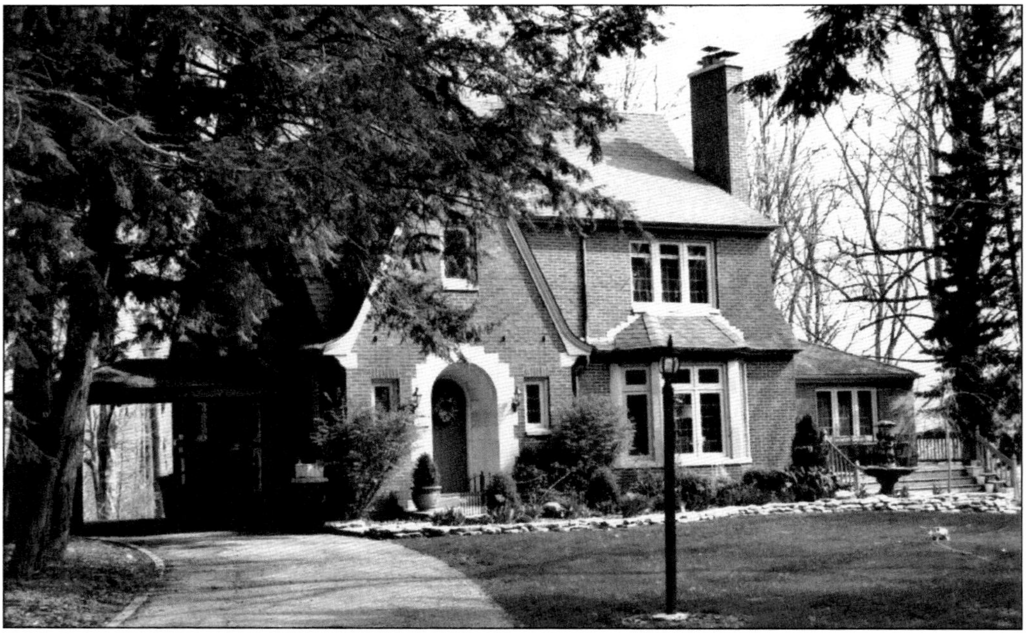

Jonathon Rigdon served Central Normal College as president from 1918 to 1929. As such, he was one of the leading members of the community. Accordingly, he built this beautiful Tudor-style house on East Broadway Street. The house looks fairly small from the street, but once inside the house has ample room upstairs and also a complete basement. (Author's collection.)

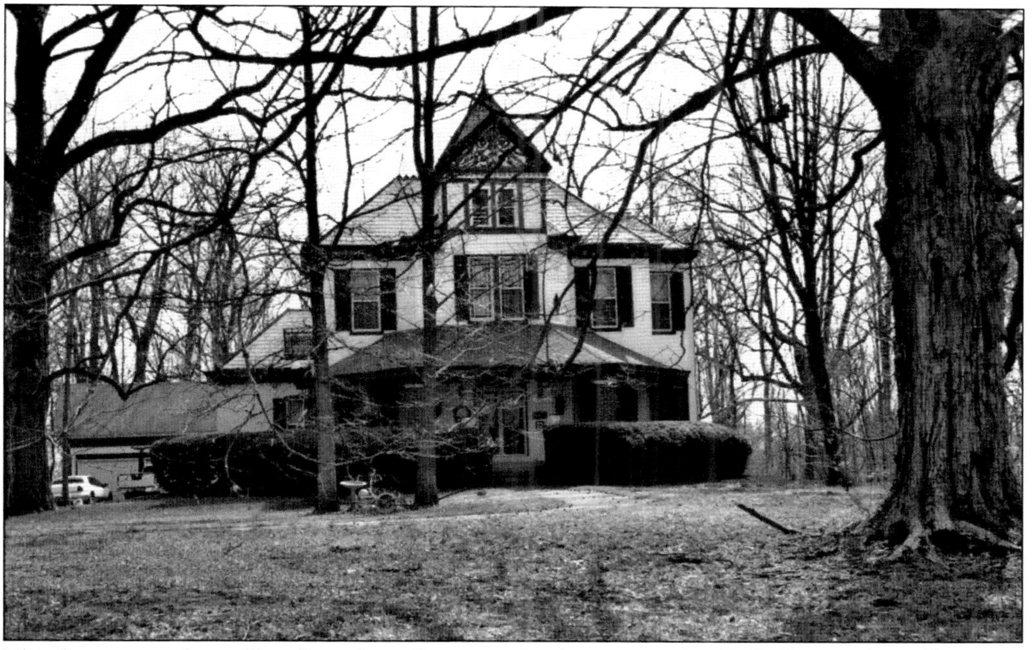

This house stands on East Broadway Street and is known as the Brill House. Actually it was built by attorney Leander M. Campbell. Behind the house, in the lowlands of the property, was a large pond. It was a beautiful spot, and the pond attracted people in both winter and summer. In 1895, Judge George Brill, who had studied law in Campbell's office, purchased the property. James Whitcomb Riley, the Hoosier poet, used to come to Danville by interurban and visit this house. (Author's collection.)

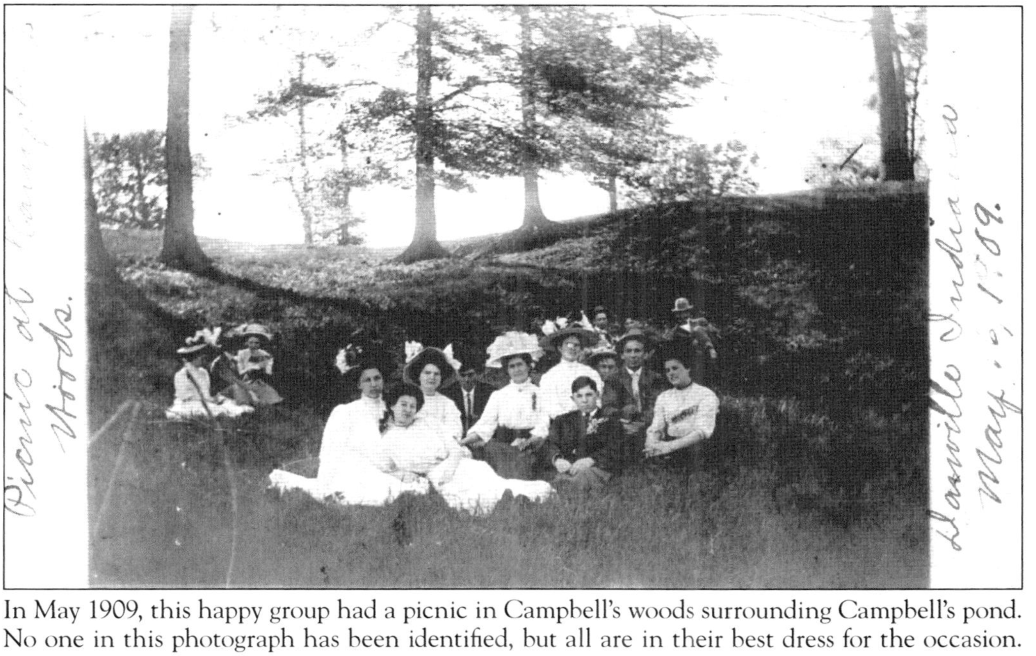

In May 1909, this happy group had a picnic in Campbell's woods surrounding Campbell's pond. No one in this photograph has been identified, but all are in their best dress for the occasion. (Hendricks County Museum.)

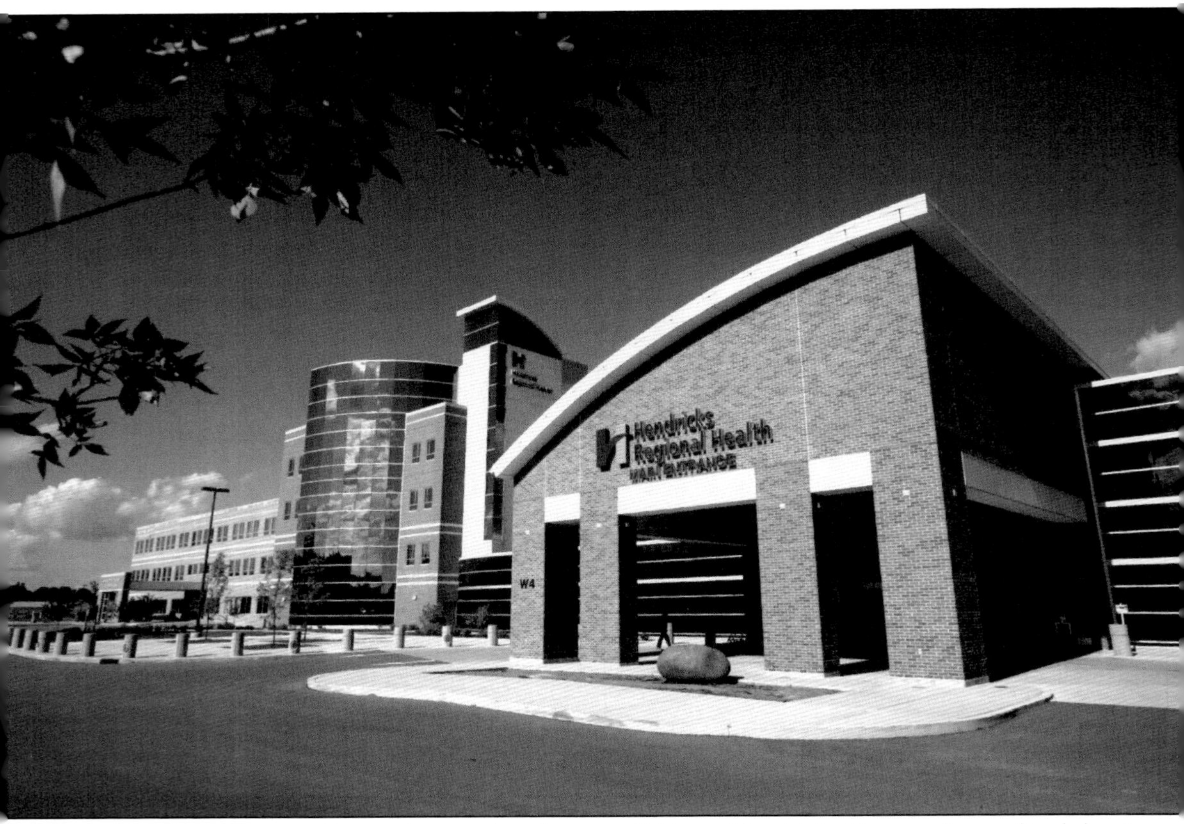

Hendricks County Hospital opened its doors in 1962 to a Hendricks County that realized that it needed medical care that was closer and more focused on the needs of Hendricks County than the Indianapolis hospitals. Over the years it has provided quality service to thousands of people, while at the same time growing and maturing to meet the medical needs of the 21st century. This is the main entrance of Hendricks Regional Health, and it is now located on the west side of the building. (Hendricks Regional Health.)

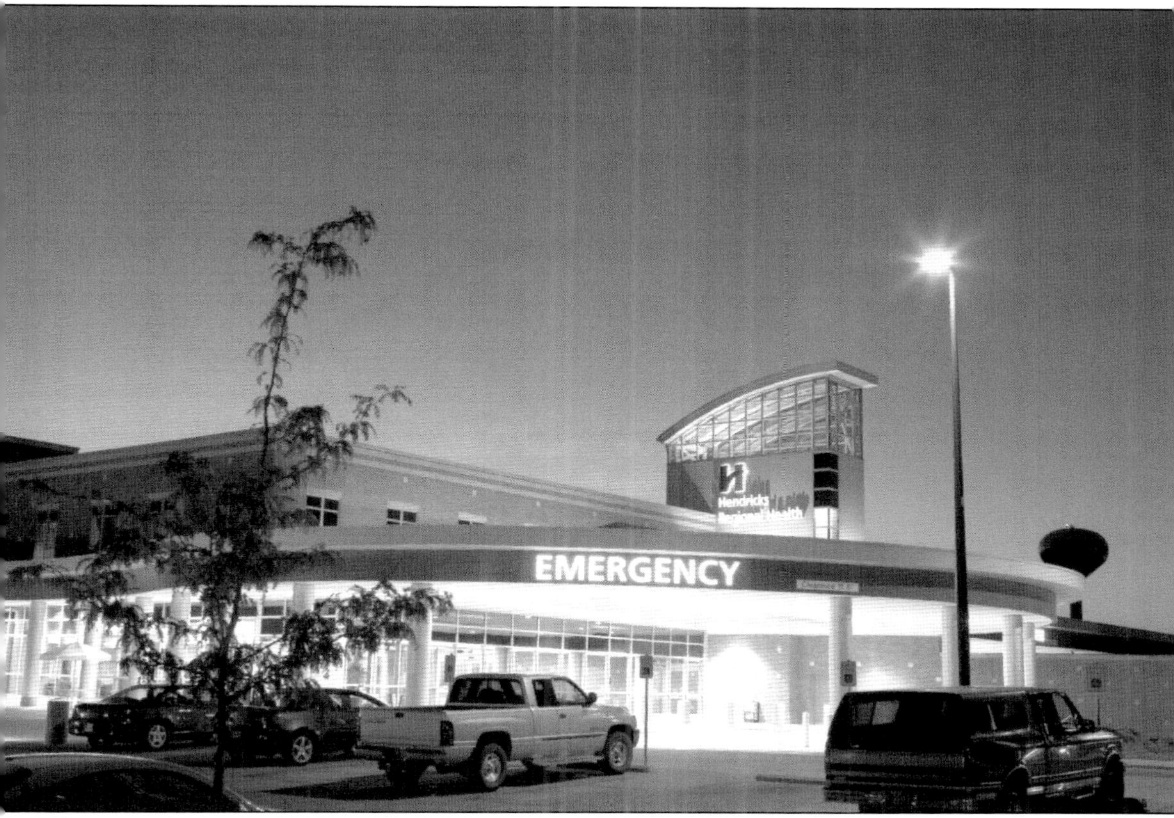

The emergency entrance to Hendricks Regional Health opens a door of technology to assist in the medical needs of those from Hendricks County and surrounding areas. The technology is aided by well-trained and caring people who are prepared to deal with whatever emergency may occur. (Hendricks Regional Health.)

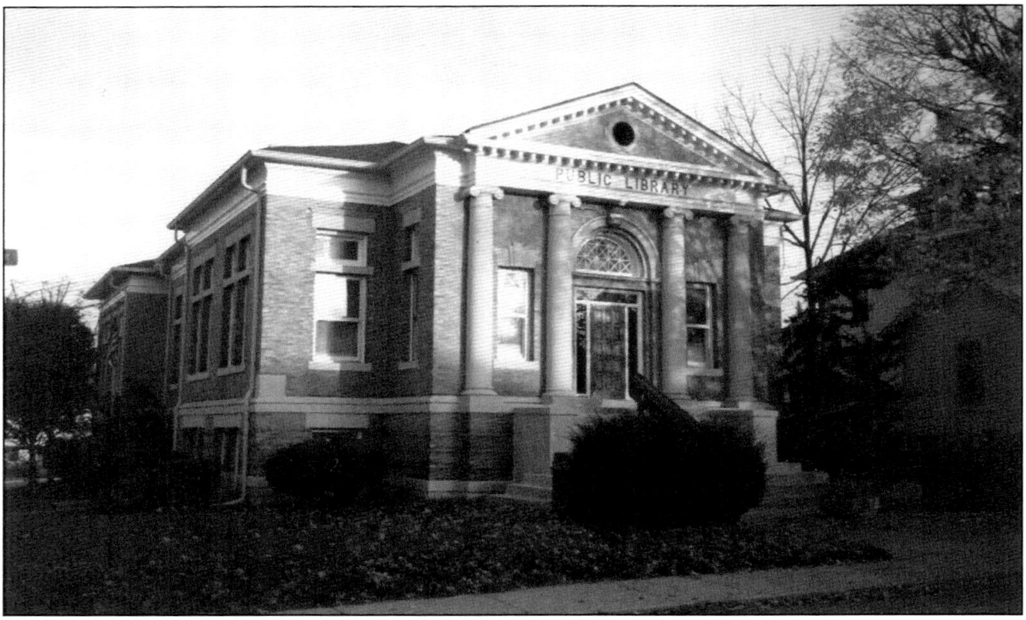

With a gift of $10,000 from Andrew Carnegie and the impetus of the Danville Commercial Club, a Carnegie library was dedicated in Danville in December 1903. For over 100 years the library has served the book needs of Danville, as well as the population of Central Normal College. (Indiana Room, Danville-Center Township Public Library.)

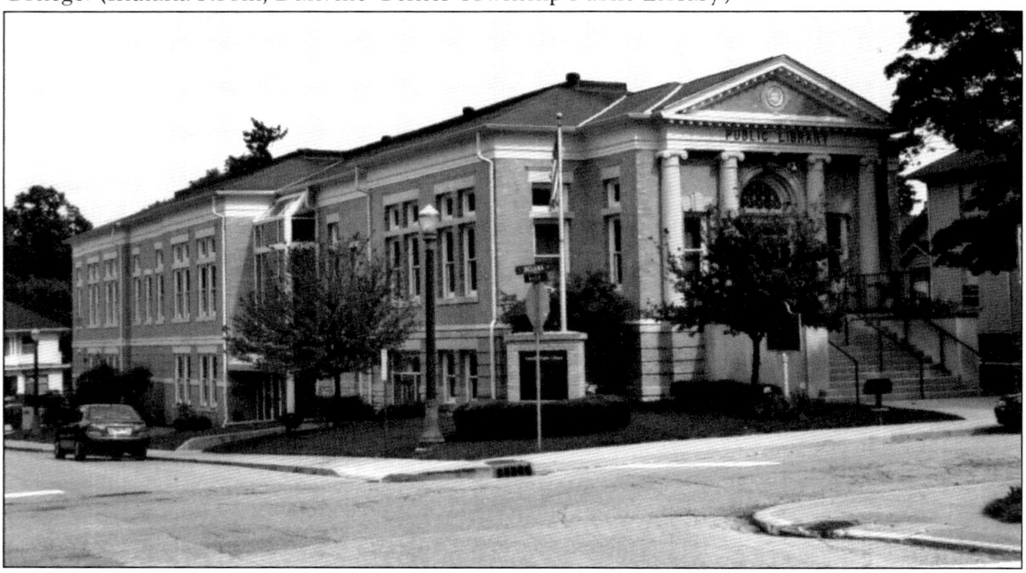

In over 100 years the Danville Public Library has grown to meet the needs of the community. The building has expanded many times in square footage, and the library has grown to include other media in its collection including videotapes, DVDs, and computer equipment and software. The public-use computers are often extremely busy, meeting the needs of those who have no computer or who are out of reach of their computer. The library has educational programs for patrons of all ages and is a real focal point of the community. (Indiana Room, Danville-Center Township Public Library.)

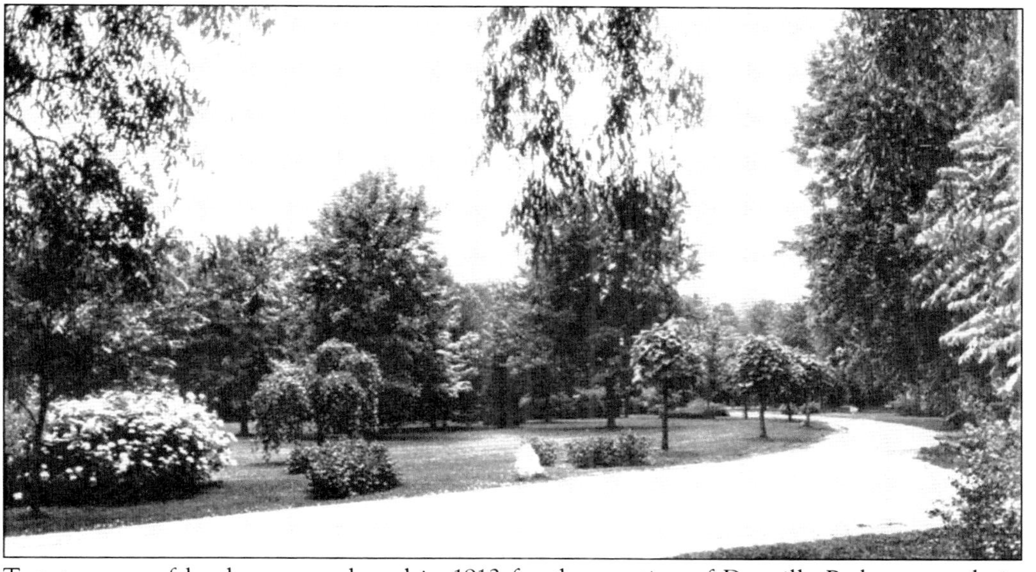

Twenty acres of land were purchased in 1913 for the creation of Danville Park, as people in the community wanted a place for public recreation. Several businessmen were involved with the Danville Browns semiprofessional baseball team, and others were interested in the welfare of athletes from the Central Normal College Purple Warriors. A deal was struck, plans were made, plants were planted, and a beautiful park was created. Danville still has one of the nicest municipal parks in Indiana. (Indiana Room, Danville-Center Township Public Library.)

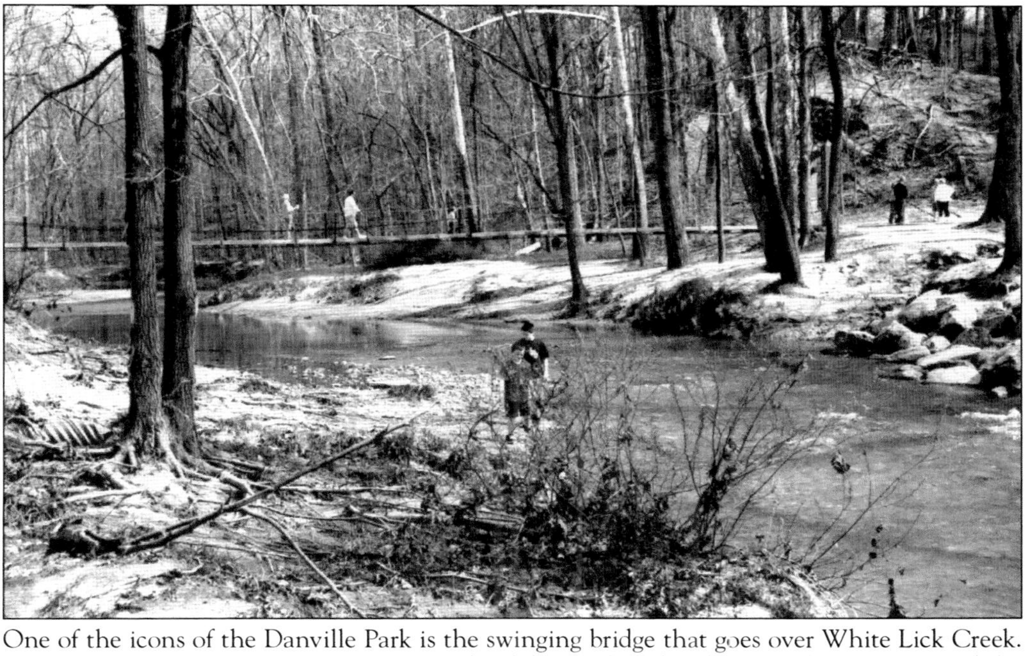

One of the icons of the Danville Park is the swinging bridge that goes over White Lick Creek. Of course, the prize for getting to the far side of the creek is the playground equipment and the picnic area. Thousands of children have played in the creek over the years, and just beyond is the woods with many trails. Besides that, there is baseball, softball, tennis, the town swimming pool, and many other joyful ways to spend a spring day. (Author's collection.)

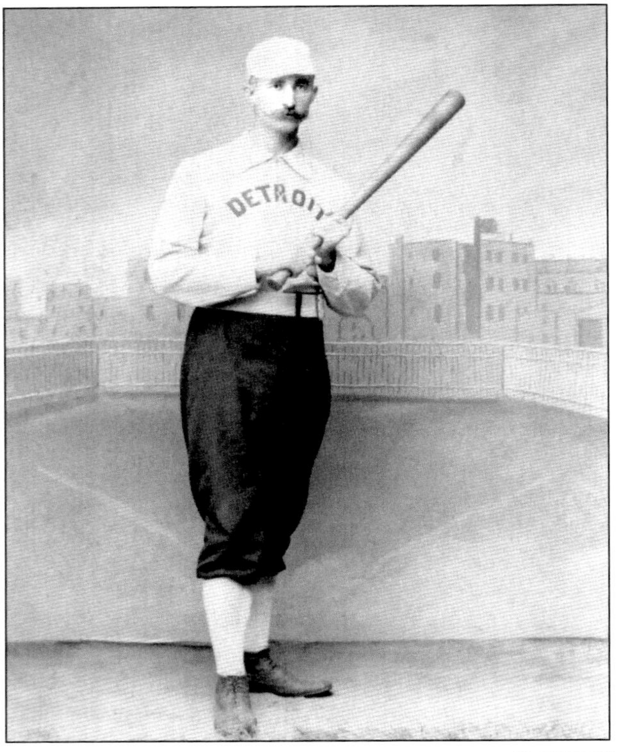

During the 1880s, the Danville Browns was one of many semiprofessional baseball teams playing in the Midwest. "Big Sam" Thompson grew up in Danville one block from where the author's law office is located and played for the Danville Browns, later making it into the big leagues. He is enshrined in the National Baseball Hall of Fame in Cooperstown, New York. Thompson remains first in runs batted in per game, edging out Lou Gehrig. (Baseball Hall of Fame.)

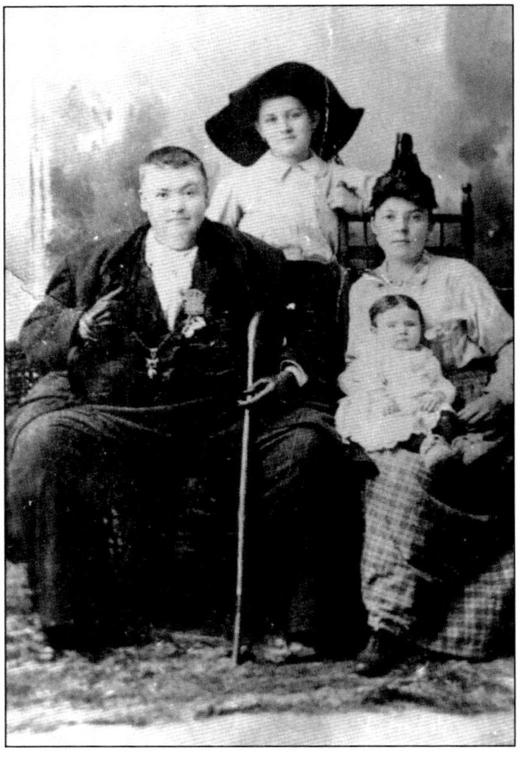

John Hanson Craig was the "heaviest man alive," weighing in at 907 pounds. He married Mary Jane Kesler, a native of Danville who became known as P. T. Barnum's "fat lady" in the 1860s. She was the largest woman in the state, weighing in at 782 pounds. The couple married in Danville and made their home here when not on tour with the circus. They are buried just outside Danville. (Guilford Township Historical Collection, Plainfield-Guilford Township Public Library.)

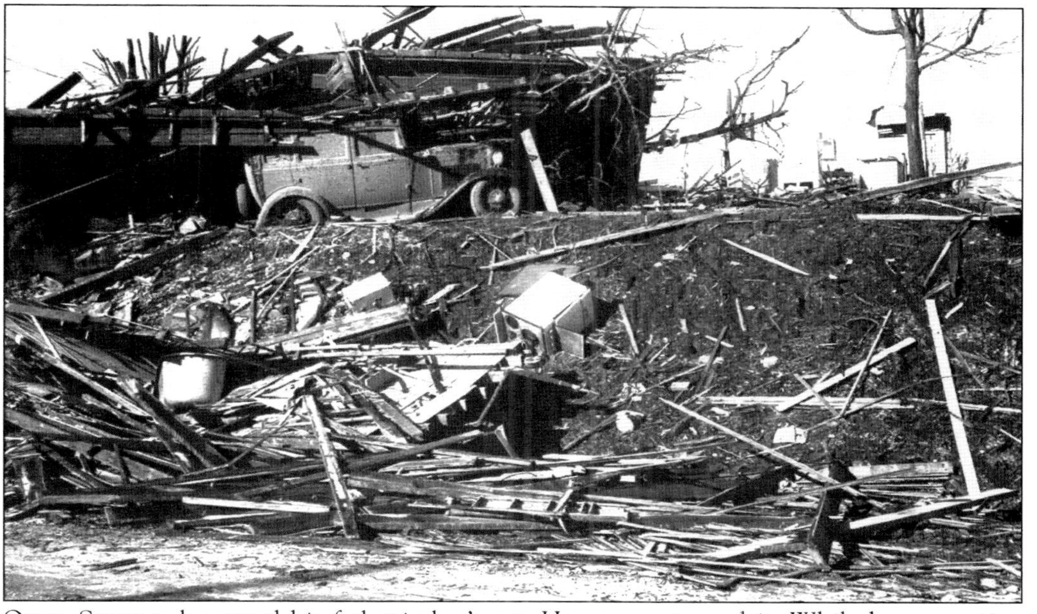

Owen Stamper borrowed his father-in-law's car. He never returned it. While he was eating supper, the Good Friday tornado of 1948 hit Danville, leaving destruction in its wake that could not be calculated and that will never fully disappear. This was at the corner of Clinton Street and Urban Street in Danville. (Indiana Room, Danville-Center Township Public Library.)

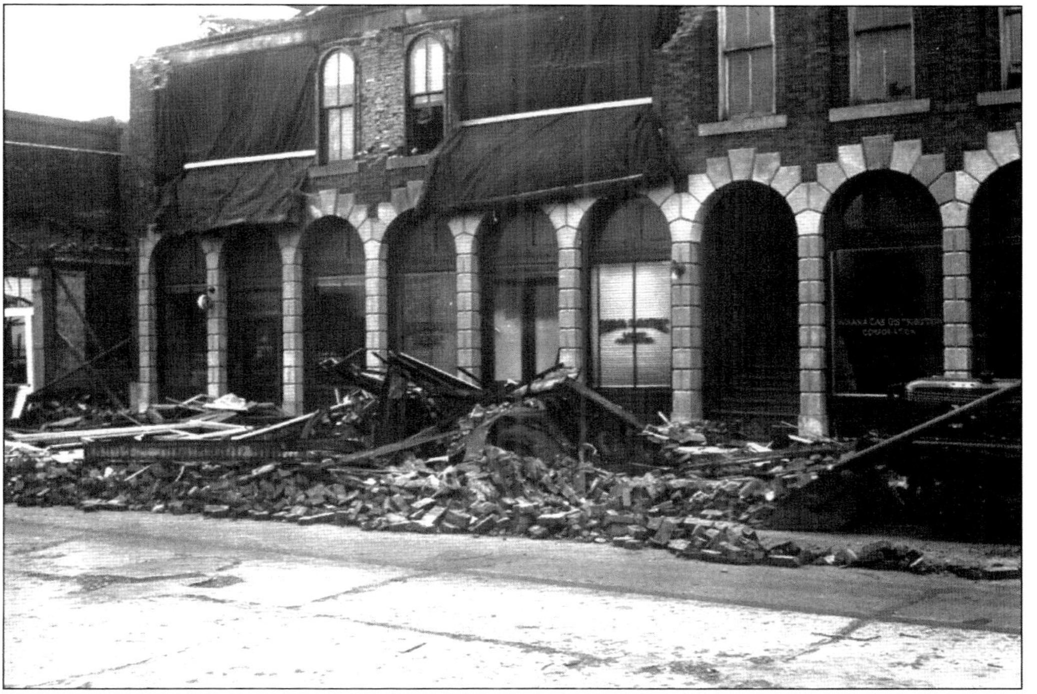

Brick rubble lines Main Street in front of the utilities building. Lots of buildings in the downtown area lost roofs and levels. Directly across the street from the utilities building the Christian church suffered major damage. (Indiana Room, Danville-Center Township Public Library.)

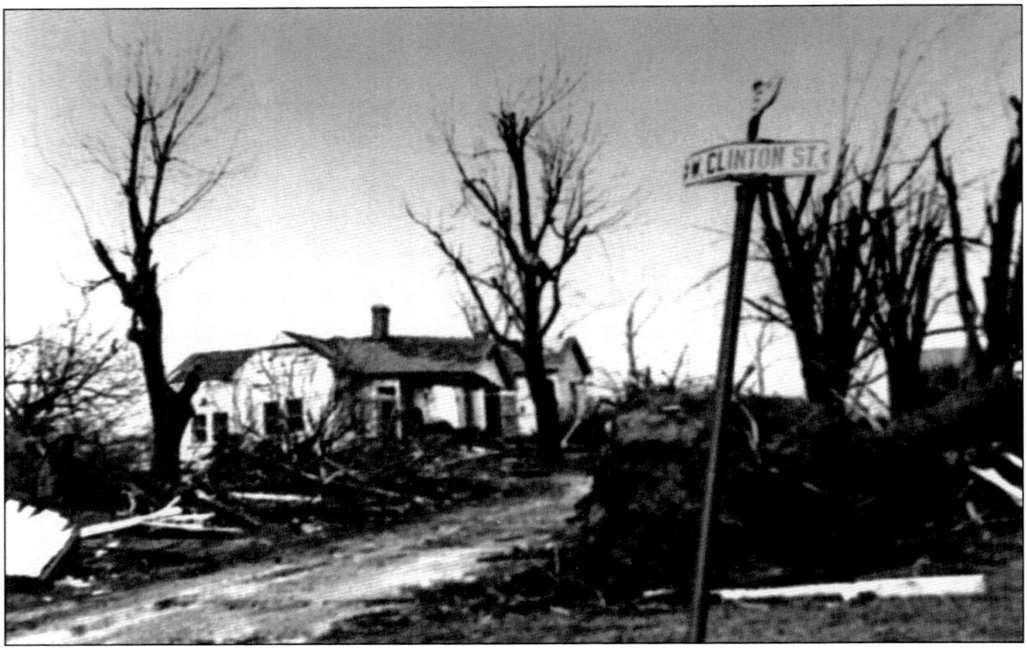

Clinton Street, parallel to Main Street, suffered substantial damage as metal was twisted, roofs were ripped off, and trees were uprooted and often shredded. (Indiana Room, Danville-Center Township Public Library.)

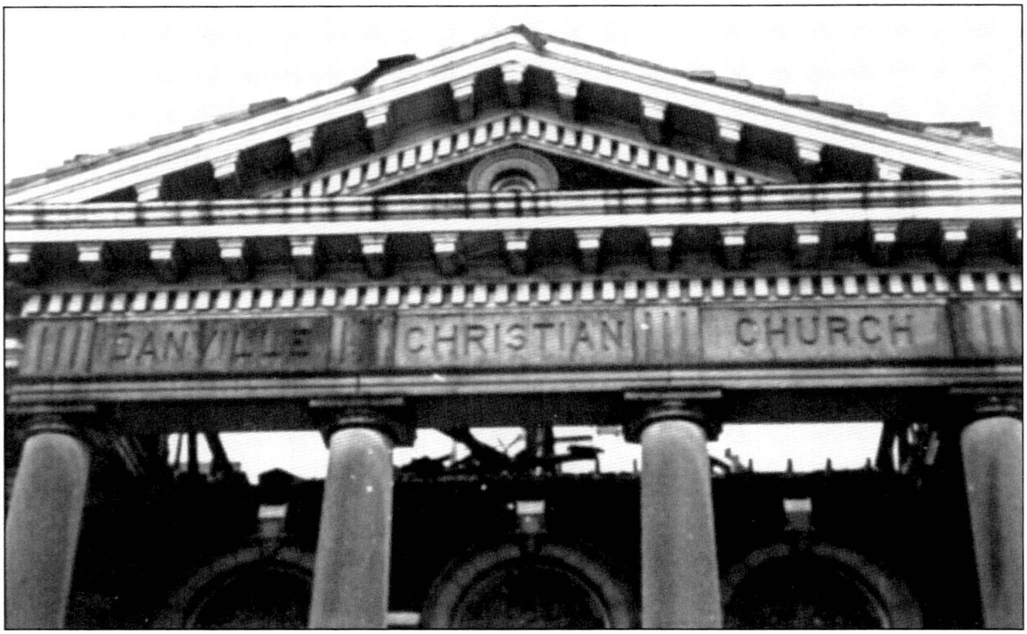

The Danville Christian Church was not intended to be an open-air church, but the Good Friday tornado made it one in 1948. Homes, businesses, and churches were all damaged, with some people taking years to recover. However, residents helped each other as best they could. (Indiana Room, Danville-Center Township Public Library.)

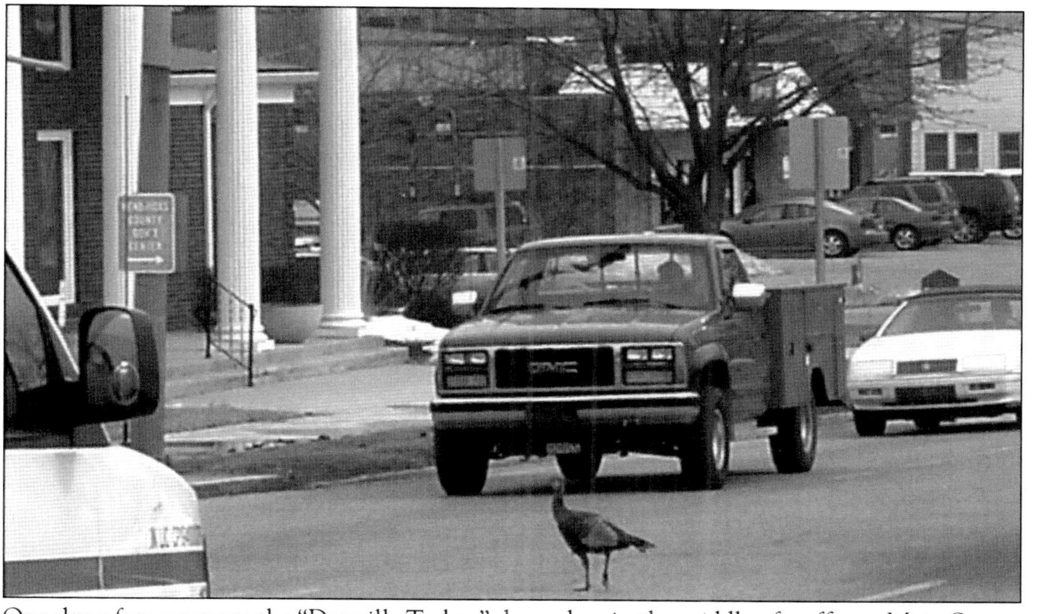

One day a few years ago the "Danville Turkey" showed up in the middle of traffic on Main Street. He seemed to enjoy strutting back and forth in front of vehicles, causing them to stop, sit, and admire him as he stopped traffic. People tried to shoo him away. He would not go. The Danville police got fairly good at chasing the Danville Turkey. He strutted around the courthouse square when traffic on Main Street was light and garnered national attention, appearing on network television news. (Danville Republican.)

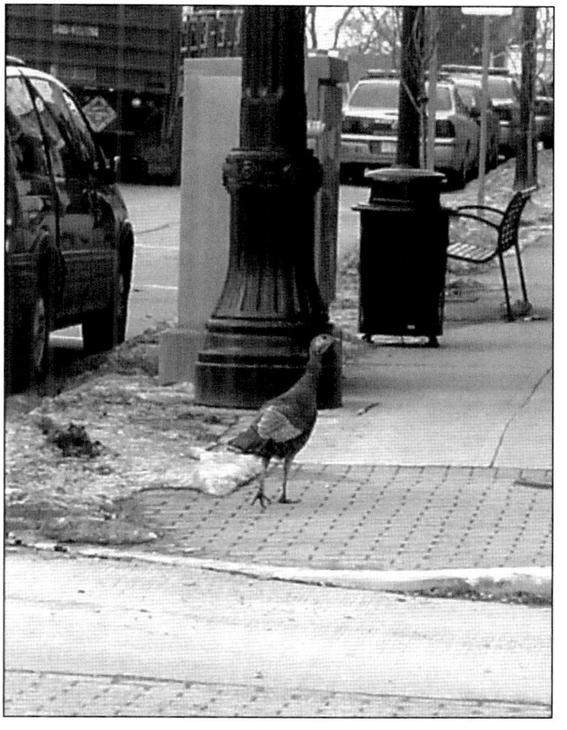

Everyone wanted to know what was going to happen to the Danville Turkey. They could not shoot him for he was not in season and he was in town. He was a protected animal so they could not adopt him. But one day the Danville Turkey was gone. No one knew where he went or how he got there. And no one knows if he is ever coming back. But Danville is still watching! (Danville Republican.)